Reframing Pilgrimage

Pilgr
has s
recen
for p
first

Pr
belo
exam
religi
religi
in ap
field
displ
'en r

Con
Hild
Schra

Simo
Durh
at the

European Association of Social Anthropologists

Series facilitator: Sarah Pink
University of Loughborough

The European Association of Social Anthropologists (EASA) was inaugurated in January 1989, in response to a widely felt need for a professional association that would represent social anthropologists in Europe and foster cooperation and interchange in teaching and research. The Series brings together the work of the Association's members in a series of edited volumes which originate from and expand upon the biennial EASA Conference.

Titles in the series are:

Conceptualizing Society
Adam Kuper (ed.)

Other Histories
Kirsten Hastrup (ed.)

Alcohol, Gender and Culture
Dimitra Gefou-Madianou (ed.)

Understanding Rituals
Daniel de Coppet (ed.)

Gendered Anthropology
Teresa del Valle (ed.)

**Social Experience and
Anthropological Knowledge**
Kirsten Hastrup and Peter Hervik (eds)

Fieldwork and Footnotes
*Han F. Vermeulen and
Arturo Alvarez Roldán (eds)*

Syncretism/Anti-syncretism
*Charles Stewart and
Rosalind Shaw (eds)*

Grasping the Changing World
Václav Hubinger (ed.)

Civil Society
Chris Hann and Elizabeth Dunn (eds)

Anthropology of Policy
Cris Shore and Susan Wright (eds)

Nature and Society
Philippe Descola and Gisli Pálsson (eds)

The Ethnography of Moralities
Signe Howell (ed.)

Inside and Outside the Law
Olivia Harris (ed.)

**Anthropological Perspectives
on Local Development**
*Simone Abram and
Jacqueline Waldren (eds)*

Recasting Ritual
*Felicia Hughes-Freeland and
Mary M. Crain (eds)*

Locality and Belonging
Nadia Lovell (ed.)

Constructing the Field
Vered Amit (ed.)

Dividends of Kinship
Peter P. Schweitzer (ed.)

Audit Cultures
Marilyn Strathern (ed.)

Gender, Agency and Change
Victoria Ana Goddard (ed.)

Natural Enemies
John Knight (ed.)

**Anthropology of Violence and
Conflict**
*Bettina E. Schmidt and
Ingo W. Schröder (eds)*

Realizing Community
Vered Amit (ed.)

Reframing Pilgrimage
Simon Coleman and John Eade (eds)

Reframing Pilgrimage

Cultures in motion

Edited by
Simon Coleman and John Eade

Routledge
Taylor & Francis Group

LONDON AND NEW YORK

First published 2004
by Routledge
2 Park Square, Milton Park, Abingdon, Oxon OX14 4RN

Simultaneously published in the USA and Canada
by Routledge
270 Madison Avenue, New York, NY 10016

Routledge is an imprint of the Taylor & Francis Group

© 2004 Selection and editorial matter EASA; individual
chapters to their contributors

Typeset in Galliard and Gill by Keystroke, Jacaranda Lodge,
Wolverhampton

British Library Cataloguing in Publication Data
A catalogue record for this book is available from the
British Library

Library of Congress Cataloging in Publication Data
Reframing pilgrimage : cultures in motion / [edited by] Simon Coleman
and John Eade.
        p.   cm.
"European Association of Social Anthropologists."
Includes bibliographical references and index.
1. Pilgrims and pilgrimages. I. Coleman, Simon. II. Eade, John, 1946–
III. European Association of Social Anthropologists.
  BL619.P5R44 2004
  203′.51—dc22

                                                            2003024747

ISBN 0–415–30354–0 (hbk)
ISBN 0–415–30355–9 (pbk)

To the memory of Michael J. Sallnow, 1949–1990

Contents

7 Coming home to the Motherland: pilgrimage tourism
   in Ghana   133
   KATHARINA SCHRAMM

8 Route metaphors of 'roots-tourism' in the Scottish
   Highland diaspora   150
   PAUL BASU

   Bibliography   175
   Index   191

Contributors

Paul Basu is Lecturer in Anthropology at the University of Sussex. His doctoral dissertation, 'Homecomings: genealogy, heritage-tourism and identity in the Scottish Highland Diaspora', represents the continuation of a long-standing interest in the symbolism of place, the relationship between landscape, narrative and identity, and cognate travel practices such as pilgrimage and heritage-tourism. He is currently developing research projects in Sierra Leone and India.

Simon Coleman is Reader in Anthropology and Deputy Dean, Faculty of Social Sciences and Health, University of Durham, England. His books include the single-authored work, *The Globalisation of Charismatic Christianity* (2000, Cambridge) and the co-edited (with Mike Crang) *Tourism: between place and performance* (2002, Berghahn) and (with John Elsner) *Pilgrimage: past and present in the world religions* (1995, British Museum Press) and *Pilgrim Voices* (2003, Berghahn).

Jill Dubisch holds the position of Regents' Professor of Anthropology at Northern Arizona University. Her research in Greece has resulted in the edited volume *Gender and Power in Rural Greece* (1986) and *In a Different Place: pilgrimage, gender and politics at a Greek island shrine* (1995), both with Princeton University Press. Her recent work on motorcycle pilgrimage is presented in *Run for the Wall: remembering Vietnam on a motorcycle pilgrimage* (2001, Rutgers), jointly authored with Raymond Michalowski.

John Eade is Professor of Sociology and Anthropology at the University of Surrey Roehampton. His single-authored works are *The Politics of Community* (1989, Ashgate) and *Placing London* (2000, Berghahn), while he edited *Living the Global City* (1997, Routledge) and co-edited (with Michael Sallnow) *Contesting the Sacred* (1991, Routledge) and (with Christopher Mele) *Understanding the City* (2002, Blackwells).

Hildi Mitchell has a PhD in Social Anthropology from Queen's University, Belfast and is an Honorary Research Fellow at the University of Sussex. Her research on the anthropology of religion has centred on the study of Mormonism, particularly in the United Kingdom. She has published on heritage and the place of the material in Mormonism, and has a particular interest in the processes and practices of belief.

Bente Nikolaisen graduated from the Department of Social Anthropology, University of Oslo, in 1993. Her fieldwork has been conducted in Istanbul, Turkey, between 1994 and 1996, and 1998 and 1999 and she is currently completing her doctoral thesis working on religious movements, particularly Sufi groups.

Eva Evers Rosander is Senior Researcher at the Department of Theology and Religious Studies, Uppsala University, and Associate Professor in Social Anthropology at Stockholm University. She has co-edited two books – *African Islam and Islam in Africa: encounters between Sufis and Islamists* (1997, C. Hurst) and *Transforming Female Identities: women's organizational forms in West Africa* (1997, The Nordic Africa Institute). She is currently working on secular and religious images of motherhood in West Africa.

Katharina Schramm teaches at the Institute of Social Anthropology, Free University Berlin, where she is completing her PhD on the encounter of diasporan Blacks and the Ghanaian state. Her research focus is on the discourse and practice of 'homecoming' in the wider context of heritage politics. She has also published on the Ghana Dance Ensemble and the changing role of cultural institutions in the postcolonial nation-building process.

Acknowledgments

This volume emerged from an enjoyable workshop held at the European Association of Social Anthropologists conference in Kraków (2000). We would like to thank contributors to that session who are not otherwise represented here, namely Ellen Badone, Filareti Kotsi, Alex Gath, Claudia Bell and John Lyall.

Sarah Pink has been a friendly, helpful and efficient series editor, and we have also received valuable feedback from Matt Wood and two anonymous reviewers for Routledge.

We would also like to thank Leslie Carlin and Caroline Egan-Strang (partners of the distracted editors) for their patience during the preparation of this volume.

Thanks to Blackwells for permission to re-publish Hildi Mitchell's chapter. A shorter version of this appeared in *Anthropology Today*, 17 (2), 2001.

Chapter 1

Introduction

Reframing pilgrimage

Simon Coleman and John Eade

Moving images?

We begin by invoking possibly the most influential text in the anthropology of pilgrimage, Victor and Edith Turner's *Image and Pilgrimage in Christian Culture* (1978). Despite the book's title, it is not, for the most part, about images *per se*. Nonetheless, at the heart of the text there are a number of photographs depicting sites discussed by the authors, covering Mexico, France, Italy, Ireland and England. A few are immediately arresting: there is one of penitential pilgrims at the Basilica of Guadalupe painstakingly moving forward on their knees; another shows a suitably grim-looking 'death-dancer' at a Mexican saint's festival, who displays representations of the nuclear bomb on the side of his skull-like mask. All repay more detailed consideration, however, for what they do and do not reveal about the study of pilgrimage. Most either depict objects (altars, *ex-votos*, paintings) or – despite the photo from Guadalupe mentioned above – people in largely static poses: kneeling in worship, sitting by statues, observing a benediction. Yet, if we look more closely we realize that there are significant if implicit stories of movement contained in these illustrations of the pilgrimage process: the pilgrims kneeling in front of Our Lord of Chalma, Mexico, are said to have approached the shrine on their knees from a distance of one mile; a plaque at Walsingham, England, tells of the distances traversed by wooden crosses that were carried to the shrine from parts of the United Kingdom; and, although the 'death-dancer' leans on his staff, we are given to understand that he customarily leaps about in grotesque fashion, scaring any young people who go near him.

Taken as a whole, these illustrations hint at some of the varieties of physical motion involved in pilgrimage, from walking to crawling to dancing. And yet, most do not show movement itself, and it is here that we see something of the dilemma facing both the photographer and the anthropologist in presenting images of pilgrimage. The act of representation – involving either the literal or the ethnographic snapshot – encourages concentration on images and issues that lend themselves most easily to the gaze of the analyst: in other words, relatively fixed rather than fluid physical and social processes. This is not to say that the Turners are unaware of the mobility inherent in most pilgrimages.[1] Edith Turner herself (1978: xiii) calls pilgrimage 'a kinetic ritual', and *Image and Pilgrimage* aims to deal with 'the interrelations of symbols and meanings framing and motivating pilgrim behavior in a major world religion' rather than a circumscribed social field (1978: xxiv). Furthermore, the theme of movement forms part of the Turners' arguments about pilgrimage as embodiment of populist, spontaneously articulated 'anti-structure'. Journeying is said to bring the possibility of creating social and/or psychological transformation, even if only on a temporary basis, and here we see the adaptation of van Gennep's depiction of life as a series of transitions.

The conceptualization of Christian pilgrimage as an often voluntary, sometimes subversive (broadly 'liminoid') rite of passage implies a greater degree of flexibility than is evident in tribal societies. There is an initiatory quality to pilgrimage, but the Turners argue (1978: 3) that it may be about 'potentiality' as well as 'transition', providing a testing ground for new ideas, and moreover one that has 'something inveterately populist, anarchical, even anticlerical' about it (1978: 32). Not only does the pilgrim to a major site escape from the everyday, but he or she 'cuts across the boundaries of provinces, realms, and even empires' (1978: 6). Furthermore, '[i]t is true that the pilgrim returns to his former mundane existence, but it is commonly believed that he has made a spiritual step forward' (1978: 15). Interestingly, the Turners hint (1978: 10) at a distinction between 'the pilgrim's new-found freedom from mundane or profane structures' during the journey itself, and the increasingly circumscribed experience of the traveller approaching a sacred destination and therefore becoming subject to religious buildings, pictorial imagery, and so on. Yet, their attention is primarily focused on major shrines themselves – usually the mid-points in complex journeys of exit and return.[2] Indeed, they even admit that 'the stress has been on the communitas[3] of the pilgrimage center, rather than on the individual's penance on the journey' (1978: 39). One can therefore argue that the anti-structural quality of the argument in *Image and Pilgrimage* is nonetheless conventional in a singular and significant respect: its largely place-centred approach to the culture of sacred travel.

The present volume also examines major pilgrimage shrines but, in addition, it provides perspectives on various forms of motion – embodied, imagined, metaphorical – as constitutive elements of many pilgrimages. We examine both movement *to* and movement *at* sites (and sometimes *from* sites as well), and in certain cases trace the ways in which mobile performances can help to construct – however temporarily – apparently sacredly charged places (cf. Coleman and Crang 2002b). In adopting this approach, we present pilgrimages as 'kinetic rituals' but we also have a further purpose. Our shift towards movement is itself intended to move the study of pilgrimage away from certain aspects of conventional anthropological discourse on the subject.[4] Just as we broaden our ethnographic gaze to take in more than the central shrine, so we attempt to widen the theoretical location of studies of 'sacred travel'.

The Turnerian notion of pilgrimage as a liminoid phenomenon, which is productive of social encounters without hierarchical constraints, has of course proved immensely resonant. Yamba (1995: 9) notes that 'anthropologists who embark on the study of pilgrimage almost all start out debating with the pronouncements of Victor Turner, whose framework they invariably employ as a point of departure' (cf. Coleman 2002).[5] However, the paradigm has also run the risk of taking studies of pilgrimage down a theoretical cul-de-sac, both in its all-encompassing character and in its implication that such travel could somehow (or at least should ideally) be divorced from more everyday social, political and cultural processes.[6] More broadly, as Tremlett has recently pointed out (2003: 24), both Victor Turner and Mircea Eliade can be seen as 'romanticist' in their attempt to secure for religion an 'ineffable inner space or realm' that can stand as a critique of modernity and its values. Although the Turners argue that pilgrimages have sometimes been associated, for instance, with political uprisings, it is not made clear how the processual, set-apart character of the institution can feed into structural change. Morinis (1992b: 2) argues further that the view of pilgrimage as extraordinary has tended to remove it from academic purview: 'Anthropologists have tended to neglect pilgrimages because they were, by definition, exceptional practices, irregular journeys outside habitual social realms.'

Even when parallels have been perceived between pilgrimage and seemingly secular institutions, such as tourism (Graburn 1977) and popular youth culture (Myerhoff 1975), the comparison has all too frequently been with activities supposedly divorced from daily life. Thus, while Sallnow (1987: 9) commends the Turnerian paradigm for taking analysis beyond a sterile functionalism, he argues that its dialectic between structure and process has provided an inflexible analytical tool, according to which the relationship between pairs of dichotomized variables is seen as zero sum – the more of one, the less of the other.[7] As we shall see later, we need to question whether pilgrimage needs by definition to be seen as 'exceptional', and to ask whether a different approach can help the topic emerge from a theoretical ghetto that is still contained largely within the anthropology of religion.

The power of *Image and Pilgrimage* and related writings by Victor Turner (e.g. 1973, 1974a, 1974b) has been such that they have influenced scholarly discourse even when their central arguments have been rejected (cf. Messerschmidt and Sharma 1981). A theoretical agenda has indeed been constructed precisely out of the shattering of the Turnerian *Image*. Eade and Sallnow's edited volume *Contesting the Sacred* (1991a) directly opposes the *communitas* paradigm, focusing instead on the role of major shrines in hosting – and amplifying – discrepant discourses among varied groups of pilgrims, thus acting as 'empty vessels' that can reflect back visitors' objectified assumptions in sacralized form. Despite their disagreements, however, both the Turners and most of the contributors to *Contesting the Sacred* implicitly focus on place in making their arguments (cf. Morinis 1992b: 3). 'Vessels' may be empty but they also have borders, boundaries that divide them from the outside, and the ethnographers in Eade and Sallnow's iconoclastic volume usually come to rest on points of arrival and dwelling at specific major shrines: Lourdes, Jerusalem, San Giovanni Rotondo, and so on. The postmodern fragmentation presented by the volume thus retains at least something of a Malinowskian linkage between culture and place.[8] Of course, as our chapters will reveal, we are not denying the importance of place in ethnography. However, we do note that even when Eade and Sallnow present a more positive agenda for Christian pilgrimage, suggesting that it can perhaps be understood as comprising combinations of 'person', 'text' and 'place' (see Mitchell, Chapter 2 this volume), 'movement' is not present in this grouping of elements.

Metaphors of modernity

Recent studies of pilgrimage have noted the contrasts between the topic's relative neglect in past ethnographic writing and its current growth both as an activity and as an object of study (Morinis 1992: 2; Kaelber 2002; Swatos and Tomasi 2002). If pilgrimage formerly eluded researchers who preferred to take small-scale, fixed socio-cultural units as their prime objects of study (Morinis 1992b: 2), explanations of pilgrimage's new-found academic popularity can draw on precisely the same problematic. Just as the introduction of historical perspectives has disrupted the notion of the ethnographic present (cf. Fabian 1983), so the realization that mobility is endemic to many current processes of culture formation has begun to have a profound influence on social scientific notions of the field. Urry (2000: 132) summarizes the point succinctly (if with some hyperbole) when he argues that contemporary forms of dwelling almost always involve diverse forms of mobility, with clear impacts on relations between notions of belonging and travelling. He therefore opposes the Heideggerian suggestion that the only form of authentic dwelling is a pattern of life rooted in a particular earth and world. At the same time, he argues (2000: 50) that travel is no longer a metaphor of progress when it characterizes how 'households' are organized more generally. Similarly, Rapport and Dawson (1998c) explore the ways in which movement plays a key role in the 'modern' imagination, with even the idea of 'home' coming to refer to routine sets of practices, rather than fixed places.

Some analysts have, therefore, come to regard 'the pilgrim' (perceived generically) as emblematic of aspects of contemporary life.[9] Clifford (1997) suggests that pilgrimage is of particular use as a comparative term in contemporary ethnographic writing, since (despite its sacred associations) it includes a broad range of Western and non-Western experiences and is less class- and gender-based than the notion of 'travel'. His use of the term relates to a broader project of exploring how practices of displacement are not incidental to, but actually constitutive of, cultural meanings in a world that is constantly 'en route', made up not of autonomous socio-cultural wholes but complex, interactive conjunctures.[10]

Similarly, Bauman's sociological work on 'liquid modernity' argues (2000: 13–14) that the era of unconditional superiority of sedentarism over nomadism and the domination of the settled over the mobile is grinding to a halt. He invokes the role of the pilgrim to make general points about contemporary identity (presumably largely in 'the West'), but his use of the term takes it in a slightly different direction to that suggested by Clifford. For Bauman (1996: 19ff.), modernity has given the metaphorical figure of the pilgrim new prominence as it comes to signify a restless seeker for identity.[11] Thus, '[d]estination, the set purpose of life's pilgrimage, gives form to the formless, makes a whole out of the fragmentary, lends continuity to the episodic' (1996: 22). Bauman's aim is then to trace the move from pilgrim to tourist, from modernity to postmodernity, since if the modern problem of identity has been to construct an identity and to keep it stable, the postmodern challenge is how to avoid fixation and thus keep one's options open (1996: 18).

Bauman's model sometimes embodies the slippery fluidity that he describes. For much of the time, he fails to acknowledge the constraints imposed by structural inequalities upon certain categories of people in the contemporary world. Asylum seekers and refugees do not enjoy the same freedom to move and to consume as wealthy tourists and cosmopolitan elites (see Massey 1994), although, as Rosander shows in this volume, we need to avoid patronizing assumptions that migrant workers cannot by definition be involved in the transnational flows of goods, information and image (cf. Appadurai 1993; Gardner 1995; Vertovec and Cohen 1999; Portes 2001).

For present purposes, the relevant aspect of Bauman's argument, in common with that of Clifford, is the assertion that 'pilgrimage' provides an analytical and metaphorical means to conceptualize the constant change that is assumed to be (variously) inherent within modernity and postmodernity. To what extent, however, might their writings actually be useful for the comparative study of pilgrimage as a religious institution? We can perhaps start with the arguments against the utility of their perspectives. In a book such as this, constituted by ethnographically based case studies of the type absent in many of Bauman's recent writings, we prefer to avoid assertions as to the nature of ideal-typical (yet rather Western, Christian-looking) 'pilgrims'.

We do not, therefore, claim that pilgrimage can be brandished as an all-purpose metaphor for 'our times'. If, as Bowman has argued (1985: 3; cf. Eade 2000: xii), the Turnerian model of pilgrimage separated interpretation from the constraints of history and society, almost the same might be said of the idea of 'the pilgrim' as archetypal seeker. We are more interested in the fact that certain forms of travel, labelled pilgrimages (or the rough equivalent) by their participants, appear to be flourishing in many parts of the world. Such journeys undoubtedly benefit from improvements in communications technology that are available to many people, but they also prompt further investigation into the specific cultural, social and economic dimensions of these examples of contemporary travel. For social scientists they raise key questions concerning informants' views and constructions of locality, landscape, mobility, space, place, the national and the transnational. In characterizing our comparative project in this way, we are not attempting to set up rigid analytical definitions. This is not to say, however, that some basic questions cannot be asked of data in order to establish the basic dimensions of the forms of travel being examined. Can they be characterized as broadly voluntary or coerced? As temporary or longer term? As local or more expansive, even transnational? As repeated or one-off? As formally marked by ritual or informal, or perhaps a mixture of both? And how are they labelled by those who undertake them – not least, how are they perceived in relation to other activities?

Finding answers to such questions requires close examination of what Urry (2000: 49) calls the 'socio-spatial practices' involved in instances of mobility. While he agrees with Clifford and Bauman that mobilities, as both metaphor and process, are at the heart of social life and thus should be central to sociological analysis, he also attempts to differentiate between forms of travel. Thus over and above communication by phone, letter and fax, he distinguishes between the physical movement of objects, imaginative travel, virtual (e.g. internet) travel and the corporeal travel of people (2002: 256). The overall point is that in contexts where so many ways of being 'on the move' are available, it becomes important to examine the complex and interwoven forms of distance and proximity inherent in many social situations: 'One should investigate not only physical and immediate presence, but also the socialities involved in occasional co-presence, imagined co-presence and virtual co-presence' (2002: 256). In many situations, intense corporeal co-presence is balanced with patterns of social life based on time–space distanciation, and Urry therefore refers to 'the globalization of intermittent co-presence' (2002: 264), as small social worlds are periodically reconstituted of those who otherwise live in geographically dispersed locations. As we shall see, some pilgrimages have the potential to provide excellent examples of such 'intermittent co-presence'.

Despite these arguments for the particularization of research into forms of movement, there are two aspects of Clifford's and Bauman's pilgrimage metaphors that are more useful for our purposes. First, the assumption that both mobility and change are chronic – or at least not unusual – conditions of many people's lives goes some way towards challenging dichotomies (evident in *Image and Pilgrimage*) between structure and process. And a corollary of the first point is that, when mobility can be regarded as mundane, pilgrimage – as either metaphor or institution – is less likely to be seen as rigidly exceptional or set apart from society. Let us therefore examine a little more closely some of the ways concepts of movement have been applied to pilgrimage.

Pilgrimage in the frame

Although 'movement' has rarely been a major focus in previous studies of pilgrimage, when it has been discussed people have adopted quite different perspectives. From the standpoint of cultural geography, for example, Bhardwaj's well-known study of *Hindu Places of Pilgrimage in India* argues that '[p]ilgrim "flows" are the connecting links between the Hindu population and its numerous sacred centres' (1973: 7). Indeed, the book is dedicated '[t]o the countless dedicated pilgrims whose footprints have given meaning to India as a cultural entity'. The work, therefore, provides an example of a functional analysis of pilgrimage: journeys of pilgrims, often across great distances, are said to help create a 'pan-Indian Hindu holy space' (1973: 173).

Bhardwaj is primarily concerned with the religious and geographical integration that may be a result of pilgrimage (cf. Wolf 1958). However, other social scientific approaches have focused on complex issues of meaning, attempting to locate pilgrimage within broader semantic fields related to journeying. Eickelman and Piscatori (1990b) look at the general category of 'Muslim Travelers', and juxtapose the *hajj* (main pilgrimage to Mecca) with *hijra* (emigration), *rihla* (travel for learning and other purposes) and *ziyara* (visits to shrines). Their approach helps to challenge the representation of pilgrimage as 'exceptional' practice, not only because they argue that motives for travel can be mixed, but also because they note how not just the sacred, but also the economic geography of Muslim travel can prompt deeply felt convictions. Thus '[t]he need to travel to saintly shrines or . . . the need of Turkish workers in Europe to travel back to Turkey, may be as compelling as the doctrinally enjoined pilgrimage to Mecca and Medina' (1990b: xiv). Similar nuances are evident in Tapper's contribution to the same volume, where she examines connections between gender, movement and exchange in a Turkish community. Tapper shows (1990: 236–7) how, in the broadest sense, *ziyaret* can be seen as voluntary movement for the purpose of paying respect to a person or shrine, whose authority is thereby acknowledged. As a term and a practice, it derives meaning not only from assumptions about the comparative mobility of women and men, but also from its place within a broader set of categories of movement, some of which have religious connotations (such as the *hajj*) while others are more secular (going for a stroll, and so on).

Travel, pilgrimage and tourism

Socially informed examination of the history of travel has also tended to
emphasize the need to understand pilgrimage in the context of other,
roughly parallel activities, and this has sometimes blurred the boundaries
between genres of mobility. Thus Erik Cohen,[12] one of the pioneers of
the anthropology of tourism, notes that there is no homogeneous tourist
type and develops a continuum where 'existential tourists' resemble
many pilgrims in the seriousness of their journey and the search for local
'authenticity' (see Cohen 1988 and cf. Meethan 2000: 93; also see
discussion of Cohen in Schramm, Chapter 7 this volume). Admittedly,
while acknowledging the pilgrim-tourist hybrid, Cohen argues for an
important difference:

> Pilgrimage and tourism differ in terms of the direction of the journey
> undertaken . . . [T]he pilgrim, and the 'pilgrim-tourist' peregrinate
> *toward* their sociocultural center, while the traveler and the 'traveler-
> tourist' move in the opposite direction.
>
> (1992: 37; italics in original)

He immediately qualifies this distinction, however, by claiming that it
applies to 'journeys to formal pilgrimage centers' as opposed to popular
pilgrimage centres, which are 'often marked by a mixture of features
characteristic of both pilgrimage and tourism' (1992: 37).

Adler's survey of 'travel as performed art' is sceptical of ambitiously
universalizing typologies that have purported to distinguish tourism
neatly from pilgrimage and also warns against scholarly narratives
suggesting unilinear temporal sequencing of travel styles.[13] She notes
that:

> The history of travel (like that of other arts) is best seen as a history
> of coexisting and competitive, as well as blossoming, declining, and
> recurring, styles whose temporal boundaries inevitably blur. When
> Goethe made his Italian journey of 1786, traveling in a manner that
> broke with many of the conventions of the *Kavaliers Tour,* he still
> found pilgrims on the road to Venice bearing the centuries-old
> insignia of scallop-shell and pilgrim's hat. Some hallmarks of an
> essentially medieval travel style were still intact at the end of the
> 18th century.
>
> (1989: 1372)

Adler argues further that any given travel style can build on earlier traditions, and gives (1989: 1373) the examples of Grand Tourists visiting Rome during the eighteenth century who carried on much of the programme established by pre-Renaissance pilgrimage, as well as the seventeenth-century English travellers to Italy who wrote with considerable scepticism about the wonder-working religious relics they were shown by their guides, but who took the road to Loreto and other pilgrim shrines with striking frequency.

In a later work, she brings supposedly sacred and secular forms of journey together under a single analytical rubric:

> The broad theoretical concern shared by those who hope to understand modern forms of travel glossed as 'tourism', as well as modern and earlier styles of travel glossed as 'religious', is with human *mobility*, deliberately shaped for expressive and communicative, rather than simply instrumental, purposes.
>
> (2002: 26)

Adler again brings the past and the present together in this work, arguing that examination of early Christian pilgrimage reveals a world whose discourses about movement bear some striking similarities to contemporary debates about tourism, relating to such issues as the moral contamination of host populations, struggles over markets, association of travel with sensual licence and the relative valorization of some places over others (2002: 27). Thus: '[a]bove all I discovered a cosmopolitan culture in which freely undertaken geographical mobility, valued as an end in itself, was endowed with rich symbolic significance' (2002: 27).

There is obviously considerable risk of historical anachronism here, and we can hardly conflate past and present attitudes to travel, explicitly sacred or otherwise. Despite Adler's remarks, there is still something to be said for identifying broad shifts in attitudes to travel over the *longue durée*. Tomasi (2002), for instance, traces the relative decline in penitential discourse within pilgrimage since the medieval period in Europe, and the increased emphasis on transformations in the self – a shift that perhaps prompts more emphasis on the experience of the journey itself than on the destination. Urry (2000: 51) also points to changing attitudes to mobility itself by stating that, before the late eighteenth century in Europe, walkers were generally seen as the dangerous 'other'. Nevertheless, Adler's approach is useful in its attempt – parallel to that of Eickelman, Piscatori and Tapper – to locate pilgrimage within wider semantic and theoretical discourses relating to mobility.

In this sense, and also in her insistence on the juxtaposition of different journeying 'styles' even on the same path, Adler provides a sociological counterpart to Frey's (1998) more strictly ethnographic account of contemporary travellers to Santiago de Compostela. Frey traces the constellation of interests that have converged in the reanimation of the pilgrimage in the past few decades, including the promotion of National Catholicism under Franco, the promptings of the Church itself, the sponsorship of New Age adherents inspired by the writings of Paulo Coelho and even the participation of long-distance hikers and cyclists, who are taking advantage of the ease of travel now available within the European Union. Certain aspects of Frey's account are striking in relation to a purely shrine-centred model of pilgrimage. First, there is her observation that distinctions between religious and non-religious travellers are not very significant to the people she encountered on the pilgrimage;[14] second, the fact that what appears to be significant to many of her informants is less the aim of reaching a specific sacred place and more the mode of travel adopted, since journeying on foot or on bicycle is valued far above car driving. Not only is walking a form of self-sacrifice involving endurance and austerity, it also allows 'pilgrims' to discover a sense of contact with the past. Many of the people whom Frey meets – often urban, educated, Western and middle class, but not necessarily Roman Catholic – are seeking to engage in bodily and temporal modes that subvert or transcend the rushing, mechanized world of modernity and postmodernity. They are choosing to move, but in a way that emphasizes a slowing down rather than a speeding up of life.

Frey's book thus becomes a genuine 'road ethnography', as she follows pilgrims through France and Spain along the Camino, the ancient and mostly rural network of pilgrim routes that stretches across Europe, and then tracks them in their homes around Europe and elsewhere (therefore incorporating the return as well as the original journey outward). Though anthropological in approach, her book is characterized by its own highly significant void: Compostela itself is a largely empty vessel in the text, though not exactly in the way described by Eade and Sallnow (1991b). Frey describes arrival at the place, but the shrine's occupancy of her text is precarious to say the least – and for Frey arrival is anticlimactic.

Intriguingly, Frey's juxtaposition of a detailed, phenomenological account of journeying with a lack of extended description of the destination parallels a much earlier attempt at road ethnography, Irawati Karve's description (1962) of participating in a Maharashtrian pilgrimage that involves the transportation of the image of Saint Dnyaneshwar from

Alandi to Pandharpur. Karve's piece – half autobiographical diary, half sociological analysis – actually ends with the words: 'I stepped inside the gates of Pandharpur with streaming eyes, weary legs, and a heavy heart' (1962: 29). In both the Spanish and the Indian cases, it seems that the intense experience of the journey almost blocks out interest in the destination, and renders overtly analytical (and necessarily distancing) techniques of writing problematic.[15]

These accounts locate their ethnography within shifting landscapes – in Frey's case, the landscapes actually cross national borders – and a similar concern is evident in Sallnow's *Pilgrims of the Andes* (1987), which examines the mobilization of people, icons and resources around holy sites in Cusco. Sallnow provides a detailed account of a group pilgrimage that is also a kinesthetic mapping of space. Thus '[b]y physically traversing the landscape, an individuated local community . . . inserts itself into a variegated macrocosmic domain, defined by collectively recognized sacred places, of greater or lesser magnitude, where theophanies are known to have occurred' (1987: 184). Furthermore, we see how the style of movement has symbolic significance:

> When dancers escort the icon to or from its place of repose, they are enclosing it within a tightly ordered, mobile ritual frame that is synoptic of the entire pilgrimage. Though actual dance is confined to these critical junctures, dance music is practically continuous throughout the journey. The ritual passage is pervaded by melody and rhythm: the pilgrimage, in a sense, is not so much walked as danced.
>
> (1987: 201)

Sallnow's coverage of the entire trip (as opposed to just the journey to the shrine) provides a broader perspective than is usually implied in the introduction to *Contesting the Sacred*. In addition, it reveals the ways in which movement can vary with directionality during the same pilgrimage. Setting off, Sallnow's companions are tense and focused on their goal; coming back, they are far less disciplined, so that the mode of journeying outward and the return are contrasted as ritualism to release, restraint to licence (here, there are indeed parallels with rites of passage). The fact that Sallnow places so much of his ethnographic focus on the 'sending' village means also that he can assess the effects of the journey on both its participants and those who are left behind, recording its impacts on kinship, neighbourhood and cycles of production as well as on the complex political dynamics of who is chosen to play key leadership roles in the journey. The result is a text that shows how pilgrimage can indeed provide a release from the everyday, but is also a recurring event, building up local memories and putting down strong roots in local networks of cooperation and competition. In this context, pilgrimage emerges as deeply embedded in peasant life, rather than as an isolated social phenomenon.

Sallnow's analysis resonates, therefore (at least in certain respects), with a critique of the Turnerian paradigm that is less often voiced than those centring around the sociological impossibility of *communitas*, but which still has validity. Morris (2002: 6) points out that many of the journeys carried out by medieval English pilgrims did not take them far from their normal contexts, since most involved a few days' travel at most. For instance, he notes that over half of the pilgrim badges recovered from a deposit in King's Lynn came from nearby Walsingham in north Norfolk. In the same volume, Duffy (2002: 165) argues that the single most important energy in late medieval English practice was its drive to localism: for many pilgrims of the time, going on pilgrimage was less like launching on a journey to the ends of the earth and more like going to the local market. Shrines mapped the familiar as much as they were signposts to the other world. Of course, as in the Peruvian case, what is being described here is relatively domestic pilgrimage, as opposed to the journeys to major shrines described by the Turners, and so we might perhaps expect there to be less opportunity to cultivate a sense of anti-structure. It might also be argued that journeys to far distant shrines are now much easier than they were in medieval England. Yet, the point remains that the Turnerian paradigm tends to assume that pilgrimage involves a distant, one-off journey rather than a more routine, regularized activity. Even in contemporary ethnographies of well-known sites, examples of localized pilgrimage can easily be found. Describing an island shrine in Greece, Dubisch notes that '[i]t is clear that pilgrims to Tinos (and to other shrines in Greece) do not sever, even temporarily, their social bonds, or leave behind the social networks that enmesh them in everyday life' (1995: 95).

'Sacred' journeys

Perhaps the most programmatic approach to analysing forms of mobility within pilgrimage is contained in Morinis's (1992b) introduction to an edited volume of essays. He starts by highlighting the immense problems in defining 'the sacred' in the wake of Durkheim's global use of the term, but concludes that '[i]t is the pursuit of the ideal, whether deified or not, that defines the sacred journey' (1992b: 2). Defining the notion of journey is equally problematic, of course, and Morinis points out that indigenous categories can merge geographical and non-geographical aspects of sacred journeying. Thus we learn that Hindu mystics and some Sufis have developed a concept of the inner pilgrimage by which the person visits sacred places within the microcosm of the mind and body. This concept provides what in Western terms appears to be a metaphorical sense of the journey, though one that is rather different to the generic analytical approaches suggested by Clifford and Bauman. Even the idea of the shrine can have its own problems of translation into English categories, as Morinis – a specialist in Indian religion – urges the reader to:

> [c]ompare the Hindu *tirtha* (sacred ford, or place of pilgrimage), which can be applied to the shrine at the end of a sacred journey, but as well to a devoted wife, a spiritual preceptor, one's parents, and virtues such as truth and honesty.
>
> (1992b: 3)

We see here that to gain an understanding of any given journey we might well need to consult a number of possible semantic fields, and not merely (as argued above) those associated with movement. Morinis therefore asserts that the analytical reduction of pilgrimages to another ritual of simpler structure, the rite of passage, cannot do justice to the complexity and diversity of the assemblages of meaning and action that constitute the phenomenon, just as strict boundaries between pilgrimages and other forms of cultural journeying cannot easily be demarcated (1992b: 8–9).

Despite these cautions concerning reductionism, Morinis does identify 'movement' as key to understanding pilgrimage. Indeed, he claims of pilgrimage that 'the term can be put to use wherever journeying and some embodiment of an ideal intersect' (1992b: 3) and that 'the essence of the journey is movement' (1992b: 12). Patterns of the overall journey may vary – sometimes taking the pilgrim from home to shrine and back, sometimes tracing more spiral or irregular movements – just as differing modes of locomotion may be adopted at various points, including crawling, dancing, and so on.[16] By a logic of opposites, the symbolic meaning of much movement may be informed by and juxtaposed with cultural representations of its opposite, stasis, and so for Morinis a good part of the meaning of sacred journeys is uncovered in culturally sensitive analysis of this central opposition:

Whether the god travels or remains fixed or the pilgrim journeys to or with the deity are important questions of symbolism at the foundation of meaning for the pilgrimage performance. Pilgrimage is woven out of the structural opposition of stasis/movement, in whatever diversity this theme might be depicted.

(1992: 16)

In the light of this comment, we might view the Turnerian opposition of structure to anti-structure/process as consisting of a contrast between fixity and fluidity that is powerful both symbolically and in rhetorical terms, even if it fails to take into account the much more complex and mutually enmeshed relations between continuity and transformation, home and homelessness, so-called 'everyday life' and sacred travel. We might also invoke theoretical perspectives from a related but different area, that of studies of globalization. Meyer and Geschiere (1999) have recently referred to the precarious balance in such contexts between 'global flows' and 'cultural closure'. Thus '[t]here is much empirical evidence that people's awareness of being involved in open-ended global flows seems to trigger a search for fixed orientation points and action frames, as well as determined efforts to affirm old and construct new boundaries' (1999: 2). Meyer and Geschiere's edited volume covers such topics as nationalism, commoditization and ethnicity, but their point about seeking fixity echoes Bauman's point about the search for identity, without attempting to construct an ideal type of the generic seeker. Rather, their point is explored and modulated through case studies that indicate the cultural specificities, entanglements and ambiguities of flows and boundaries.

When applied to pilgrimage, as we shall see, this theoretical apparatus can suggest that many pilgrim sites, rather than being contexts for the cultivation of anti-structure, can provide arenas for the rhetorical, ideologically charged assertion of apparent continuity, even fixity, in religious and wider social identities. As Swatos notes in his reflections on pilgrimage (2002: 120), processes of globalization can stimulate the rediscovery of different kinds of particularism and localism. Similarly, we might argue that the rhetorical construction of ideologies of localism in pilgrimage discourses may act in opposition to the seeming globalization promoted by the 'non-places' of super-modernity (Augé 1995).

Re-framing pilgrimage: linking different understandings of movement

These perspectives on movement clearly do not yet add up to a discrete analytical debate, in contrast to the ways in which *communitas* and contestation have often been explicitly juxtaposed in pilgrimage studies. Instead, we can discern a number of different, though not necessarily mutually exclusive, understandings of the topic, which can be summarized as follows:

1   *Movement as performative action.* By this, we mean the sense that movement can effect (not always consciously) certain social and cultural transformations. Bhardwaj explores the idea of movement as integrative in creating a pan-Hindu sacred space; Sallnow is less functionalist in orientation but sees Peruvian pilgrimage as involving the kinetic mapping of space (compare Schramm, Dubisch, Nikolaisen, this volume). More generally, we see resonances here with Urry's deployment (2000: 53) of de Certeau's notion that walking can be constitutive of social space in the way that speech acts constitute language.

2   *Movement as embodied action.* The phenomenology of Karve and Frey, as well as Sallnow's ethnography, indicate the importance of seeing pilgrimage as providing the catalyst for certain kinds of bodily experiences (see especially Dubisch, Mitchell, Nikolaisen, Coleman, this volume). And, as Urry points out (2002), corporeal co-presence as well as corporeal testing – putting the body through its paces – may sometimes explicitly be valorized.

3   *Movement as part of a semantic field.* This refers to the need to contextualize the meaning of 'pilgrimage' within local cultural understandings of mobility (Eickelman and Piscatori, Tapper, Adler) or such terms as space, place and landscape. In addition, a given style of mobility may take on particularly charged meaning as a marker of difference (just as the label 'pilgrim' may be adopted in rhetorical contradistinction to that of 'tourist'). Frey's pilgrims ideally walk rather than drive, accumulating cultural capital that can be glossed as either sacred or secular; Sallnow's companions dance within, but also to some extent across, the landscape. We shall see in virtually all of our chapters how the movement involved in pilgrimage may invoke, play on, appropriate, domesticate, sometimes even negate another form of journeying, such as tourism or migration. The broader point is of course that we must avoid essentializing movement as a category (Rapport and Dawson 1998c: 23).

4   *Movement as metaphor*. Here, we refer less to Bauman and Clifford and more to the ways in which pilgrimage-related discourses may evoke movement rather than require its physical instanciation. Morinis referred to the concepts of the inner pilgrimage and 'life as a journey' cultivated by Hindu mystics and Sufis. Examples taken from other religious traditions might include the notion of pilgrimage as a metaphor for the journey of the Christian soul (Morris 2002: 2) or even Bawa Yamba's striking discussion of West African Muslims based in the Sudan (also discussed by Rosander), who do not move as such, yet regard themselves as being in transit to Mecca, thus perpetuating 'an ideology of pilgrim-ness' (1995: 120).

Is there any connecting thread that might link these dimensions of mobility? One is that we see both informants and ethnographers coming to regard movement as a marked activity: it becomes an object of attention and reflexivity, and is transformed from a largely taken for granted physiological act into a cultural performance (Morinis 1992a). Much of this book is precisely concerned with such processes of translation, within a framework that seeks to understand actors' own models of pilgrimage or sacralized travel but does not assume that such marked travel is, by definition, divorced from other aspects of social,[17] cultural or indeed religious life.

If pilgrimage can be seen as involving the institutionalization (or even domestication) of mobility in physical, metaphorical and/or ideological terms, such a focus can be located on various levels. Within the macro-context of the political economy of travel and the globalization of (religious) cultures, dynamic interplays between transnational, national and regional processes may be evident. Theorizing around themes of mobility and movement can also be located within – and integrated with – micro-level examinations of the embodied motion inherent within pilgrimage practices, combined with analyses of the sacred geographies and architectures that provide the material and symbolic background to such motion. In such cases, the focus on pilgrimage as ritual and performance is to the fore, with it involving sometimes unpredictable encounters between liturgical forms, personal imagination and memory translated into acts of the body.

We confess that the notion of a 'frame', invoked in the title of this book, is a rather static metaphor for describing a phenomenon that can be so fluid. Our aim is not to force pilgrimage into a Procrustean category of our particular devising, but to view examples of the phenomenon from one perspective. We are certainly not arguing that a 'movement frame' is the only means of encapsulating pilgrimage: there are many other ways to examine sacred travel in relation to wider social theory – involving, for instance, consumption and material culture studies (McDannell 1995), popular culture (Reader and Walter 1993), postmodern contestation of symbols (Eade and Sallnow 1991b), exchange (Tapper 1990), the gendering of spatial practices (Dubisch 1995; Morrison 2000) and the notion of anthropology itself as a pilgrimage (Dubisch 1995). If pilgrimage is to be brought back into the analytical mainstream, there are many paths for us to trace.

Pilgrimage and 'meta-movement'

Both the Turners (1978) and Eade and Sallnow (1991b) focused on Christian pilgrimage. In putting together this volume, however, we decided not to restrict ourselves to any particular region or religion. Our aim is more to explore the interfaces between forms and representations of mobility within diverse cultural and religious contexts. Of course, one obvious connecting theme is that each case study involves diverse processes of sacralization of movement, persons and/or places. We prefer the verb 'sacralize' to the noun 'sacred' since we wish to emphasize the often partial, performative, contested character of appropriating something or someone as 'holy'.[18] In addition, each contribution explores dimensions of what we call here 'meta-movement' – the combination of mobility itself with a degree of reflexivity as to its meaning, form and function. Thus, not only do many of our authors explore movement within movement – particular styles or episodes of motion within the broader framework of a journey – they also show how pilgrimage can provide opportunities to reflect upon, re-embody, sometimes even retrospectively transform, past journeys. We therefore examine journeys that are about journeys, and which in the process often turn history into both myth and ritual.

Hildi Mitchell examines British Mormons who visit 'Mormon country', the sacred American homeland of the religion and a landscape that many of them will never have visited previously. Although the focus of the piece is not directly on movement *per se*, its central argument makes a vital point concerning the relationship between everyday religious activity and that of pilgrimage. Mitchell shows how Mormon travellers' experiences of religio-historical sites are deeply informed by physically embedded memories taken from other Mormon situations. Before they make their journey, members have already been taught how to relate to the material objects and sacred articles of historically important sites in the 'correct' Mormon manner. Engagements with museum artifacts echo more obviously ritualized interactions with such objects as the *Book of Mormon* and temples.

Pilgrimage becomes, therefore, one of a number of techniques through which Mormon theology and cosmology are experienced through practice rather than disembodied belief. However, the experience of travel is also converted into testimonies that are a vital part of the common currency of Mormon identity and commitment. Being there – having made the journey in order to be physically present – is both a sign and a reinforcement of commitment, and the effects of travel continue in narratives recounted on return to the UK. Towards the end of her piece, Mitchell provides a striking example of the power of the Mormon disposition when she contrasts her cynical view of a Mormon film with the deeply engaged response of 'pilgrims'. We also note that the film she mentions depicts a journey, which involves the tribulations of Joseph Smith and his followers in the early days of the faith. An important part of her informant's trip is, itself, a reflection on the meaning of movement for the foundation of the faith.

Simon Coleman's chapter also examines engagement with landscapes of broadly Christian history by juxtaposing two radically contrasting styles of pilgrimage, based on diverse sub-cultural assumptions concerning the interactions among persons, places and movements. Many Anglo- and Roman Catholic visitors to Walsingham ('England's Nazareth') see themselves as recalling the past in their measured movements along liturgically charged pathways. Contemporary pilgrimage for these Christians is a mimetic act, bringing tradition and personal memory into the present, just as the biblical landscape is translated through ritual performance to a remote part of rural England. Catholic journeys therefore partake of self-consciously sacramentalized articulations of the body and its motion. Swedish charismatics, by contrast, are engaged in explicitly globalizing and commoditized forms of mobility that valorize speed and effacement of history, and express a horror of stasis. Missionizing pilgrimages to Jerusalem become a means not only of appropriating the 'real' Holy Land, but also of taking charge of the future (in the form of a hastening of the Second Coming) through a kinesthetic appropriation of landscape. They also belong to a wider range of charismatic activities that cultivate the sacralized travel of people, objects and images.

If our first two case studies involve examining variations on Christianity, the next two invoke different dimensions of Sufism. Eva

Evers Rosander examines Senegalese women who are members of the Islamic Sufi order of *El Mouridiyya*, and traces their movements in both Senegal and the diaspora (the Spanish island of Tenerife). In line with Eickelman and Piscatori's (1990b) exploration of the semantics of travel, she shows that travel is an integrated part of Mouridism in ideology and practice, and one that invokes overlapping meanings connected with such themes as hard work, financial dealings, the *hajj*, exile, exodus and death. Furthermore, Mouridism itself is connected globally through religious, economic, social and political networks. Women who remain in the homeland organize journeys to pilgrimage sites, which both provide annual breaks and contribute to their moral capital. The situation for migrants, however, is more complex. Women who move to work in a non-Muslim country risk exposure to slander and loss of respectability, but at the same time diasporic Mouridism offers such people a key moral space that is activated through forms of mobility. Money – associated metonymically with the self – acts as a core link between diaspora and homeland, as it is sent home by migrant traders to support family and religious causes. While migrants cannot usually afford to go on annual pilgrimages to Senegal (and lack the visas to do so), their donations can contribute to forms of pilgrimage by proxy. Rosander therefore shows how pilgrimage can entail physical immobility in combination with movement, cultivated by the religious imagination and realized through the transportation of objects. In the process, apparently secular networks of trade take on sacralized dimensions.

Nikolaisen also investigates the interactions among a Sufi order, a homeland and diasporic activity, but her focus is on Mevlevi dervishes and masculine forms of motion. Central to Mevlevi teaching and cosmology are notions of *turning* movements (involving the performance of *sema* – the whirling dance – to reach unity with God), as well as *returning* movements (performing pilgrimages and journeying to and from new worlds). Sacred travel inland and abroad to perform *sema* has been a major activity among Mevlevi dervishes from Istanbul since the 1950s, partly prompted by the ban on Sufi orders which has been in force since 1925 and which has restricted possibilities for this type of religious activity within Turkey itself. Alongside such reconfigured mobility there has developed an increased focus on the performance of the ritual to international publics. In describing Mevlevi organization and disciplining of spaces considered appropriate for the performance of *sema*, Nikolaisen also discusses the way in which embodied knowledge is used to transform secular space into ritual space, creating a form of temporary home in relation to a ritual *habitus*. As in the case of Senegalese migrants, the anonymity of transnational space is being domesticated, and forms of mobility deployed to redefine the self in relation to changing economic and political circumstances.

Jill Dubisch takes us out of the realm of explicit religion, but she describes a journey that is claimed by many of its participants to be a pilgrimage. We follow Vietnam veterans and their supporters as they ride their motorcycles across the United States from California to Washington, DC, in an annual Memorial Day pilgrimage known as the Run for the Wall. Their destination is one of America's most prominent shrines, the Vietnam Veterans Memorial ('The Wall'). Unlike many pilgrims, however, the riders are not greeted at the end of their journey by enthusiastic hosts – such receptions are more likely at points along the route – and so it is during the journey itself that the Vets receive the 'welcome home' they feel was never granted them (or indeed the dead) as they returned immediately after the war itself. The pilgrimage thus recasts the warrior as hero, instead of the ignored or despised participant in an unpopular conflict. Journeying is redefined on a number of levels: 'We're not tourists, we're pilgrims' is a claim that indicates the seriousness of the trip, and one that helps to convert two marginal roles – of biker and Vietnam War veteran – into more central figures in a reclaimed American imaginary. While this journey is voluntary and based within the USA, it evokes some of the trauma and contradictions surrounding a less willingly undertaken trip to a foreign land.

The form of movement is clearly important, as well. Motorcycling creates a visceral connection with machine and landscape, and while it plays on core American values of independence and self-reliance it also permits a swift and collective reclaiming of the homeland – a performative construction of place through movement that we also see, for instance, in the chapters by Coleman and Nikolaisen. In common with the Mevlevis, a sense of frustration with attitudes at home is proving a catalyst for a journey that attempts to create a favourably disposed audience. Admittedly, as Dubisch points out, this is a case study that, unlike many of the other examples in this volume, is more rooted in national than transnational networks of connection. However, the Vietnam War itself was an expression of global power-broking, while the run is beginning to show signs of its own forms of transnationalism, with Australian, Canadian and Irish veterans becoming involved.

Schramm's piece again deals with the expression of US identity in relation to the remaking of a homeland, but in her case the pilgrims are black Americans seeking connections with Ghana as a site of past slavery and present heritage. As in Rosander's case, we see the emergence and confirmation of a diasporic identity wherein economic flows and emotional investments reinforce each other, and similar complexity is involved in Schramm's conclusion that she is observing 'pilgrim tourism' – a form of pilgrimage that is incorporated into a tourism infrastructure. In promoting this kind of trip, the Ghanaian state brings two issues to the forefront. First, within the framework of African American discourse of homecoming, slave-sites are portrayed as sacred grounds and the voyage of African descendants back to the 'motherland' is conceptualized as a sacred journey within the ideological context of Pan-Africanism. Second, these sites are clearly identified as major tourist attractions. Thus, in the process of commemoration of the slave experience, the sacred is staged on a tourism platform. Schramm describes the choreographic mapping of 'slave stations' of the route – involving for the pilgrim something of a dialectic between observing and becoming a spectacle – and emphasizes a key link between motion and emotion, movement and engagement, for many of the visitors.

This case study parallels the one developed by Dubisch in encapsulating a journey that is constructed as a means of dealing with unfinished historical business and evolves from one-off occasion into recurring event. The visit to Ghana evokes not a past war but a traumatic ripping of Africans from their homeland, and (as we see in Mitchell's and Coleman's examples) travel involves getting literally and metaphorically in touch with a history that is also a physical enactment of perceived origins.

The volume concludes with Paul Basu's powerful exploration of route metaphors and the quest for 'roots' by heritage tourists in the Scottish Highlands. Like the African Americans encountered by Schramm, these tourists come from a diaspora and return 'home' to get in touch with traces of their past. Their nostalgic journeys are suffused with the same intense emotions that Schramm describes, and again we see the strong feelings of expulsion and exile, even if this attitude conveniently glosses over the ambiguities of Scottish involvement in colonial expansion. Academics may be correct to doubt the objective reality of the past that these 'exiles' hungrily devour (cf. Rapport and Dawson 1998c). However, such objectivity fails to appreciate the subjective reality of the myths, which provides these exiles a degree of ontological security in the whirl of contemporary local/ global change. These travellers want to reassert the ties of blood and territory rather than celebrate their freedom from fixity and roots. Homecoming, quest and pilgrimage serve as the three 'route metaphors' that ground them in a mobile world and differentiate them from other, pleasure-seeking tourists.

Basu journeys far and wide in disciplinary terms to analyse what he has observed. He begins with Victor Turner, drawing on *Dramas, Fields and Metaphors* (1974c) rather than *Image and Pilgrimage* (1978) and to the 'appropriateness and potential fruitfulness' of root metaphors rather than *communitas*. He draws on other major anthropological influences (Barthes, Clifford, Morinis, Ray and Strathern, for example), but trawls sociology through the work of Nisbet, and Smith, the classic text by Berger, Berger and Kellner, *The Homeless Mind* (1973), and Giddens' more recent explorations, as well as philosophy (MacIntyre), medieval history (Locke) and psychology (MacAdams and Maslow). This wide-ranging exploration is intended to uncover the ways in which metaphor enables us to look beyond the language of words to understand other languages associated with objects, landscapes and practices and how such languages are articulated in 'roots-tourism'. These diasporic tourists draw on the metaphors of homecoming, quest and pilgrimage to generate 'a composite grammar' and to develop 'a repertoire of appropriate actions and attitudes for their journeys . . . and their vague, incommunicable longing is thus given form'.

Basu draws on both structuralist and postmodern perspectives and indicates the limitations of the postmodern celebration of hybridity and movement for an emic understanding of the tourists he encountered in the Scottish Highlands. His approach is in the spirit of this volume where we bring together diverse forms of movement across territorial and ideological boundaries and engage with people who identify themselves with such multiple embodied, imagined and metaphorical places as homes and sacred sites. 'Cultures in motion' are the focus of our desire to offer a reframing of pilgrimage studies in the knowledge that our desire to know can only move the discussion so far. The frame does not constitute a panoptic box within which all knowledge about pilgrimage can be gazed at by the professional observer. We are engaged in an analytical journey without end.

Notes

1 We need also to be aware of the textual justifications for movement in pilgrimage. For instance, in Christianity, see the Old Testament model of Israelites spending 40 years in the wilderness, Christ's wandering and the journey to Emmaus (Coleman and Elsner 2003).

2 There are, of course, parts of their text where they do refer explicitly to mobility. Thus (1978: 22–3) they briefly refer to the ways in which way

stations intensify the pilgrim's approach to the shrine; and their description of St Patrick's Purgatory in Lough Derg describes movement at the island itself.

3   The Turners' term of 'social antistructure', or '[a] relational quality of full unmediated communication, even communion . . . which arises spontaneously in all kinds of groups' (1978: 250).

4   Although this introduction will cover some of the literature on pilgrimage, we do not aim to be all-encompassing. For critical summaries of the anthropology of pilgrimage, see Morinis (1984), Eade (2000), Coleman (2002).

5   Of course, we are doing the same but the point is that our agenda is not primarily constructed around either defending or deconstructing the notion of *communitas*.

6   One can also argue, as Chapters 2 and 3 in this book reveal (Mitchell, Coleman), that the Turnerian paradigm misleadingly sets pilgrimage apart from more 'everyday' religious processes.

7   Sallnow (p. 9) therefore quotes Werbner's point (1977: xiii) that the paradigm tends to represent as mutually exclusive alternatives what are, in fact, aspects that combine in a variety of ways in a range of actual cases.

8   We perhaps see here instanciations of the depiction of place as a trope of scholarly authority, both a locus of the ethnographic gaze and a part through which cultural wholes can be presented (Rapport and Dawson 1998b: 5).

9   Looking up books about pilgrimage on Amazon.com in September 2003, we found 1,616 entries. The top three were *The Life You Save May Be Your Own: an American pilgrimage* by Paul Elie (Farrar Straus & Girouxm, 2003), an inspiration book by a Roman Catholic; *So Strange My Path: a spiritual pilgrimage* (Bloch Publishing Co., May 1977), an autobiographical account by Abraham Carmel, a Jewish teacher; and *The Pilgrimage* by Paulo Coelho (Harper; reprint edition September 2000), a text that recounts the trials of Paulo Coelho as he journeys across Spain to discover personal power, wisdom and a miraculous sword that seals his initiation into the secret society of 'the Tradition'.

10 Clifford expresses the impact on ethnographers by asserting that '[i]n the history of twentieth-century anthropology, "informants" first appear as natives; they emerge as travelers' (1997: 19).

11 In certain respects, Bauman's characterization does resonate with Tomasi's view (2002: 13ff.) that there has been a shift from pilgrimage to religious tourism. The journey as demonstration of freedom, unconstrained by a search for salvation, thus moves from an emphasis on suffering to one of pleasure, as well as the pursuit of knowledge. *Curiositas* is no longer to be discouraged.

12 Cohen is one of the few anthropologists to have explored the complex relationship between pilgrimage and tourism in contemporary society. As Malcolm Crick (1995) suggests in his provocative paper 'The anthropologist as tourist: an identity in question', anthropological wariness or hostility towards studying tourism may be due to the uncomfortable similarities between anthropology and tourism. Adrian Franklin (2003) has produced a stimulating discussion of tourism where he rejects the view that it is simply an addition to everyday life – rather he shows how it permeates society as a

whole. While he argues that tourism and pilgrimage blend with one another, he still retains the Turnerian view of pilgrimage as a journey away from the everyday.

13 Given Adler's view, it is interesting and perhaps ironic that Bauman dedicates his 'From Pilgrim to Tourist' chapter to her.

14 Rojek and Urry claim that the failure of attempts to distinguish clearly between travel, tourism and pilgrimage can be explained by the move from organized to disorganized capitalism. Organized capitalism was characterized by a 'differentiation of social practices, each presupposing their own mode of judgment, hierarchy and authority' (1997: 2). Since the 1970s this form of modernity (Modernity 1) has given way in the de-industrializing West to Modernity 2, where rigidities and boundaries are rejected for a pick'n'mix approach towards identities. They refer to the process of de-differentiation, where a wide range of distinctions have broken down – 'high/low culture, art/life, culture/street life, home/abroad' – and, with them, the social practices which bounded 'different social/spatial locations' (1997: 3).

15 Unlike Karve, Frey does spend much time examining the impact of pilgrimage on 'home' life after pilgrimage, including indeed the impact on her own marriage.

16 Furthermore (1992: 16) there may be a broader temporal referent for movement: sacred journeys are often timed to occur within monthly, annual, seasonal or other cycles.

17 Thus activities termed pilgrimages may sometimes look more like, say, migration than they do other examples of sacred travel.

18 We concede that there is no inherent reason why a comparative study of mobility should necessarily confine itself to cases involving processes of sacralization, but doing so in the context of this volume allows us to comment directly on the anthropological discourse of pilgrimage – a discourse that exists whether or not one concedes that there is any 'essential' element to 'pilgrimage' as a human activity.

Chapter 2

'Being there'
British Mormons and the history trail

Hildi Mitchell

This chapter explores some aspects of Mormon relationships with their historical past, and thus with their theology (Davies 1989). It situates the relationship that British Mormons have to various places in (Mormon) America within a framework of relationships of persons, places and texts, as suggested by Eade and Sallnow (1991a), and elaborated by Coleman and Elsner (1995). The way in which this relationship is played out in this Mormon case reveals the importance of embodied knowledge, which, I argue elsewhere (Mitchell 2000), is central to the way in which Mormonism works. Here I contend that visiting Mormon historical sites, museums and key buildings is another way in which Mormons are able to actively participate in their theology and cosmology. Mormons interact with the material remnants and reminders of their history through embodied memories of their engagement with the objects, buildings and narratives of their theology. We begin to see how, for Mormons, history works as theology (Davies 1989), and the ways in which embodied practice, rather than belief, forms the basis of their religious life.

The chapter is divided into three interrelated sections. The first deals with Mormon history, showing how it is central to Mormon theology. The centrality of a particular type of historical consciousness reveals a complex interplay between different kinds of places, texts and people. The second part shows how this relationship echoes the interplay between persons, place and both text and object in wider Mormonism, most especially in Mormon temples and in the Mormon practice of testimony bearing. The final section shows how this Mormon engagement with temples and testimonies works to shape their interaction with historical sites, thus illuminating the extent to which pilgrimage activities are different or similar to everyday religious action (cf. Coleman and Elsner 1998). This section draws on ideas about memory, which have been usefully explored by other authors in the analysis of religion (Whitehouse 1992, 1996; Mitchell 1997), to suggest a development of some apparently contradictory ideas. In the move away from exploring archetypal structures of pilgrimage associated with both Durkheim and Marx,[1] there has been a tendency to privilege the fluidity of the pilgrimage events and the creativity of the individual pilgrim (Eade and Sallnow 1991a; Coleman and Elsner 1998). This chapter seeks to show how embodied memory acts as the interface between individual experiences and wider religious structures, which perhaps helps to integrate the apparent opposition of the individual/structure dichotomy.

The place of history and the history of places

'This is the place!'
>Attr. Church President Brigham Young, on arriving in the Salt Lake Valley, prior to establishing a Mormon community there

In addition to the Bible, Mormons have a number of other books of scripture. The best known is the *Book of Mormon*, which tells the story of the ancient inhabitants of the Americas (generally believed by Mormons to be the ancestors of Native Americans) who left Jerusalem around 600 BC and were led by God to the 'promised land' of America. It is a history of these people and of God's dealings with them. Mormons believe that the kingdom of God on earth existed among these people – in other words, that the Church was in existence at that time. Members in the modern dispensation can therefore learn about how they should behave and organize themselves from reading this history, much as Christians of other denominations look to the New Testament. The *Book of Mormon* is for Mormons both an historical document, and a central 'player' in the history of the Church. As missionaries passed around copies among potential converts, it was this 'gold bible' that first attracted adherents to the movement (Shipps 1987: 33).

There is another book of scripture that perhaps has even more significance for Mormon history. Much Mormon scholarship has attempted to discover historical evidence for events in the *Book of Mormon* and to map the places mentioned onto modern America. However, for most Mormons, the book is of importance as a historical and religious text, rather than as a signpost to specific places.[2] The *Doctrine and Covenants*, in contrast, is a book of 'modern' scripture (i.e. dating from the early years of the Church, in the mid-nineteenth century). Mormons take it to be transcriptions of revelations given to Joseph Smith as he established the new Church. As such, this book of scripture is intrinsically linked to the unfolding of the history of the new Church, and often to events as well as the places in which these events occurred. Some brief extracts will illustrate the point:

> From Section 24, '*Revelation given to Joseph Smith the Prophet and Oliver Cowdery, at Harmony, Pennsylvania, July 1830 . . .* '
> 1. Behold, thou wast called and chosen to write the Book of Mormon, and to thy ministry; and I have lifted thee up out of thine afflictions, and have counseled [sic] thee, that thou hast been delivered from all thine enemies, and thou hast been delivered from the powers of Satan and from darkness!
> 2. Nevertheless, thou art not excusable in thy transgressions; nevertheless, go thy way and sin no more.
> 3. Magnify thine office; and after thou hast sowed thy fields and secured them, go speedily unto the Church which is in Colesville, Fayette, and Manchester, and they shall support thee; and I will bless them both spiritually and temporally.

> From Section 82, '*Revelation given to Joseph Smith the Prophet, in Jackson County, Missouri, April 26, 1832 . . .* '
> 13. For I have consecrated the land of Kirtland in mine own due time for the benefit of the saints of the Most High, and for a stake to Zion.

> From Section 84, '*Revelation given through Joseph Smith the Prophet, at Kirtland, Ohio, September 22 and 23, 1832 . . .* '
> 2. Yea, the word of the Lord concerning his church, established in the last days for the restoration of his people, as he has spoken by the mouth of his prophets, and for the gathering of his saints to stand upon mount Zion, which shall be the city of New Jerusalem.
> 3. Which city shall be built, beginning at the temple lot, which is appointed by the finger of the Lord, in the western boundaries of the state of Missouri, and dedicated by the hand of Joseph Smith, Jun., and others with whom the Lord was well pleased.

Not only does the *Doctrine and Covenants* contain references to people and places that figure in Mormon history, it also details occasions when heavenly visitations occurred, including visitations from God himself, thus linking particular places in America with both Mormon history (cf. Bracht 1990 on the sacralization of America) and divinity itself.

> From Section 110, '*Visions manifested to Joseph Smith the Prophet and Oliver Cowdery in the temple at Kirtland, Ohio, April 3, 1836 . . .*'
> 1. The veil was taken from our minds, and the eyes of our understanding were opened.
> 2. We saw the Lord standing upon the breastwork of the pulpit, before us; and under his feet was a paved work of pure gold, in color like amber.
> 3. His eyes were as a flame of fire; the hair of his head was white like the pure snow; his countenance shone above the brightness of the sun; and his voice was as the sound of the rushing of great waters.

The integration of historical 'fact' into present day faith is important here. When Church courses of study examine the *Doctrine and Covenants* (*D&C*), they usually do so alongside an examination of the period of Mormon history when it was written. Thus, the principles of doctrine and organization set out in the *D&C* gain an authority guaranteed by connection with the key founding fathers of the Church. This process also works to sacralize history, and to allow for centralized Church control over what versions of this history are taught. In Mormonism, then, we have identifiable places in contemporary America appearing in sacred scripture – which Mormons can visit, in the process identifying themselves with both Mormon history and transcendental 'truths' (see Mitchell 1998 on the difference between historical and religious 'truth').

Persons, places, objects – bearing testimonies, moving through temples

The *Doctrine and Covenants* illustrates to Mormons how principles of Church organization were revealed in response to particular historical events. Further, the history of the early Church, which is recorded in another Church scripture, the *Pearl of Great Price*, serves as an 'origin myth' (see, for example, Eliade 1964) in which members can participate. Members participate in this myth primarily through the practice of testimony bearing, which they do at least once a month as part of a special Sunday service. Testimonies allow the incorporation of personal experiences into cultural values (Knowlton 1991, 1994). A common theme is the assertion of belief in the story of Joseph Smith's 'first vision', which began the chain of events leading to the publication of the *Book of Mormon* and the founding of the Church (cf. Shipps 1987: 31). This narrative involved the young Joseph Smith seeking guidance at a time of religious confusion and being answered by heavenly visitations and the promise of restoration of ancient and everlasting truths.

Davies argues (1989: 170) that the practice of referring to this story in bearing testimony shows a commitment to a particular theory of history in which God is a central character and force, as all history becomes the history of the Church itself. However, the use of the story also allows individual Mormons to enter into the myth themselves. As Knowlton says, it 'links the formative myth of Mormonism and the Saints' daily lives' (1991: 21). The first vision story is a symbol which is:

> sufficiently multivalent to serve, on the one hand, as a 'shared community experience . . . that every Mormon must respond to personally', and, on the other, as a disseminator of agreement about things historical and a preserver of unity about matters doctrinal.
> (Allen 1980, cited in Shipps 1987: 32)

The following testimony, borne at a Fast and Testimony meeting during my fieldwork in Manchester in 1996 by Elder Smith, a young missionary in Manchester, is typical in this respect.

> Brothers and sisters, I am so grateful to be here on my mission. It is a wonderful feeling being able to share the gospel. I just found out that someone I baptized right at the beginning of my mission is now preparing to go through the temple for the first time. This was such special news, because it shows that he's been faithful to the Church since he was baptized. It is my desire that everyone in the Church can know the joy that comes through bringing the gospel to someone. I pray that everyone here will be able to share in bringing someone to the Church. I know this Church is true. I know that it is the only true Church on earth and that it was restored by Joseph Smith, who was a prophet of God. I know that, through prayer, everyone can receive a witness that the Church is true. You may not have a vision, or angels, or anything like that, but you will know. I'm grateful for the opportunity to be here in Manchester, and I say these things in the name of Jesus Christ. Amen.

Elder Smith stresses the importance of sharing the gospel by emphasizing that it is true, restored by Joseph Smith. He also identifies contemporary converts and members with the figure of Joseph Smith, through his assertion that they too can receive confirmation that the Church is true.

In bearing testimony, however, the link with the origin myth and thus with the community is made not merely as a metaphor or narrative, but through bodily feeling. The foundation of a testimony is first gained through interaction with Mormon scripture. Carol, an informant in Manchester, had her first contact with the LDS Church through a chance encounter with the missionaries, who give her a copy of the *Book of Mormon*. As she narrated her experience in one testimony meeting,[3] she showed how reading the book transformed her relationship with the missionaries, making her eager to see them and to join the Church. The *Book of Mormon* is, of course, a written, and therefore linguistic, item. But its power in this situation is its ability to produce an emotional response in the reader. Carol's testimony related:

> When I was first given the *Book of Mormon*, I sat down to read it in my room and started to cry, well, more like sob. I'm not an emotional person, I never get emotional or cry when reading a book, but I did then. My yearning and hunger for religion was changed. I knew the *Book of Mormon* had to be true, and was a testament of Jesus Christ.

An affective response to what is experienced in Mormonism is of key importance in both gaining a testimony and the process and narration of conversion (cf. Davies 1987). Change, or conversion, for Mormons is not, as Stromberg suggests (1993: 15), 'constituted above all in talk' and 'sustained only to the extent that it is continually constituted' through the retelling of the conversion story, since it actually precedes the learning of the new language of the adopted religion. Instead, it is constituted in feeling, in an emotional response to Mormon artefacts and rituals, and it is continually reconstituted in the feelings experienced in moments of testimony bearing. One of the stated reasons for bearing testimony is that the bearing actually strengthens the testimony of the teller, as well as of the listener.

A concern with the significance of emotion in the understanding of belief (see, for example, Christian 1982; Whitehouse 1996; Mitchell 1997) can be identified with increasing concern in anthropology about over-linguistic approaches to belief, which have been manifest in the development of embodiment or practice-oriented theories (for example, Bourdieu 1977, 1989; Csordas 1989). Christian's examples of '*collective* religious weeping' in early modern Spain (1982: 100; my emphasis), and Lyon and Barbalet's reminder of the significance of the notion of the '*body* of the Church' (1994: 55; my emphasis) suggest that emotion should be viewed as an embodied and collective phenomenon. As Davies points out (1987: 131), the emotions displayed during the bearing of Mormon testimonies, 'depend on the awareness that all Mormons are united in their shared commitment'.

This contrasts with traditional theories suggesting that emotions are essentially individual and consist of an inner experience or feeling, which has a physiological basis. Nineteenth-century writers such as William James and C.G. Lange argued that these inner physiological entities were accompanied by outward manifestations, which were observed as evidence of the existence of an emotion (see Solomon 1984: 238). Such a view has been increasingly challenged. Solomon, for example, argues that '[a]n emotion is not a feeling (or a set of feelings) but an *interpretation*' (1984: 248; original emphasis), while Jon Mitchell explores how particular interpretations come to be applied to particular feelings. In examining Maltese informants' memories of being con-firmed, in which many of them recall 'shock' and 'tingling' emanating from the hand of the Archbishop, he says:

> It is significant here that their descriptions of the feeling were very similar. Presumably, they had no way of judging whether their own feelings were the same as other people's. Yet there was agreement about what it felt like to be confirmed. The individual memory of a particular feeling was collectivised, in the process of establishing a common explanation of what each individual had felt.
>
> (Mitchell 1997: 86)

We will come back to Mitchell's use of the concept of memory in inter-preting and experiencing religious moments in the next section of this chapter. But for now we will note his suggestion that the interpretation of feelings experienced during religious rituals, or the interpretation of events as religious or spiritual, depends in a large part on the appro-priateness of a particular interpretation within a given context. This parallels Stromberg's suggestion that conversion involves making sense of new experiences through the shared language of a religious community (Stromberg 1993), but suggests a more central role for felt experience than Stromberg allows.

A good example is Thomas Csordas's analysis of a Charismatic healing conference (1989). He describes how members of the conference were invited to participate in activities which encouraged a variety of multi-sensory images. As well as being healed, participants displayed a variety of emotions and 'somatic manifestations', including vibrating of hands and arms, sensations of lightness or heaviness, power or love flowing through the body, heat, tingling, weeping and laughter (Csordas 1989: 18). These sensations were interpreted by the leaders as representing an incorporation of divine power. Further, the leaders' enumeration of the physical accompaniments of divine power that some participants would experience (heaviness, heat, tingling) recapitulates a repertoire acquired from their own experience and from reports of participants in similar events (Csordas 1989: 20).

Mormon recollections of, or comments on, the feelings which accompany the inception and the retelling of a testimony also display similarities. Mormons speak of a 'thumping heart', or a 'warm feeling' in the bosom/stomach/chest. Often they describe warmth, or glowing – 'My heart burned within me' is a common turn of phrase. They also talk of peacefulness or calmness, and identify feelings of confusion or anger as incompatible with feeling the spirit. Sometimes, there are visible tears. Much as weeping was interpreted as evidence of spiritual communication in early modern Spain (Christian 1982), these sets of descriptions of feelings are interpreted by Mormons as evidence of the presence of 'the spirit'. One can both feel the spirit and have the spirit, depending on one's status within the Mormon community,[4] but both are identified by the feelings described above. It has been suggested that the Holy Spirit is invoked to describe feelings which are difficult to explain in terms of a commonly understood symbol, which again suggests the importance of community-wide interpretations and modes of expression (cf. Lyon and Barbalet 1994).

The shared experience of the community of Mormon believers has its pinnacle in the Mormon temple experience. Unlike chapels, which are used for Sunday worship and are open to all members and interested non-members, Mormon temples are reserved for the carrying out of sacred and secret salvation ordinances, and entrance to them is restricted to members of the Church who meet strict entry requirements.

According to my informants in Manchester and London, the temple is such a key part of Mormonism that it cannot be understood without it. Participation in the rites of the temple is *essential* for exaltation after death, and these rituals, together with the temple itself, form what Davies

(1987: 38) calls a 'root metaphor' for Mormons. Even for those who are not temple-goers, the temple still plays a central role. Preparation for first attending the temple is taken seriously, and suspension of temple-going privileges may be used as a sanction for incorrect (especially immoral) behaviour.

Mormon temples are special buildings reserved for the purposes of performing sacred rites, which are considered essential to exaltation. All Mormons are expected to undergo these rituals, for which they wear special clothing. The covenants (which include a vow of secrecy concerning what goes on in the temple) made as part of these rituals are remembered by the subsequent wearing of special undergarments (known simply as 'garments') which are worn at all times under everyday clothing. These are marked with symbols found in the temple. In addition, temples are built to represent the Mormon cosmos – having, for example, rooms which represent earth and different parts of heaven. As the main ritual of the temple, the 'endowment', progresses, initiands move through these rooms, representing their own moving through the cosmos (for more detail see Talmage 1966; Dolgin 1974; Buerger 1994; Mitchell 2000).

As we saw regarding other religious feelings, again we see how the interpretations available influence the feelings that participants have in a particular religious context. Temple rituals depend for their effectiveness on embodied recollections of previous experiences as well as on reports from other participants. Although initiates are forbidden to discuss the content of temple rituals, the one thing that people do speak about is the fact that participation is an intensely spiritual experience. Comparisons that they make between this and other occasions of feeling the spirit, such as baptisms or testimony meetings, ensure that, despite lack of spoken exegesis about the meaning of the temple, attendees are able to interpret it in accordance with previous and expected experiences. Further, temple rites are embodied through the adoption of certain clothing and bodily behaviour, thus ensuring that their bodies are 'taught' to feel certain things which Mormons interpret as indicative of belief. From this perspective, the question becomes not, as Needham (1972: 100) would have it, how can we know from the performance of a rite that the participant believes the ideological premise which underlies it? But, how does participation in 'the conventional externals of religious belief' produce belief as a socially informed category?

In the context of the temple, two things stand out as being of key importance: personal participation in ritual (both as a saving act and as a testimony building activity) and the body. Since the 1980s, the body has become an increasing preoccupation of anthropological analysis. However, this trend has tended to confine itself to an analysis of either the way in which the body is culturally constructed (e.g. Blacking 1977) or the way in which it is symbolic of the social (e.g. Douglas 1970). Embodiment, as mentioned earlier, and as outlined by Csordas (1989, 1994b), differs significantly from this kind of anthropology of the body (see also Jackson 1983). Seeing the *formation* of the body as connected to the *representation* of the body, it does not simply make the body an object of anthropological study, but argues that the body is actually the subject of culture (Csordas 1989: 5; 1994b: 269). From this perspective, culture is viewed as grounded in the body, as one exists as a body in the world, and one comes to comprehend the world through bodily existence in it. In this way, the socially informed body is an object of interest, not because it is a symbol of the cultural (cf. Douglas 1970), but because it is its very basis. As Davies has pointed out (1987: 131), a testimony of the truthfulness of Mormonism depends upon an intuitional and emotional response to what is experienced, rather than on an intellectual comprehension of doctrine, and it is through participation in ritual and engagement with the Mormon world that the individual Mormon's body becomes receptive to the religion's truths. It has been suggested that traditions of religious rituals appropriate the body, through the suspension of natural attitudes, movements and postures, in order to facilitate the emergence of a more spiritual awareness and create a metamorphosis of our very being (Levin 1985: 180). This metamorphosis begins with rituals of preparation (for example Mormon washings and anointings as a preparation for the main rituals of the temple) and continues through control of bodily attitude in the performance of ritual, and in regulation of bodily behaviour.

There is a long association of temples with bodies, in many religious traditions. Temples may be said to represent the body of God, the body of the Church, the human body or the embodiment of the universe. In Mormonism, the design of the temple is an iconographic representation of the Mormon cosmos, through which individual bodies move; second, the temple and the human body are compared, especially in relation to ideas of bodily purity; third, the temple rituals are incorporated into the Mormon individual's experience of the body through the wearing of sacred clothing, both during the temple rituals and afterwards at all times. In addition, restriction of admission into the sacred space of the temple through the implementation of strict behavioural require-ments allows a powerful control over Mormon bodies outside of the temple, as well as within it. As the pinnacle of Mormon ritual experience is incorporated into mundane life through the experience of the body, the cosmological and theological ideas represented by the temple become part of an embodied experience. Bodies and temples operate within Mormonism as symbols of each other. But the significance of the temple is not merely as a symbol. If we aim to decode the signs in a study of ritual, and insist on separating the social or theological meaning of the rites from the psychological state of the bodies participating in them, we may fail to recognize a significant way in which these rites work. As Asad points out, 'the body's knowledge of the real world is not always dependent on signs' (1997: 43).

This idea of 'the body's knowledge' is what I mean by arguing that the temple ritual is embodied. I draw both on Bourdieu's notion of *habitus* (see Bourdieu 1977, 1989), and on that of Marcel Mauss (1950). *Habitus* in this context refers to the way in which bodies become accustomed to behaving in certain ways. Such a concept invites us to analyse 'the body', not as a system of symbolic meanings, but as a series of embodied aptitudes. Anyone who, like me, has spent years studying a musical instrument, will see this clearly in Asad's explanation of Mauss's *habitus* as being:

> About the way a professional pianist's *practised hands* remember and play the music being performed, not about how the symbolizing mind 'clothes a natural bodily tendency' with cultural meaning.
>
> (Asad 1997: 47)

Or, in other words, an *anthropology of practical reason* – 'a self developable means for achieving a range of human objects' including spiritual experience (Asad 1997: 47–8). This development can be achieved by entering into the performance of certain tasks and rituals, which 'teach' the body how to achieve the end of, in this case, spirituality. For Mormons, the temple is key in this process, since it represents a central point of theology and experience.

As the pinnacle of Mormon ritual experience is incorporated into mundane life through the experience of the body, the cosmological and theological ideas which the temple represents become part of an embodied experience. Entrance to Mormon temples is restricted to those Mormons who have been interviewed and approved by their Bishop and Stake President. Members who are found to be 'worthy' of entering the temple are given a 'temple recommend', which has to be shown to gain admittance to the temple, and must be renewed every year for subsequent visits. Getting a recommend assumes some degree of an ideal Mormon body, since bodily regulations form significant criteria which must be satisfied. For example, two important criteria are keeping the word of wisdom and moral cleanliness. Individuals who have already been to their temple for the 'endowment' ritual[5] must also confirm that they wear their temple garments at all times. Other criteria also focus on action and behaviour, such as being honest or meeting maintenance payments. The temple recommend operates as a signifier of proper Mormon status – all Mormons, even those not intending to attend the temple in the near future (for example, youths, or women married to non-members), are supposed to live their lives so that they are eligible for a temple recommend. The Church can also stipulate that only temple recommend holders may work for its institutions (e.g. Brigham Young University in Utah).

Although the temple is the pinnacle of Mormon religious life, offering both the rituals required for eternal salvation and a profoundly sacred experience as Mormons enact the principles of their theology, the temple experience lacks exegesis, since the rites and feelings had there cannot be discussed outside of its walls. Unlike Mormon testimonies, which are reiterated daily and weekly, the only repetition of the sacred feelings had in the temple comes within the temple itself on subsequent visits. Without elaboration of what the rituals mean, there is often confusion regarding the temple, and some new initiates find it deeply disturbing, since the form of its rituals varies considerably from the rituals of non-temple Mormonism with which members are already familiar. So how are these initiates prepared to experience the rituals, and how do they come to experience them as the pinnacle of their religious experience?

The answer lies in the ways in which the temple experience mirrors the experiences had in other Mormon contexts, such as the testimony meeting. The temple experience, like the testimony experience, is associated with certain religious feelings. One informant recalled, for example:

> Even sitting out here in the gardens I feel really peaceful. The trees and flowers are so beautiful, and it makes me feel close to God. Sometimes I like to spend time sitting here when I'm going through a difficult time. When I was inactive and didn't have a temple recommend I found that I could still feel close to God when I was in the temple grounds and it really helped me with some important decisions.

Members often state that the Celestial room is an especially good place for reflection and for communion with God. They use the time they spend there to think through problems of both a spiritual and a temporal nature. One of my informants recalled that she had even felt this 'peace' when in the vicinity of the Preston Temple, which, at the time was still under construction and resembled a building site more than a religious place.

> I was really depressed and upset about something, so I went for a drive to clear my head and to just get away from it all. After I'd driven for a while I realised I was near the Preston Temple, so I decided to go there. I stopped the car near to the entrance of the area and sat in it for a while. I felt so peaceful and close to God. I sat there in the car for ages, outside the building site. People driving past must have thought I was crazy, but I felt that it was already a spiritual place.

People who have recently returned from their first visit to the temple narrate their experiences in vague terms of 'feeling spiritual' and 'warm feelings', and often display the 'signs' of religious feelings associated more generally with testimonies, such as tears. This is partly due to the conditions of secrecy, and partly because they have learned that this is what Mormon sacredness is – an interaction with material objects and sacred space which produces a strong emotional and bodily feeling. Embodied memories of testimony meetings and other sacred events are carried into the temple to help make sense of an experience which has no other explanation.

Embodied memories

It is this learned, embodied and remembered sacredness which informs the motivations for and the experiences had on religious travel, in particular to historical sites in the USA. My ethnography for this section draws on interviews with informants in Manchester and London about their trips to these sites and also on my own visits to some of the sites in the Salt Lake area. The findings suggest that embodied memories of everyday Mormon religiosity play a key role in understanding Mormon religious travel.

Let us re-examine Jon Mitchell's analysis of his Maltese informants' descriptions of being touched by the archbishop. He says:

It is significant here that their descriptions of the feeling were very similar. Presumably, they had no way of judging whether their own feelings were the same as other people's. Yet there was agreement about what it felt like to be confirmed. The individual memory of a particular feeling was collectivised, in the process of establishing a common explanation of what each individual had felt.

(1997: 86)

In Mormonism, too, there is collective agreement about what constitutes signs of the spirit. These 'depend on the awareness that all Mormons are united in their shared commitment' (Davies 1987: 131). Mitchell's argument for the importance of considering feeling in the analysis of belief centres on the concept of collective memory. He argues, in line with Solomon and others who have challenged accepted views of emotion, that the interpretation of a feeling is an integral part of the feeling itself, and, further, that this interpretation is shared through the process of collective memory, through comparing feelings to recollections of previous feelings, and through talking about them to establish a shared embodied memory.

Here I argue that British Mormons who go to Salt Lake City and other important sites in the USA take with them their embodied memories of concepts such as 'the spirit', 'testimony' and 'sacredness', which have been shaped in their everyday religious lives. Because subsequent experiences on the history trail or in Salt Lake City can then be experienced in terms of these memories, they are able to be experienced as sacred and testimony-building experiences, however apparently mundane or secular. Thus, while individual Mormons may construct their own paths through Mormon heritage, and feel personal feelings whilst on them, they are highly likely to experience these places, events and objects in a hegemonic, culturally constructed way.[6]

The next sections examine some aspects of Mormon visits to Salt Lake City, showing how they depend for their interpretation as 'religious' experiences on embodied memories of other Mormon religious experiences.

'Being there' – doing it for yourself

A frequent feature of British Mormons' narratives of going to Salt Lake City and other places along the Mormon history trail is the motif of 'being there'. One of my informants told me why she went to Salt Lake City – 'I suppose because every member of the Church feels a need to see where it all started.' Although she was technically incorrect in that the Church started some way away from the Salt Lake valley on the east coast of America in upstate New York, her sentiments echo not merely a wish to 'see' and 'feel' history, but also an acceptance of the perceived need for every member to gain his or her own testimony. Not only is going to historical sites a way to enhance one's testimony, but the practice of doing this is also moulded on the testimony model.

The effect of seeing for oneself also applied in the case of this informant to other experiences (i.e. not to do with historical sites). As she told me about all the things she had seen and done it was clear that everything was experienced as increasing her testimony – however small and insignificant, and however 'secular'. These things ranged from the fact that the road is laid out on the original grid system worked out during the presidency of Brigham Young, to seeing the current president of the Church in person. She told me:

> On a lot of postcards I sort of wrote on the back of it that the Church is true, the gospel is true. Because that made you feel like that, that made you feel so good, you know, while you were there. And when I go to conference here, erm, the satellite conference, you know, that's always good and something always touches you, and makes you believe and makes it more sort of concrete inside you that you know it's right, but actually being there, was far more . . . how can I put it, erm, that brought it home to you far more than just seeing it over television, to be there in real life.

A similar sentiment was expressed to me on two occasions when I discussed my future fieldwork with informants in Manchester, England. In the first I was deliberating over whether to go on a visit to the temple with some of the women in my ward. This would involve (at the time, before the Preston Temple was completed) a long drive from Manchester to Surrey, and as I would not be able to go in I was not sure how useful it would be to me. The 'usefulness' of the trip was obviously interpreted rather differently by one of the other women, who told me that it would be beneficial for me to go, since being in the vicinity of the temple would bring me enlightenment and help me think through things which had been bothering me. The second was when I was talking about going to Salt Lake City. Almost without exception, members I told of this planned trip told me it would be 'good' for me, it would 'help [me] understand' and that I should 'see for [my]self'. In the same way that the temple teaches the most fundamental and important truths of

Mormonism without words, simply through one's participation and being there, Salt Lake City, it seemed, would enable me to know things about Mormonism which I didn't already know.

Interaction with objects

During my visit to Salt Lake City I explored one of the main tourist attractions which lies to the west of Temple Square,[7] the Museum of Church History and Art. The museum is housed on three levels. The ground floor is devoted to Church history, from the First Vision through the establishment of Salt Lake City to the growth of a 'Worldwide Church'. A number of media are used in this exhibition: video presentations, touch sensitive screens, reconstructions (e.g. Nauvoo Temple, a covered wagon), models (e.g. of Joseph Smith's family farm, the layout of Salt Lake City) and artefacts (e.g. part of the *Book of Mormon* manuscript, death masks of Joseph and Hyrum Smith, John Taylor's watch).[8] The first floor contains portraits of the presidents of the Church, together with artefacts from the period of each one's presidency, and a brief outline of their contributions to Church history. There are also some portraits of important leaders (not presidents), and of the current Quorum of Twelve and First Presidency.[9] The art of the museum was located in three main places, and was of two main types. Also on the first floor was a room containing Native American art, together with an exegesis stating that Native Americans have a special relationship with Mormons because they are the descendants of the *Book of Mormon* peoples. In addition there were two art competitions, one on the first floor showing celebrations of 150 years of pioneers, and one in the basement of depictions of 'pioneers' by children.[10]

Interactions with the artefacts in this museum are conducted in ways comparable with those evident in relation to other objects such as the *Book of Mormon* and the temple. Again it seems very much a case of the importance of 'being there' and seeing for oneself. While I was in the museum a mother showed her two young children John Taylor's watch. She quizzed them about the story attached to it. Did they remember why it was important? Did they remember how it saved John Taylor's life by deflecting the bullet? 'Oh, yes!' they cried, clamouring for a better look, and exclaiming how 'neat' it was to see the 'actual watch'. Two teenagers had a similar reaction to the page of the original *Book of Mormon* manuscript. These 'actual watches' and original manuscripts are, like the temple and its associated paraphernalia, tangible witnesses to a Mormon reality. Their physicality 'bears witness' to the truthfulness of the faith of

Mormons. Such physical witness ranges from Joseph Smith's death, commonly seen as a martyrdom in which he sealed his testimony with his blood, to the burning in the bosom experienced by all who gain a witness of the truthfulness of the *Book of Mormon* – a physical record of God's dealings with a chosen people. Like the *Book of Mormon*, which sacralizes American history (cf. Bracht 1990) and the *Doctrine and Covenants*, which sacralizes places in the American landscape, encounters with these various physical emblems allow sacred feeling in the individual.

Legacy – feeling and spirituality

As we saw earlier regarding both the testimony and the temple, certain feelings are considered important evidence of the presence of the spirit. When a lot of people cry in a testimony meeting it is often pronounced a very spiritual meeting.[11] The same thing arises in Mormon historical appreciation centres – most clearly through the medium of film. Although a number of films in the Museum of Church History and Art seemed designed to elicit an emotional response, particularly those which portrayed the hardship of the emigration from Liverpool to Salt Lake City, the emotional/spiritual film *par excellence* was *Legacy*, shown daily in the Joseph Smith Memorial Building, to the east of Temple Square.

   This feature film tells the story of a pioneer family, centring on a young woman called Eliza, her brother Johnny and her husband David. It follows them as they join the pioneer trek to the 'promised land' of Salt Lake City. The film introduces key elements from Mormon history, having Eliza's husband join the Mormon battalion, showing missionaries going to Liverpool and English immigrants joining the pioneer groups, and depicting the persecution suffered by the pioneers in hostile territories. It also features events of healing and other prayers being answered, including one incident where Eliza is healed by the Prophet Joseph Smith himself. These 'faith-promoting' events occur generally around incidents of hardship, death of family members and illness, but the film also contains shots of beautiful sunsets and breathtaking landscapes. I recorded in my notebook that it was 'very sentimental', indeed many of the audience (who comprised both members and non-members of the Mormon Church) were sniffling into tissues by the time the lights came up at the end of the film. But such sentimentality, as we saw earlier, is often considered to be the feeling of the spirit. Contrast my cynicism with the recollections of one of my informants concerning the same film.

I think nearly everybody came out of there in tears. I mean, the minute that it started, it was showing you how they travelled, like across and everything and they died, and things like that, and the tears were just pouring down my face . . . Oh that really brought it home to you, the suffering, the stuff they had gone through, by Joseph Smith and the early members of the Church to give us what we've got now.

For this woman, watching *Legacy* was not merely an emotional experience, it was a spiritual one. We see how the cultural template within which emotions are interpreted as signs of the spirit had been laid down, internalized and remembered by the body from previous emotional/spiritual experiences. While non-Mormons such as myself experience *Legacy* as overly sentimental and contrived, Mormons such as my informant, who inhabit correctly taught bodies which contain memories of previous experiences, find them testimony-building and spiritual.

Conclusions

The aim of this chapter has been to begin to provide a theoretical framework for making sense of both British and American Mormons' relationships to historical things and places, to understand how these are experienced, not merely as secular travel, but as faithbuilding explorations of sacred places and feelings. I have argued that a significant way in which this is accomplished is through embodied memories of other religious moments. Although to some extent the paper is also about history, it is not making an argument about how social memories construct history, but about how embodied memories are important in giving rise to religious feelings. However, through these embodied memories, individual Mormons are able to enter into their history in much the same way as they enter their origin myths through bearing testimony, and their cosmology through going through the temple. In each of these, the sacredness and Mormonness of the experience depends, as does, for example, the healing described by Csordas (1989: 20), on the recapitulation of a repertoire acquired from their own experience and from reports of participants in similar events.

Notes

1 This has been developed in the study of pilgrimage in a variety of ways, for example Turner's (1978) structure/anti-structure model and correspondence theorists' attempts to explain pilgrimage in terms of political and economic structures.

2 I have never encountered anyone trying to visit a historical site from the *Book of Mormon*.

3 Stromberg (1993) and Caldwell (1983) have both discussed the form of the testimony or conversion narrative as a particular genre. It also receives historical consideration in the Mormon context, in, for example, Harrison (1989).

4 Following baptism into the LDS Church, individuals are confirmed. This is a blessing from Melchizedek Priesthood holders and confirms the individual a member of the Church, as well as bestowing upon him or her the 'gift of the Holy Ghost'. Once one has been given the gift of the Holy Ghost, one has the right to his presence at all times, depending upon one's righteousness. Any individual without the gift of the Holy Ghost can still feel his influence. Indeed, it is through the influence of the Holy Ghost's witness that converts come to know the Church is true.

5 The 'endowment' is one of the rituals (or 'ordinances') which an individual must do in order to gain admittance to the Celestial Kingdom after death. Since *all* individuals must 'receive' their endowment, as well as the other ordinances, living members of the Church who have already received their own endowment go to the temple to act as proxies for dead relatives in these rituals.

6 I do have an essay written by a now ex-Mormon reflecting on his visits to Mormon historical sites. While he is clearly able to experience these in a counter-hegemonic manner, his experiences too are influenced by the existence of these hegemonic discourses.

7 Temple Square houses the Salt Lake Temple, the Tabernacle and a number of other buildings, including visitors' centres.

8 John Taylor, an Englishman, was the third president of the Church. He was with Joseph Smith in jail when he was shot. The story goes that he was also shot, but that his life was saved because the bullet aimed at his heart was deflected by his pocket watch. This preserved him for his ministry later in the Church's history.

9 The only portraits of women from Church history are on the ground floor, tucked away near to the gift shop. This mirrors not only the fact that women are excluded from holding the priesthood, and thus from general leadership in the Church, but even the seating arrangements at General Conference – where the female leaders of the Church's organization for women (Relief Society) sit away from the main male leaders' seating, at the top of the choir stalls.

10 The year I visited (1997) was the 150th anniversary of the arrival in Salt Lake City – a number of activities, events, TV programmes, and so on commemorated this.

11 The extent to which this can be seen by the cynical as, in fact, engineered would have to be the topic of another paper.

Chapter 3

From England's Nazareth to Sweden's Jerusalem

Movement, (virtual) landscapes and pilgrimage

Simon Coleman

Colliding worlds?

Every May, the Anglican shrine of Walsingham in north Norfolk stages its 'National Pilgrimage'. Thousands of Anglo-Catholics descend upon the picturesque village, exploring its sacred sites as well as its tea shops and pubs. Amid this celebration of both religion and Englishness another 'traditional' part of the social landscape can usually be found, though it is one that contradicts the celebratory tone of the day. Lining the roads of the High Street, and therefore framing the formal procession of Anglicans as they walk through the village, stands a small band of evangelical Christians, as liturgically 'low' as the pilgrims are 'high', and rather more dowdily dressed. Their banners do not bear images of Our Lady; instead, they direct accusations of 'idolatry' and 'Papism' towards the pilgrims, railing against what they regard as a 'cult' of Marianism.

This annual scene recalls Eade and Sallnow's core metaphor of 'contesting the sacred' in describing behaviour at shrines (1991b): two rival sets of believers are locking theological horns within an arena of great symbolic significance. A few Anglicans have even (half) jokingly told me that they regard the regular presence of the protesters as constituting a kind of Protestant pilgrimage in its own right. Nonetheless, the image reinforces conventional sociological assumptions concerning Christian pilgrimage: that it is essentially a 'Catholic' (or Orthodox) activity, involving expressions of devotion to particular places and objects that are anathema to Protestants.[1] Yet, in this chapter I wish to complicate this picture by presenting an alternative view of the apparent oxymoron of 'Protestant pilgrimage'. I shall be juxtaposing Anglo- and Roman Catholic pilgrimage to Walsingham with forms of travel carried out by Christians who are even more aggressively evangelical than those turning up to attack the National Day. The conservative

Protestants I shall examine belong to the 'Word of Life' (*Livets Ord*) ministry in Sweden, one of the leading European centres for the Faith or 'Prosperity' movement of charismatic Christians,[2] and part of my analysis focuses on the regular journeys to the Holy Land put on by the Word of Life for its supporters. If Catholic pilgrims to Walsingham visit a place that they sometimes call 'England's Nazareth', Faith Christians from Sweden frequently go to the Holy Land itself.

My initial aim in examining these two Christian constituencies is partly, and unsurprisingly, to show how they reveal significantly different attitudes towards ritual, time and materiality. However, I also want to show how they are united in their focus on movement itself as a marked activity, as a cultural performance that incorporates performative action.[3] From an analytical point of view, concentrating on movement provides one way to avoid the self-limiting argument that Protestants eschew pilgrimage. After all, the latter is about much more than the sacralization of relics or images, and if we focus on its sometimes metaphorical, but sometimes literal, evocation of mobility, it emerges as an immensely resonant aspect of Protestant as well as Catholic thought and practice. Of course, we cannot essentialize movement *per se*, and the significance of a 'semantic' approach to pilgrimage is that it seeks to understand the phenomenon in the context of broader cultural assumptions concerning travel and mobility (cf. Eickelman and Piscatori 1990b). The two constituencies I examine can, therefore, be seen as providing significantly divergent ways of negotiating the relationship between macro-processes associated with the political economy of travel and micro-level forms of actual physical mobility.

My argument is further that, in both of the case studies, we are witnessing forms of action that are as much about reinvoking behaviour taken from 'home' as they are about engaging in the 'exceptional'. Indeed, what is occurring in both the English and the Swedish pilgrim groups is, in part, a complex reconstitution of home, involving the staging of familiar ritual action in carefully chosen temporal and spatial arenas. Here, I draw on Rapport and Dawson's argument (1998b: 6) that 'home' may be located less in a single place and more in routine sets of practices, forms of habitual interaction and memory. I also adapt an argument developed by Thomas Csordas (1994a; 1997; cf. Coleman and Collins 2000: 318) in his work on Catholic charismatics. Csordas (1997: 74) refers to the process of dissolving boundaries between church and everyday activity as the 'ritualization of life', and draws on Bourdieu's notion of *habitus* (1977) to show how rigid distinctions between supposedly sacred and supposedly secular actions cannot be sustained once one sees how forms of worship become embodied dispositions that cannot be shut off once the believer leaves a service (see also Mitchell, Chapter 2 this volume).

If the thrust of Csordas's argument moves our gaze from nominally set-apart worship to more everyday activities, mine encourages us to look in the opposite direction as well, since I explore how 'non-pilgrimage' activities[4] and assumptions leach into those making up sacralized travel, not as forms of 'impurity' but as constitutive aspects of the travel itself. In this sense, I support Eade and Sallnow's (1991b) emphasis on the ways in which behaviours and attitudes developed away from shrines inevitably loom large in pilgrims' interpretation and appropriation of sacred shrines. However, what I want to leave flexible is any claim about the extent to which the Christians I examine consciously deconstruct the boundaries between pilgrimage and other aspects of their religious lives. As we shall see, for much of the time believers assert that they are going on journeys that are special, while simultaneously perceiving the behavioural and theological overlaps between the trip and other aspects of life to be of vital significance.

Setting the scenes

Walsingham is one of the premier pilgrimage sites in Britain. The village and its environs contain an Anglican and a Roman Catholic shrine, and both denominations have set up dedicated offices to cater for the many visitors who come in the spring, summer and early autumn. Perhaps a quarter of a million pilgrims come each year (Williams 1996: vii), though the contemporary popularity of the place masks a fragmented history that is not entirely erased in the present.[5] According to an anonymous fifteenth-century ballad,[6] the shrine was founded in 1061 when an aristocratic widow, Richeldis, was granted three 'visions' of the Virgin (Gillett 1946: 1; Turner and Turner 1978: 177). The Virgin took Richeldis in spirit to Nazareth and showed her the House of the Annunciation, while also demanding that an exact copy of this house be built in Norfolk. Once the replica was completed, Walsingham was visited by royalty as well as more ordinary pilgrims, and grew extremely wealthy – indeed too wealthy for its own good, since it provided a tempting target for Henry VIII's iconoclastic commissioners in the 1530s. With the destruction of the shrine, pilgrimage activity all but stopped for over three centuries.

In 1896 a wealthy benefactress, Charlotte Boyd, became interested in the ruined site of the original shrine. Boyd could not persuade the owners to sell up, but she did purchase a small fourteenth-century chapel situated just over a mile from the village, in Houghton-le-Dale. The chapel had provided the last stop for medieval pilgrims before they arrived at the shrine, and it, rather than the ruins at Walsingham, became the site of the first official Roman Catholic pilgrimage since the Reformation. In 1934, the English Bishops named it the 'Roman Catholic National Shrine of Our Lady'. Since then, the shrine at Houghton-le-Dale has continued to develop, a Chapel of the Holy Ghost being consecrated in 1938 and a large, barn-like Chapel of Reconciliation in 1982.

Roman Catholics were soon caught up by High Anglicans, led by the local parish priest, Hope Patten. In 1931, Patten obtained land in the village bought privately by a benefactor. Here, he built his own replica of the Holy House as well as a surrounding church, and also claimed to have found a holy well associated with the original shrine.[7] Extensions were added in later years as more pilgrims came to the site. Patten also decorated the walls of the house with stones taken from the monasteries dissolved by Henry VIII, implying that the fabric of medieval Catholicism could literally be reconstructed and unified in his new building.

Early relations between Anglo- and Roman Catholics were strained. Both, after all, were constructing pilgrimage traditions that were consciously national in their appeal. Both drew on a liturgical vocabulary involving embodied engagement with sacralized landscape through processions and stations of the cross, behind which could also be discerned reflections on such somatically related theological themes as Annunciation, Incarnation and sacrifice. Patten encouraged cells devoted to Walsingham to be set up around the country and abroad, while from 1948 the Roman Catholic shrine boasted crosses taken to the site from various parts of the United Kingdom. Both sides claimed that Walsingham was 'England's Nazareth', and Roman Catholics in particular emphasized Richard II's presentation of England as 'Our Lady's Dowry'. However, if the fundamental problem for Patten was to find an influential place for his shrine in relation to mainstream Anglicanism, for Roman Catholics the main problem was that their faith was clearly less 'established' than that of the Church of England: returning England and Walsingham to the true Catholic religion therefore implied reasserting the rights of a once-dominant religious minority rather than fighting battles with low-church Anglicans. In both cases, distinct identity in the present was being legitimated with reference to a somewhat idealizing medievalism, which asserted the possibility of reviving, even reincarnating, the past through contemporary forms of worship.

Even today, High Anglican pilgrimage to the village establishes liturgical differences from the rest of the established Church, and is often associated not only with 'smells and bells' but also with certain ideological positions, such as disapproval of women priests. However, the very popularity of pilgrimages to the place has also transformed their meaning and organization. Larger and more varied constituencies have acquired a stake in the shrines, and as the role of Christianity itself has changed in British society, so the significance of these journeys has become more ambiguous. Both Anglicanism and Roman Catholicism form part of a more pluralistic religious environment than that evident in the first half of the twentieth century (cf. Swatos 2002). It is clear that old boundaries of opposition between the shrines are much less closely marked than before, and have given way to more flexible relations of cooperation and ecumenism. Such sharing is replicated in virtual space, with both shrines featured on the home page of the official website for the pilgrimage.[8] The first picture the cyber-pilgrim sees is not that of a particular shrine but that of the remains of the east window of the Augustinian priory that had been built next to the original Holy House – a suitably uncontroversial image. More than ever before during its revival, Walsingham now offers a multitude of routes to pilgrims seeking spiritual experiences.

The village has also become something of a 'heritage' site. Local shops selling food and agricultural equipment have been replaced by souvenir shops and cafés. Many of the houses in the middle of the village are also now owned by pious incomers who are attracted to Walsingham for its sacred associations. The centre caters to the expectations of believers who expect to find an 'authentic' medieval village (cf. MacCannell 1976; Boissevain 1996: 12), and who often stay in hostels provided by shrine organizations, but it also accommodates a much wider constituency of visitors, including secular day-trippers from the nearby seaside. In this sense, it illustrates the trend in European pilgrimage highlighted by Voyé (2002: 124) towards more and more pilgrimages (broadly defined), but proportionately fewer 'institutionalized' visits.

Contemporary Walsingham is not particularly known for its healing cures unlike, for instance, Lourdes. Rather, its ruins and its revival, its hosting of devout pilgrims alongside not only evangelicals but also tourists, prompt questions concerning religious identity which may receive answers through particular forms of movement within and between its sacred spots. While some visitors browse aimlessly or idiosyncratically around its sites, others know precisely where they are going. Indeed, in an interview I conducted in 1995, the then treasurer of the Anglican shrine estimated that the number of recurring residents at the two shrines ran into many thousands. For these believers, the Turnerian model (1978) of pilgrimage as a dramatic and often unique journey to a great site is not strictly relevant: Walsingham becomes a landscape that is special yet deeply familiar as they move with some deliberation through its streets, shrines and shops.

Pilgrimage is a recognized category of behaviour among Roman and Anglo-Catholics, but it receives far less positive acknowledgement in Protestant circles. Part of the problem for the latter is the institution's apparent infringement of the Second Commandment, since it can be interpreted as bestowing upon objects, places and people the veneration due to God alone (cf. Keeble 2002: 239). Reader (1993: 4) nevertheless argues that pilgrimage is transposed by Protestants onto a metaphorical plane by imagining individual life as a spiritual journey though a hostile world towards God. Biblical models of wandering can be found in figures ranging from Abraham to Jesus himself, while what Keeble (2002: 241) describes as the most influential and enduring imaginative product of early English Protestantism, Bunyan's *The Pilgrim's Progress* (first published in 1678), juxtaposes a world of stability with that of seemingly reckless movement: the Celestial City and spiritual transcendence are the ultimate goals of Christian the Everyman. In these terms, 'home' as embodiment of stasis becomes a trap, a hurdle to be overcome if spiritually improving mobility is to be achieved. Bunyan's book not only contains the famous image of Christian running away from his family, crying 'Life, life, eternal life' but also, in its very first lines, another evocation of movement: the narrator's initial description of the dream he had 'as I walked through the wilderness of this world'. Similarly, in their description of the vocabulary of early Protestant spiritual autobiographers, Peacock and Tyson (1989: 216–17) note: 'Their favorite allegory is the sojourner, the pilgrim and traveler in this world which is not home, for the pilgrim is only here en route to a final destiny.'

Movement, then, is crucial to such Protestant depictions of the spiritual life, alongside an ambivalent juxtaposition of earthly with spiritual home. Yet, it is surely too limiting a perspective to see Protestantism as transposing sanctified travel on to a purely metaphorical plane. Physical movement itself has often been a deeply resonant element of the Reformed religious life. Many early English Protestants were constantly on the road, with walking and wayfaring expressing ideals of action against inaction, restless dynamism in opposition to self-satisfied stasis (Keeble 2002: 241). Puritan settlers in North America may have seen the whole of life as a symbolic journey, an exile in the wilderness with themselves as Israelites close to Zion (Covey 1961: 13), but of course many of them had actually made a journey themselves, and a similar blend of the symbolic and the physically enacted – literally and metaphorically domesticating the wilderness – could be seen in missionizing and colonializing enterprises in Africa (Comaroff and Comaroff 1991: 173ff.).

The nineteenth century saw a growth in actual Protestant pilgrimage to the Holy Land (Hummel and Hummel 1995; Coleman 2002).[9] In Jerusalem, Protestants might walk along the Via Dolorosa but would not incorporate the Stations of the Cross. Bible reading at significant sites was naturally important, but the choice of spots to focus on was also important. For instance, the Sea of Galilee was a Protestant favourite, not only because it was here that the teaching and preaching of Jesus mostly took place, but also because it represented an empty landscape rather than a building encumbered with icons or other religious paraphernalia (Hummel and Hummel 1995: 15). The Holy Land was ideally regarded not as sacred in itself, but as a powerful catalyst for the cultivation of spiritually powerful experiences rooted in the interaction between believer and Bible. For some believers, also, there was the quasi-messianic aim of redeeming the area from the degeneration evident in its primitive population (cf. Hummel and Hummel 1995: 37).

Today, pilgrimage motifs can be discerned in North American Protestant kinship-based revivalist gatherings and prayer meetings (cf. Neville 1987), as well as in annual evangelical gatherings such as 'Spring Harvest' in England. Meanwhile, the Christian Zionist movement has refocused attention on Jerusalem as a key location for millenarian predictions of Christ's Second Coming. Other developments reflect the ability of evangelicals to take advantage of new communications technologies. During the 1990s, the 'Toronto Blessing' entailed many thousands of Protestant charismatics visiting Toronto Airport Christian Fellowship in the hope of gaining access to a large-scale manifestation of the 'anointing' of the Holy Spirit, some describing this journey as akin to a pilgrimage experience. The Blessing spread to ministries and congregations around the world, and news of its diffusion was relayed by word of mouth, television images, faxes and the Internet.

Although apparently highly contemporary and specific to a certain branch of Protestantism, the Toronto Blessing revealed characteristics evident in much of the history of Protestant travel and pilgrimage.

Specific objects were not deployed as the focus of worship and the locale of the Toronto Fellowship was not considered to be holy in itself: a dismal setting, it was almost akin to a 'non-place' constituted by constant movement (cf. Augé 1995). The tendency of the Blessing to break out very quickly into new locales around the world perhaps also indicated a Protestant deconstruction of place as container of sanctity. Percy (1998: 281) sees it as reflecting a Protestant religious attitude shaped by discourses of journeying and striving. He describes Toronto Airport Vineyard Fellowship as a shrine to postmodern revivalism, lacking relics but imparting a particular type of individualized religious experience that was transferable back into more localized ecclesial contexts.

My own work has investigated the emergence, since the early 1980s, of the Word of Life ministry based in Uppsala, Sweden (e.g. Coleman 2000a, forthcoming). The ministry was founded by Ulf Ekman, a former priest within the Swedish Church who trained at Kenneth Hagin's Bible Center in Tulsa, before resigning his clerical post and setting up as an independent pastor. Since the mid-1980s, the Word of Life has been the object of considerable criticism from Christian and secular groups in Sweden, who condemn it as an over-Americanized and aggressively missionizing organization. Yet, the group has continued to expand its operations. It now runs a university based on the model established by Oral Roberts in Tulsa, possibly the largest Bible school in Europe (taking in both Swedish- and English-speaking students), schools for primary and secondary education, a congregation with over 2,000 people and an extensive media business producing books, audio-cassettes, videos, a website, radio broadcasts and both terrestrial and satellite television programmes. No particular class or gender patterns are yet discernible among its constituents, but many are young. Although the group's headquarters are in Uppsala, it has proved an important catalyst for the development of many other ministries in Scandinavia (Skog 1993), and runs offices and/or Bible schools in other parts of Europe as well as in the USA. Furthermore, while it is formally an independent foundation, the group regularly hosts preachers from other Faith ministries located around the world. It even contains a travel agency under its organizational umbrella, which assists in organizing trips to such places as the Holy Land.

Although housing a larger permanent organization than the Toronto Airport Fellowship, the Word of Life functions in a similar way in that it is constantly funnelling people through its various operations: Bible school and university students, conference delegates and customers at its shops are all encouraged to visit, even re-visit, but not necessarily to stay on a permanent basis. Toronto Fellowship is located in an industrial zone by an airport, and the Word of Life – as its promotional literature points out – is also situated in an industrial area, just a motorway's drive from Sweden's largest airport. Thus in the Swedish group a sense of charismatic flow and permanent inspiration is maintained through the physical movement of people through its doors and out again. Movement, mobility and travel are actions with high symbolic capital in Faith circles. A brochure advertising the Word of Life Bible Centre talks of how members create 'revival in their own lives and "to the world's outermost limit"', of how even the congregation's work is mostly directed outwards, both locally and internationally. It quotes a Word of Life slogan: 'Each member prays, gives and goes.'[10] Even ordinary congregation members who live and work in Uppsala are encouraged to sponsor missionary work overseas; they attend conferences at which the guest speaker will talk of just having flown in from, say, Atlanta or Lagos the day before, and where they are likely to meet Faith delegates from Russia or Germany who are taking advantage of the group's simultaneous translations of its services into other languages; they might also sign up to the group's monthly video library, and thus receive taped updates of the group's activities in Sweden and beyond.

We can see being developed here a charismatic theory of idealized global action, a sense of how to create an arena of influence that is transnational in scope. In such a context, the reputation of preachers is at least partly constituted by their ability to give the impression of straddling the globe in their operations and activities. Thus Ekman is characterized by Word of Life members as a 'world-wide' man of God, demonstrating that even a preacher from a country as small as Sweden can build up a global reputation. In travelling to all continents, Ekman and other Faith believers are delineating a landscape of evangelical agency, where faith is shown to transcend barriers of culture, territory and nationhood.

So all travel, all movement, is framed by a set of charismatic assumptions about the meanings of motion, of transcending space through time, and the linkage of such activity to ideas about agency and influence over others. If we are to regard some of what these Christians do as akin to pilgrimage, we must first understand that pilgrimage is not an activity that stands apart from all others. It belongs to a range of activities that cultivate the sacralized movement of people, objects and images, and that see such people and objects as gaining in sacred power precisely because they travel across great distances.

I have therefore moved in this section from a broadly Catholic to a distinctively Protestant sensibility, but in both cases we have begun to see how mobility becomes a means of both traversing religious landscapes and remaking them in one's own image. This section has also spent some time examining Jerusalem and especially Walsingham as arenas for pilgrimage, but I have attempted to contextualize such a place-centred appreciation of Catholic and charismatic perceptions of pilgrimage by locating it within sub-cultural understandings of landscape, home and travel. It is now time to look more closely at the pilgrimages themselves.

Movement, mimesis and home

Pilgrimages to Walsingham[11] differ from their medieval counterparts in at least one significant respect: the journeys from home to shrine and back tend to occur swiftly and without great exertion. A few pilgrims choose to walk or to take a non-motorized form of transport, but most come by car or bus. While particular styles of journeying *to* the place are not usually perceived as demonstrations of authenticity, journeying *within* the village and its environs has acquired considerable symbolic weight. In the High Street, and to some extent down the 'Holy Mile' – the lane that leads from the Slipper Chapel into the village – cars have to compete with the numerous pedestrians who stream between significant points throughout much of the day during the pilgrimage season.

In discussing mobility as both metaphor and process, Urry (2000: 54) contrasts the insouciance of the strolling *flâneur* with more overtly choreographed practices of walking. Both types of movement are evident at Walsingham, and many others in between, but here I focus on the more formal routines of 'habitual' pilgrims. Anglo- and Roman Catholic parish groups frequently return to the village at the same time each year, year after year. Engagement with the place can involve the choice to move from a given starting-point along a strictly delimited path to one or other of the shrines, ignoring all distractions. In such cases, stately and meditative movement through the stations of the cross may be complemented by the solemn, ambulatory mode of a procession through the village. This type of pilgrimage is not only a (usually) self-conscious attempt to adhere to Catholic tradition, it also 'reproduces' aspects of pilgrimage from a model assumed to have been established in the past. It is a means of dwelling in a form of movement that is also a type of embodied replication.

Membership of some of these parties can remain remarkably stable. Within the great tradition of the medieval pilgrimage a parish can create a little tradition of its own continuous and regular, if temporary, appropriation of Walsingham: such self-referential mimesis becomes a kind of ritual within a ritual. The idea of recurrent return may be built into the structure and the experience of the journey. In response to my question of whether she and her parish ever went on pilgrimage anywhere else, one Anglican woman's reply was that this rarely happened, since 'Walsingham is *ours*, yes, we just kind of do that.' Just as the parish belongs to Walsingham, so Walsingham belongs to the parish.

This sense of ownership is sometimes expressed by pilgrims who describe Walsingham as a second home. Thus, a Roman Catholic woman who has actually bought a house in the village commented on her lack of desire to go on pilgrimages elsewhere:

> I don't see the need really because I do feel that I've been brought here and this is where it's going to happen for me. I watch other pilgrims that come. Some pilgrims – it becomes *home* for the week, and I relate to that.

For many pilgrims, the visit to Walsingham involves going to a place that is ostensibly very different to their towns of origin (and the majority of such pilgrims are urban and working or lower middle class). However, one cannot describe Walsingham as an unfamiliar or novel environment for them. Rather, their regular visits to its sacred spots constitute a predictable and, for some, semi-obligatory part of the liturgical calendar. 'Locating' the 'dwelling' self within the pilgrimage site is not just a matter of seeing Walsingham as a idealized microcosm of (some version of) the Catholic world; it is also a process of self-conscious repetition, a reinvocation of past visits to the site that draws upon interactions between (individual and group) memory, bodily dispositions and the liturgical scripts provided by the shrine. This form of pilgrimage is thus a rhetorical and reflexive assertion that certain connections between space, time and identity can be re-established through mobilities that link, and even at times constitute, contexts of potential 'dwelling'.

Processing through the village, and in particular going up the Holy Mile, can therefore become an embodied metonym of pilgrimage as a whole, and one that takes on extra significance not only because travel to and from the village is normally motorized, but also because walking along the Mile contains an element of 'witness'. Here is an elderly

Roman Catholic woman, describing her perambulation from the village
to the Slipper Chapel with her parish:

> Really it's making a sort of . . . stand that you believe in it . . .
> I mean . . . walking along the road saying the rosary, with the
> traffic going past, can be very funny and you always have to see the
> funny side . . . and I think Catholics are very good at laughing at
> themselves anyway.

Here, she expresses a common sense that, while penance may underlie
some of the contemporary pilgrimage, it is equally concerned with
proclaiming a religious identity to the self and to others; and also her
awareness of what the procession might look like to others, since we see
how what seems so solemn can also be regarded with a degree of irony
(Coleman and Elsner 1998).

Another elderly female Roman Catholic from the same parish (based
in the north-east of England) revealed further dimensions of the walk,
again related to its character as a form of movement:

> We hadn't come to Walsingham to sit on a bus . . . we were going
> to do it properly . . . and . . . to do something . . . to give something
> to Our Lady . . . as sort of in return for, you know . . . what we . . .
> get . . . So we did, just the two of us . . . and we said the rosary as
> we walked along and we sang hymns . . . and then we got to the
> Slipper Chapel and lo and behold . . . a Hexham and Newcastle bus
> came.

Evident here is a distantly penitential sense of 'proper' walking as gift,
but also the implication that such walking establishes difference from
Christians who merely drive directly to the shrine. Such walking acts as
a kind of liturgical frame, distancing the site temporally and spatially from
the everyday in one sense, but at the same time invoking actions familiar
from both parish life and previous pilgrimages.

Both the Roman and the Anglo-Catholic sites also incorporate mini-
pathways within themselves, encouraging perambulation around points
of interest or stations of the cross. In this regard, the replica Holy House
of the Anglican shrine is deeply resonant, and indeed the house is
often visited by Christians from both denominations. It is a small brick
construction, located within the Anglican shrine church, and contains
a statue of the Virgin and Child. In one sense, it is a material symbol of
an idea of home displaced and then emplaced – both Jesus' biblical

dwelling translated to Norfolk and a sacred spot literally 'grounding' an idealized vision of Catholic English faith. Intimacy is built into the construction through its modest size, low lights and location within another building. At the same time, the impression that the Holy House provides a literal and figurative form of dwelling in movement is illustrated by the physical acts of most of the people who enter it from the shrine church. The house is subject to the constant flow of visitors in and out of its confined space, and such flow is encouraged by the presence of two entrances, opposite each other, adjacent to its back wall. Visitors tend to come in and pause, kneeling in front of the statue of the Virgin and Child and perhaps lighting a candle, before leaving. It is a place of both stillness and movement, situated in the centre of the shrine.

The image of Walsingham as 'home' is rendered complex by the presence in the village of two versions of Catholicism. Whether they choose to ignore the 'other' side or not, pilgrims are almost always aware of the presence of parallel rituals. Differences in theological affiliation are expressed through subtle distinctions in custom as well as explicit statements. Roman and Anglo-Catholics are even said to favour different pubs in the village, while a Roman Catholic woman notes: 'Well . . . Anglican vicars dress in a different way . . . often they are more . . . what word would I use? . . . the Anglicans are probably more Catholic than the Catholics!' Her statement illustrates the point that Anglicans are constructing a liturgical tradition, a *habitus*, that is self-consciously orchestrated and articulated not only in relation to the 'Romans', but also in opposition to low-church modes of self-presentation.

Admittedly, pilgrims' expectations of 'homecoming' are sometimes disappointed. An elderly Roman Catholic woman, originally from southern Ireland but living in London, expresses her frustration vividly in the following passage from an interview:

> We started as Henry VIII started . . . out at the Slipper Chapel. We walked in our bare feet in the '50s, which of course pilgrims did. We did that at home as well, I mean you climbed Croagh Patrick in your bare feet; if you are a sinner you climb in your bare feet . . . I said: 'We will walk in our bare feet.' Because the road wasn't made up, it was an old road in those days and it was just a mile long from the Slipper Chapel to Walsingham and you started there and you walked in. *Now*, of course, when I went with the Church down here, All Saints, to the National Pilgrimage, they started *inside* Walsingham and they walked *out* . . . I think that the

[Slipper] Chapel itself is beautiful. I loved it but the only thing that bothered me was that they brought us into Walsingham and brought us out and then brought us home from there.

As is often evident in narratives of past pilgrimages, we see here a jumble of places, times and associations juxtaposed in the person's recall. The pilgrim begins by describing a procession she undertook over 40 years earlier. The decision to walk in bare feet evokes the medieval past but also suggests the penitential expiation of sin through physical suffering. In addition, it provides the narrator with an echo of pilgrimages carried out 'at home' in Ireland. The symbolic power of movement is made even more evident as the woman goes on to describe a recent pilgrimage to Walsingham. Her complaint is that the procession involved motion *away* from the centre of the village (starting at the Roman Catholic pilgrim bureau, situated in the market square), towards the Slipper Chapel. Such movement follows the medieval pathway, but in reverse, thus expressing the current peripherality of the Roman Catholic shrine and implying that the past cannot always fully be revived in the present.

If the village still exhibits tendencies towards segmentary opposition between the two camps, many pilgrims to both shrines are united in the conviction that Walsingham provides a bastion against secularization. In this respect, tourists play a key symbolic role as they exemplify visitors to the village who may have no faith and almost certainly have no previous experience of its shrines. Pilgrims are not strictly 'locals', but they are not transient passers-through either, and in response to my question as to whether pilgrims are easily distinguishable from tourists, interviewees often refer to patterns of movement. An Anglican shrine priest described the contrast in the following way:

I can sometimes tell people who are definitely not pilgrims . . . There's a . . . class of people . . . who have no sense of the numinous, or, of place, of boundaries . . . This . . . came home to me earlier on in the summer when I was sitting in the shrine saying the Office or something, and watching one of Father X's cats . . . And it walked *through* the sanctuary . . . And I thought: 'Why has the cat crossed those boundaries and not gone round in the way that everybody else does?' And, of course, it's because the cat doesn't *see* the boundaries. And I suddenly thought: 'Oh yes, *that's* what it is about these people, these poor folk who come into this place, they don't know the boundaries, they don't know that they've crossed the threshold into something else, and they're wandering around here as though it ought to be Marks and Spencer's and it isn't.' . . . But actually there are lots of boundaries which are unmarked physically, but which are marked mentally, emotionally, in the minds of people who know.

The description of the tourist/cat who rides roughshod over boundaries expresses the idea of a visitor unschooled in the pilgrim *habitus*. Those 'people who know' are relative insiders to the workings of the shrine, and include pilgrims as well as officiating priests. An auratic sense of the numinous is produced through the ability to proceed along well-established pathways that are marked by embodied and habitual practices as much as by material signs or borders.

Speed can also become a signifier of secular outsiderhood. Here is a middle-aged Roman Catholic man, who has come to live in the village, commenting on tourists:

> They drive up through the High Street at ridiculous pace sometimes and stop . . . and really haven't a clue what's going on here at all, or they go straight through and they don't register that this is Walsingham and the history of Walsingham and they are on their way to Wells or somewhere else.

Such behaviour implies ignorance and an attitude that treats Walsingham as an anonymous waystation or 'non-place' (Augé 1995). Interestingly, the same man also recounted a story of an event he witnessed at the Roman Catholic shrine:

> I was in . . . the big Reconciliation Chapel . . . When you walk in . . . you go down on your knees and bow and so on and [there is] absolutely no talking whatsoever and obviously many people go in and that happens, that halo happens, but in come the tourists, open the door, and there was this . . . obviously elderly couple and their son and daughter or whatever and this particular young [woman] . . . And they walked in and . . . they were drawn towards the front of the church and they sat and they were looking round and they were taking photographs; then they came to the altar and, of course, the candles and . . . this girl, I remember she was fascinated, she had been chatting and she went right up to it, she went right up to the altar and said: 'Isn't that lovely, it must be special.' Then she

went down on her knees as if she realized . . . they were overawed, in fact, by what was going on there.

Here we see what is almost a Catholic conversion narrative, expressed through describing movement. In their initial engagement with the shrine, these tourists take photographs rather than responding to it as a place of liturgy. Soon, however, they are not only drawn to the altar but one of their number expresses her attitude by kneeling, presumably in silence.

Of course, it would be wrong to assume that visits to Walsingham consist of only two extremes: rigidly orchestrated pilgrimages or touristic browsing. Still other visitors to the sites may be Christians who are less committed to the fixed liturgies of orthodox Catholicism of either variety. Such pilgrims tend not to see themselves as located within the recurring and predetermined temporal and spatial boundaries so important to parish groups, but are usually more liturgically sophisticated than casual visitors. People may choose to explore the village alone rather than stay with their group; they may attend services of a liturgical tradition that is not their own; some actually stage alternative liturgies such as processions or stations of the cross in spaces adjacent to but not within the established pathways and shrines (Coleman and Elsner 1998). Yet, even as these pilgrims subvert the liturgical boundaries of the shrine, they are usually deploying movement as a form of half-mimesis, a distorted echo both of the past and of the actions of their more conservative contemporaries.

Back to the future

To Faith Christians, all nations can seem at times like generic units: all contain souls that must be saved, irrespective of particularities of culture, landscape or political system. Even so, some countries, such as the USA, are regarded as particularly advanced in reaping benefits and blessings from God. In addition, one country and one city are at the centre of charismatic understandings of their mission and indeed their relationship to sacred text: Israel and Jerusalem.

Particularly from the 1990s onwards, the Word of Life has maintained contacts with Christian Zionist organizations, including the International Christian Embassy, a non-denominational pressure group founded in 1980 and based in Jerusalem. Writing about the role of Christian Zionists in organizing pilgrimages to Jerusalem, Glenn Bowman (1991: 118) quotes one of them, Merv Watson, from an interview:

Our role is to speed up the day in which the ultimate destiny of the day is realized . . . If our faith is anything it's not just nodding our heads to prophecy but getting off our butts to do something to help.

Watson thus expresses, in North American, evangelical idiom, the link between personal agency and eschatology. Such agency can be expressed in a number of ways, often associated with the creation of forms of sacralized mobility. For instance, Christian Zionists interpret the Bible as instructing them to bring God's chosen people, the Jews, back from the diaspora to re-establish the kingdom of Israel (Bowman 1991: 117). Members of the Word of Life certainly seem to have taken the hint. Ulf Ekman claims to have received a personal call from God, during a trip to the Holy Land, to 'Take the Russian Jews Home'. By the end of 1993 the Swedish ministry had obtained a boat with room for up to a thousand people, and its members were paying visits to Russia to encourage Jews to return to their homeland before anti-Semitism, itself a sign of the coming apocalypse, became rife in the diaspora. Swedish charismatics were encouraged to support the project financially for at least a year, and in return they would receive a gift from the ministry that indicated the temporal urgency of the mission: a watch with the prophecy from Jeremiah 16: 14–16 printed on it.[12] Among other things, the verses refer to the children of Israel returning to their land, and coming from the land of the north. Such work is seen as vital because the world itself is moving in linear fashion towards imminent End Times and the return of Jesus. The sooner the whole world is reached by the Gospels, and the Jews have returned to Israel, the sooner Jesus can return. The logic of this position is that the Messiah's return is actually dependent upon the agency of charismatics, who must straddle the globe in order to complete the divine plan for humanity.

The operation to take Jews back to Israel involves the movement of others to the Holy Land. At the same time, Faith ministries such as the Word of Life have been developing extensive programmes to make visits to Israel by believers a regular occurrence. Tourism, in the form of camel rides or driving jeeps in the desert, is combined with tracing Jesus' footsteps around the country. Much of Bowman's (1991: 118) description of evangelical pilgrimage to Jerusalem is relevant here. He notes that visits are not just about tracing Jesus' life historically, but also preparing for His return in the future. Visits are combined with lectures and prayer sessions, marches through the city, as well as consideration of how current and recent events – not least the re-establishment of

Israel itself – are putting contemporary flesh on biblical prophecies. As Bowman points out (1991: 119), the pilgrimage is about enabling pilgrims to feel that they are integrally involved in the divine redemptive project. Often, the pilgrims arrive during the Feast of Tabernacles for a pilgrimage sponsored by the Christian Embassy. Bowman interprets this as allowing them to locate themselves in the history of the Jewish people, who are celebrating Succoth at the same time. But of course this is a form of mimesis that also points to the future, since restoration of the Jewish people means the return of Jesus.

'Pilgrimage'[13] to Israel has become institutionalized within the Word of Life year through the annual tradition, started in the late 1980s, of taking Bible school students on a trip to the Holy Land as a way of rounding off their education (in the future, university students will also probably be involved). A leaflet provided for Bible school students in the mid-1990s notes: 'Many have described how they have gained a whole new view of Israel and a clearer understanding of God's plans for the End times.' It is also claimed that God will talk to each individual believer 'in a special way' in Jerusalem, indicating a characteristically conservative Protestant view of place as catalyst for personal experience. In the first year the journey involved almost 300 students, while a particularly large group involving 900 people visited Israel in 1991.[14] The group's literature noted that it was the largest pilgrimage to Israel since the (first) Gulf War;[15] furthermore, the plane carrying one of the groups was apparently also the one that a few days earlier had brought some Jews back to the country from Ethiopia. The pilgrims were invited to the Knesset where they sang the pilgrims' theme song 'We bless you Israel', and at a huge concert in Jerusalem guests of honour included the mayor of the city and a former speaker of the Knesset. Ekman was even photographed meeting Prime Minister Shamir during the trip.

Note the various ways in which the pilgrimage I have just described demonstrates charismatic agency. The large numbers of people indicate strength of support; the visit involves conventional holy sites as well as a kind of ritual appropriation of parliament;[16] events are staged not just by local people in Israel, but also by the Swedish visitors themselves, who thus bear witness to others of the power of their faith; indeed, the theme song 'We bless you Israel' does not initially mention that Israel, the pilgrimage site, is blessing the pilgrims, but rather the reverse. As a later description of the event put it: 'The Word of Life with this unique journey had the opportunity to proclaim God's view of the land and cry out: "We bless you, Israel!"'[17] According to Faith ideology, God blesses those who bless others, so that the act of blessing Israel is expected to redound upon the self, but it is also significant that the initiative is being taken by pilgrims, not their hosts. Finally, lest we forget the apocalyptic significance of Israel and the forces that are converging upon it, we note the coincidence – though surely it is interpreted as much more than that – of the plane, a prime instrument of modern mobility, that within a few days carries both Swedish pilgrims and returning Jews to the Holy Land.

My description of Faith pilgrimage shows how Rojek and Urry's assumption (1997: 145) that mobility authorizes an increased stance of cosmopolitanism is a little too confident in its assumption of widespread applicability.[18] Sacred travel for these charismatics does not exactly broaden the mind, but reinforces a sub-cultural perspective on inspired agency – an agency that is channelled through a global landscape of missionization oriented theologically and imaginatively, temporally and spatially, towards Jerusalem. Charismatic pilgrimage as I am describing it is a kind of witness to others as well as to oneself, and it seems significant that the Word of Life has set up seminars in Israel aimed at 'educating' locals as well as visitors about the principles of Faith Christianity.[19]

There is much discussion in literature on Jerusalem of how various Christian denominations compete over control of the Church of the Holy Sepulchre (Bowman 1991); however, charismatic attempts to take over space are often more mobile and removed from the confines of a single church. For instance, the march through the streets of Jerusalem arranged by such pilgrims is a means through which to claim temporary occupation of space that is both sacred and part of people's everyday lives. (It also echoes action closer to home, in the form of the annual Word of Life procession through the streets of Uppsala.) In his piece, Bowman (1991: 120) notes how the culmination of the week's celebration of the Feast of Tabernacles is a 'Praise Procession' meant to enact before the eyes of the Israeli people the 'coming up of the nations to Jerusalem' (Leviticus 23: 33–6, 39–43). This sense of occupation of a single city, Jerusalem, by believers who are united yet come from all parts of the globe, certainly seems to be present in Word of Life discourse. For instance, an advert proclaims the opportunity to 'Celebrate the Feast of Tabernacles in Jerusalem together with thousands of participants from the whole world.'[20]

There is, however, another dimension to such pilgrimage. These Christians frequently travel in parties that are led by important pastors.[21] Ekman has been a frequent tour-guide around Israel, and he claims to have visited the country with his wife Birgitta over 40 times since 1987.

Adverts for the pilgrimages juxtapose descriptions of the places and activities offered with enthusiastic mention of the charismatic personalities (frequently from different countries) who will be coming along to preach and teach. We therefore see how place is juxtaposed with, and interpreted through, persons (cf. Eade and Sallnow 1991b: 9) who are not just ordinary believers, but powerful charismatic preachers who embody the mobility that is so valued by these Christians (Coleman 2000a). In thinking about this charismatic juxtaposition of place and person, I am distantly reminded of Jock Stirrat's (1991) analysis of the shift from place-specific Catholic shrines to new person-centred shrines in Sri Lanka over the past century. Stirrat's argument is that locating sacred power in mobile persons removes authority from clerical hierarchies, not least since places are easier to control than individuals who claim direct relationships with the divine. The Church as mediator is therefore bypassed. (A similar problematic was evident in the Hummels' discussion [1995: 15] of Victorian Protestants' liking for empty landscapes rather than buildings.) In the Word of Life case, charismatic ideology is by definition suspicious of 'the Church' in its incarnation as over-institutionalized religion. Yet, structures of authority are clearly embodied in mobile preachers who constitute the new establishment, the new hierarchy of access to divine power. Thus preachers take pilgrims to Jerusalem, but it is a Jerusalem that is created and represented on their terms, through their images and words, with agency primarily located in the actions of leading charismatics who both bear witness of their faith to local inhabitants of the city and act as vehicles for the inspiration that will hasten the return of Jesus to His earthly seat of power. The juxtaposition of Jerusalem the place with charismatic preachers is captured perfectly in a cut-and-paste image produced for a newsletter by a young Word of Life supporter.[22] Emerging from the city we see giant depictions of Ulf Ekman and Lester Sumrall, in classic charismatic poses of mobile inspiration, located definitively and authoritatively within a holy place – indeed, dominating it.[23]

This image has already proved to be something of a fulfilled prophecy. Since the beginning of 2002, Ekman and his wife have actually been living in Jerusalem, engaged in setting up a Word of Life study centre in the city. As they argue on the Word of Life website: 'For a number of years we have felt a calling to establish the Word of Life in Israel so as to be a blessing for the nation.'[24] The aim is for the centre to provide information as well as education, and to act as a base for journeys to Israel, either of immigrants or of more temporary visitors. In the future, it seems likely that functionally-specific visits will also be arranged, such as study journeys, prayer journeys, visits for youth or for pastors and so on. Thus Ekman and Birgitta conclude: 'We want both to take Israel to the faithful and the faithful to Israel.'[25]

If Turner has famously referred to Christian pilgrimage as involving a journey to 'the center out there' (1973), Ulf and Birgitta Ekman appear to be making themselves and their organization a permanent part of the centre itself, as well as facilitating movement to Jerusalem for others. Different kinds of mobility are juxtaposed – ranging from permanently-staying immigrants to short-term travellers – with all contributing to an overall goal of speeding the 'End Times'. Other journeys organized by the group also evoke an eschatological sense of the significance of Jewish history, for instance the visits to World War II concentration camps that the ministry has arranged.[26]

Last words: variations on a theme of movement

Catholic pilgrims to Walsingham seek legitimacy for their vision of nationhood and religion by invoking history. Their deliberate movements replicate what is assumed to be past activity at the site, but take on further dimensions through the establishment of differences in relation to alternative appropriations of the site, including the boundary-breaking impatience of tourists and the iconoclasm of protesting evangelicals. By contrast, Word of Life members explicitly valorize the speed associated with hyper-modernity. 'Pilgrimage' is part of a much wider charismatic repertoire of mobilities that provide spiritual justification for transnational practices (cf. Coleman 2000a). If Catholics seek a kind of 'recurrence' of history, charismatics look more to metaphorical and literal 'progression' towards a future that leads ultimately to the Last Days.[27]

Despite such differences, both constituencies use pilgrimage less as a classic means of penance (although this element is present in some Catholic accounts) and more as a form of witness, a defence of identity in relation to religious and secular alternatives. They therefore invoke sub-culturally specific forms of agency, appropriating place via movement *to* and movement *at* symbolically charged spots. In addition, both constituencies exhibit something of a tension between movement to and dwelling at shrines: just as many Catholics have decided to retire to Walsingham, making it their domestic as well as their spiritual home, the decision of the Ekmans to settle in Jerusalem indicates a charismatic

desire for long-term association with a 'strategic' site. In both cases, distinctions between home and away are collapsed, as is the idea of a return to 'normal' life after pilgrimage.

The forms of movement adopted by Catholics and charismatics can fruitfully be juxtaposed with those described by Frey in her ethnography of contemporary journeying to Santiago de Compostela. According to Frey (1998), complex tensions exist among Compostela pilgrims, centring on the relationship between perceived 'authenticity' of purpose and mode of transport. Travelling by foot across ancient European pathways into northern Spain has the highest status, and car travel the lowest. The bodily and temporal modes involved in slow, effortful travel appear to subvert the rushing, mechanized world of the present, allowing space a kind of victory over time (see Urry 2000: 53, influenced by de Certeau) and helping to produce a sense of contact with the past. If the contemporary world appears to be about the compression of time and space (Harvey 1989), pilgrims to Compostela are entering a kind of sacred decompression chamber.

Both Frey and I are interested in analysing sacred travel in terms of pilgrims' own categories of time, space and movement. The attempt to 'slow down' the world that she describes is reminiscent of many Walsingham pilgrims, but an important difference is that Frey's account focuses almost entirely on journeys to and from Compostela, whereas I have examined the mini-journeys constructed at Walsingham itself. Furthermore, we have seen how members of the Faith Movement (who do admittedly have processional traditions of their own) are on a permanent search for means of personal and collective acceleration, and see such movement as the ultimate expression of an agency that must permeate all of life and not just time in church. Thus, while Urry has noted (1995: 141) that the 'modern subject' is a subject on the move, I hope to have shown that there are many ways to move, just as there are many ways to be modern.

Notes

1 See, for example, Turner and Turner (1978) and the comments by Percy (1998).
2 Over the last 30 years or so Faith or Prosperity Christians have developed a high, and often controversial, profile within neo-Pentecostal, revivalist circles. Combining forms of Positive Thinking, post-war healing revivalism and contemporary charismatic trans-denominationalism, preachers such as Kenneth Hagin, Kenneth and Gloria Copeland and Lester Sumrall have

had considerable success in setting up televangelical ministries and global networks of believers united by fellowships, Bible schools, conferences and consumption of media.

3 See the Introduction to this volume for a discussion of 'performative' pilgrimage.

4 Of either a 'religious' or a 'secular' character.

5 Much of the following summary of Walsingham's history is adapted from Coleman (2000b).

6 Printed by Richard Pynson, located in Magdalene College, Cambridge.

7 In fact, neither shrine possesses the site revealed by excavations in the 1960s to be the probable location of the original Holy House: it is situated much closer to the ruins of the Augustinian priory in the centre of the village.

8 http://www.walsingham.org.uk/

9 An important figure in organizing 'secular' tours of the Holy Land was Thomas Cook, himself a former preacher.

10 1994–5 Brochure for the Bible Centre, pp. 5–7.: 'Varje medlem ber, ger och går'.

11 Some of my argument here is taken from Coleman (2000b).

12 *Word of Life Newsletter*, 1994, 2.

13 The word 'pilgrimage' is not normally used; 'resa' or 'journey' is more common. My account relies on fieldwork in Sweden rather than in Israel.

14 *Word of Life Newsletter*, 1991, 3: 6–7. To date (September 2003), the Word of Life claims to have transported a total of 6,000 people on these visits to Israel.

15 A claim made before the outbreak of the second Gulf War.

16 Organizers often try to arrange meetings with local people who are regarded as being 'strategically' important in Israel, such as pastors and businessmen.

17 *Word of Life Newsletter*, 1991, 3: 7.

18 Similarly, I think that constructing a dichotomy (drawing on Bauman 2000) between Walsingham pilgrims as seekers after fixity, and charismatics as engaged on a quest for open-ended identity, would be too crude. For instance, we see how these conservative Protestants do not embrace pluralism or contingency in their construction of an orientation towards transnationalism.

19 This desire to educate local people in God's plan as well as in Faith ideology perhaps contains a distant echo of nineteenth-century Victorian attempts to enlighten the inhabitants of the Holy Land.

20 *Word of Life Newsletter*, 1991, 3: 12.

21 Variants of this are present in many pilgrimage traditions, of course.

22 *Nyhetsbrevet Blås i Trumpet på Sion*, April 1987, p.1.

23 This image perhaps provides a definitive charismatic example of Eade and Sallnow's pilgrimage 'trio' of person, place and text (1991b: 9).

24 September 2003.

25 September 2003.

26 The group also keeps a record of Jewish visitors to its headquarters in Uppsala, including former Prime Minister Benjamin Netanyahu.

27 This is not to say that future-oriented discourse is absent from Walsingham pilgrims. For instance, a few people have spoken to me of the place's potentially key role in bringing Christian denominations together into one unified body of Christ.

Chapter 4

Going and not going to Porokhane

Mourid women and pilgrimage in Senegal and Spain

Eva Evers Rosander

Religion and gender

This chapter deals with Senegalese women, members of a Sufi *tariqa* (Arabic: 'way', order) called Mouridism, and their religious ideas and practice in both Senegal and Tenerife, Spain.[1] My main aim is to compare women's religious practice in Senegal and in the diaspora. I want to examine two key themes: (i) the ways in which women's access to fairly large financial resources in Tenerife influences their religiosity and changes their position in the Mourid community in Senegal and (ii) how Mouridism – a genuinely Senegalese Sufi form of Islam – has adapted to the hectic tourist ghetto activities in Tenerife's Playa de las Américas.

Mouridism offers a moral space for the women in this diaspora – a space both religious and secular (cf. Evers Rosander 2000). In this situation, what new and hybrid forms of Mouridism are we referring to? Does access to money give women a new form of agency? And, if this is the case, is the main arena for the display of status and prestige of these female Mourid migrants located in Senegal or in Spain? In which geographical or social field is their moral reputation contested, negotiated and confirmed?

Interpreting Mouridism and its main events, the pilgrimages, as one form of embodied and gendered social movement opens up new aspects of religious practice. My approach is inspired by Sered's focus (1992) on women's religious practice as characterized by caring for others. Mourid women in Senegal, just like the Kurdish Jewish women in Israel studied by Sered, set out on organized journeys to pilgrimage sites, including Porokhane, a major focus of this chapter. They seem to share the belief that the journey from start to end is a religious event. They also appear to enjoy the journey as an annual break and an attractive excursion, with a legitimate and respectable purpose, offering a mixture of both new and well-known sensations. Women's pilgrimages contribute positively to their respectability and moral reputation; morality being, according to Sered, a vital part of female religiosity (see also Tapper 1990; Evers Rosander 1991; Gemzoe 1999).

When Eickelman and Piscatori assert (1990: 15) that social scientists have until recently downplayed the transnational dimensions of pilgrimage, they draw attention to something important but hitherto not examined: the travel element. Paying particular attention to travel fits my theoretical approach just as much as it occupies the minds of my Mourid informants in both Senegal and Spain. If, as Eickelman and Piscatori suggest (1990c: 3), we think of travel as a specific form of social action within Muslim religious traditions, we will get a better understanding of the female preoccupation with going and not going to Porokhane.

Urry's recent discussion of travel (2002) is helpful here. He asks why people travel at all, given their access to new communication technologies. He distinguishes between four types of movement – the *physical* movement of objects, which in my context could refer to women sending money to Porokhane, *imaginative* and *virtual* travel by people (in my context this would refer to the use of videos, listening to other people's stories and remembering earlier pilgrimages) and *corporeal* travel (this would refer to the women who actually go to Porokhane as pilgrims or journey transnationally as a form of 'embodied social life' (2002: 255) or even a 'way of life' (2002: 256).

Urry also considers another concept which is relevant to my analysis – co-presence. He distinguishes between *occasional* co-presence, and again *imagined* and *virtual* co-presence (2002: 256). The women who go to Porokhane can be said to belong to the first category, those who do not could be included within the second category, while virtual co-presence is created through gifts of money taking the women's place in the pilgrimage. My point is that in this particular case women's corporeal absence is compensated by the physical co-presence of money, which increases their social capital and is converted into moral capital. This constitutes, therefore, an interesting combination of the variables of co-presence outlined by Urry.

Although pilgrimage is usually associated with strong and well-known elements of mobility, it may actually entail physical immobility combined with religious imaginary mobility (cf. Eickelman and Piscatori 1990c). Both corporeal and imaginative co-presence in pilgrimage open up ways of becoming someone else to generate increased moral capital. This entails discarding and leaving behind one's former identity and entering a state of raised consciousness about something beyond the everyday, routinized self, and remaining in this state for an unlimited period of time. It means achieving an identity as a pilgrim in life, as a way of being in the world (cf. Yamba 1995). Diasporic Mourid women's religious practices show the relevance of paying attention to this aspect of pilgrimage.

I also want to complement earlier political and social scientists' statements about Mourid women's invisibility or passivity in religious life (Cruise O'Brien 1971; Copans 1988). While recent research has examined women's marginality in religious life (cf. Callaway and Creevey 1994), the vast field of Mourid women's religious traditions, ideas and practices has been ignored until recently. Surprisingly little has been written on areas of Sufi Islam where women are involved, in general, and the underlying beliefs and 'sacred strategies' that motivate Mourid women's agency, in particular.

A theme conspicuous by its absence in the research on Senegalese Mouridism concerns the ways in which religious faith – expressed in religious acts or rituals – is tightly connected with economic resources and the generation and accumulation of such resources. The study of Mourid traders abroad has fortunately resulted in studies such as the works by Ebin (1995, 1996), Carter (1997), Riccio (2001, 2003) and Tall (2002). Carter, in particular, deals with commerce among Mourids in Italy in a way similar to what Parry and Bloch describe as 'a relationship between a cycle of short term exchange which is the legitimate domain of the individual – often acquisitive – activity, and a cycle of long term exchanges, concerned with the production of the social and cosmic order' (1989: 2). Yet little attention has been paid so far to Senegalese women traders in the diaspora and their religious practice.

Mouridism in Senegal

Mouridism as a religious institution and/or movement is a characteristic part of Senegalese civil society, held together by the *khalif général*, a son of the founder, and other close family members. The hierarchical structure has a base of disciples, organized in religious associations (Wolof: *daira*). The religious associations function as moral, religious and social spaces for Mourids in Senegal as well as abroad. The *daira*'s economic activities constitute the core of its existence. A previously agreed financial contribution (Wolof: *addiyya*) is regularly collected, usually at the monthly meetings. The Mourid religious leader (Wolof:

shaykh; French: *marabout*), to whom the activities of the association are dedicated, receives the money at the annual feast in the *marabout*'s house, where all his disciples assemble. A *shaykh*, who displays great wealth through the size of his house, his cars and his bejewelled wives, also has much blessing (Wolof: *barke*). Such a *marabout* has great resources to share with his disciples in the form of money, spiritual power and blessing (cf. Ebin 1995).

It is the duty of the religious leader to return something of his blessing and his well-being to each disciple. The reason I write *he* (the disciple) is that all the Mourid *marabouts* and disciples are supposed to be male. Only if a *marabout* has no sons may his daughter, under very special conditions, take over from her father as religious leader. The daughters of the *marabouts* and women who are married to *marabouts* are called *sokhna*. There are examples of women who have their own disciples (cf. Coulon and Reveyrand 1990; Jean 1997) and who have become famous because of their piety or high position – as a daughter of the founder, for example. These women are comparatively few, however. Mourid women are expected to have the same kind of relationship to their men folk that their men have to their religious leaders, i.e. they should be obedient and subservient.

I have chosen the pilgrimage (Wolof: *magal*) to Porokhane, where the mother of the founder of Mouridism is venerated, because my focus is on Mourid women and their religious practices. Mam Diarra Bousso, the mother of the greatest personality in Mouridism, Shaykh Amadou Bamba, is a female mystic 'saint', who inspires all Mourids, particularly the women. She is an ideal model for male disciples in their relationship with their *marabouts* but, for the women, she is also an ideal mother and wife, with whom they can identify in their various familial roles: as daughters-in-law, or as the second or third wife in a polygynous marriage.

Yet although men always put Mam Diarra's son first in the religious hierarchy, Mourid women assert that the two – the mother and the son – are one. Mam Diarra is just as sacred and highly ranked a religious personality as the son. Moreover, they argue, in accordance with the current ideology of the dominant Senegalese ethnic groups Wolof and Halpulaar, that it is because of the mother's morally stainless behaviour that the son has achieved such great moral and spiritual qualities. Mourid women also state again and again that, as a mother, Mam Diarra gives more generously than her son. She does not deny the pilgrims anything when they visit her tomb in Porokhane. Whatever the size of the gift or the favour that the pilgrims ask from her, her generosity is 'like the sea' or 'without limits', as the women put it.

Sacred travel

Mouridism is a *tariqa* with universal missionary ambitions, connected globally through rapidly expanding religious, economic, social and political networks. The Mourids' strong religious identity and their efficiently coordinated transnational networks certainly encourage Mouridism. Expansion is also facilitated by the financial resources that emigration offers, not least because of the contributions of the diasporic associations to the Mourid establishment in Touba. From the well-organized centre in Touba, Senegal, the Mourid leader and his collaborating disciples coordinate the *tariqa*'s activities in Senegal and follow the diasporic activities. This is done through frequent and distant journeys undertaken by the *marabouts*, who visit the Mourid diasporic associations in different parts of the world, giving advice, blessing disciples and collecting money. The *physical* movement of money from Tenerife to Senegal constitutes the core link between the two countries and the centre around which all activities circle.

Spain constitutes just one of many Mourid diasporic arenas for religious and economic transactions between Senegal and Europe (Italy, France, Spain), Senegal and the USA (New York, Chicago, Atlanta) and between Senegal and other Mourid groups scattered around the world. It is fascinating to see how these constellations of Mourid immigrants, living abroad, are to some extent culturally hybrid and dynamic, while they are also sustained by an emphasis on the compelling nature of obligations and social control. This is something which the Mourid migrants and disciples strongly feel across space and national boundaries. Mourids have an existential connection with other co-diasporics elsewhere and in the home country (cf. Werbner 2002: 251f.).

In the history of Mouridism, as well as today, sacred travel, forced travel, travel and trade and travel and miracles are important ingredients which have powerful religious meaning for the believers. Sacred travel in Mouridism involves the institutionalization of mobility in physical and also ideological terms. The expulsion of the Mourid founder by the French and his various exiles in other African countries provide contemporary Mourid migrants outside the homeland with images and references, which are expressed in a religious idiom. The Mourids think of their travels in terms of exile and pilgrimage, underlining hard work, suffering and sacrifice as religious duties. In his book on Senegalese Mourid men in Italy, Carter (1997) reflects on this migration as a new form of *hijra* or sacred journey of the Senegalese Mourids. The exile into which the founder of Mouridism was forced serves as an example for the Mourids to follow in the contemporary European diaspora – '[t]ravel and the hardships associated with it have become a core of the Mourid imagination and a justification for the political importance of the Mourid' (1997: 63).

The emigrants identify themselves more with their Mourid 'saints', such as Shaykh Amadou Bamba and Mam Diarra, than with other Muslim saintly personalities and the pilgrimage to Touba is for many Mourids of greater importance than the *hajj* to Mecca. As in tourism practice, the essential character of space in Mourid migration to other countries lies in its combination of the material and the metaphorical (cf. Crang 2002: 207).

The *magal* and *communitas*

The *magal* in Porokhane can be analysed in different ways, following the dominant theoretical discourses in anthropology concerning pilgrimage. It is easy enough to find the Turners' ideas about *communitas* (Turner and Turner 1978) confirmed in the pilgrims' attitudes to each other and in their enactment of the *ziyara* (the walk around the pilgrim site), their visits to the holy places and participation in the commemorative activities. Equality is stressed at all social levels and non-kin men generally make an effort to show respect to women they do not know in Porokhane.

The Turnerian idea of *communitas* (1978) has been challenged by Eade and Sallnow (1991a), who argued that *communitas* was just one idealizing discourse about pilgrimage. Yamba (1995) also distances himself from the Turnerian model. He criticizes the way in which many anthropologists have allowed the Turners' varied and complex pronouncements on pilgrimage to provide 'what amounts to an uncomfortable yardstick for every prospective analysis of the phenomenon' (1995: 9). For Yamba a better anthropological approach is to 'hide behind one's own ethnography' (ibid.), in order to avoid what he calls 'that seminal, if rather overworked, model of "structure" and "anti-structure" which most anthropologists, who embark on the study of pilgrimage, inevitably adopt as the main theoretical model for their analysis' (ibid.). The West Africans in Sudan, studied by Yamba, live there as 'permanent pilgrims'; they see themselves as pilgrims on their way to Mecca, even though they never actually arrive there. They *do not* share a sacred goal for a limited period, set by religiously determined dates, and they *do not* set out on a journey with a well-defined group of co-pilgrims. Pilgrimage follows these West Africans through the various life processes. They live in a pilgrimage continuum, in both time and space.

Despite these criticisms of the Turnerian model, some Mourids may fit into this model, at least partially. They go once a year on a two-day pilgrimage (from a Thursday morning to a Friday late night, including the journey) to the *magal* of Mam Diarra Bousso in Porokhane. Each year the date of the pilgrimage is decided by the Bousso family in agreement with the Mourid leader in Touba. Most of the women go as members of their regional religious associations and most of them carry the same name – the *daira* of Mam Diarra Bousso.

Mourid women in Playa de las Américas

Senegalese women started their 'exodus' to Spain on a small scale during the 1990s. Before then, men mostly migrated alone (Sarr 1998). The first women to join their husbands went as housewives, not as professional traders. In 2001 about 20 per cent of the Senegalese in Playa de las Américas were women (around 50 women). Many, who lived without their husbands, stayed with female family members or with other Senegalese women migrants. Some came originally to Tenerife as members of an African dancing group and remained to survive from trading and braiding, like those who came after them. Today quite a number of these women are cosmopolitans whose lifestyle is based on travelling for commercial purposes.

All Senegalese migrants' lives are affected by the Spanish requirements of valid visas and residence and labour permits. Those who do not have valid papers are always anxious and afraid of being caught by the police. They are permanently ready to run away and have their merchandise loaded up in bags and bundles for a speedy departure. Indeed, trading with clothes and with *madera* (Spanish: wooden sculptures) or making braids in the streets produces bad nerves and aching bodies. Women dream of earning enough money to be able to travel freely between Senegal and Spain and to have access to both 'worlds', trading both ways. If they can afford to go back to Senegal after three months, they renew their visa for another three months. They can then stay legally in Spain for shorter periods, avoiding problems with the Spanish authorities. They would like to put their Tenerife goods on sale in Senegal in their own shops or in the large houses, which they build or plan to build with the money they earn from trading. Since they are used to travel and need to maintain their commercial networks, they would prefer to hire someone to care for the shop so that they can be 'on the move' periodically throughout the year.

Women complain about the lack of free time in Tenerife, compared to

Senegal. The fact that the more time they spend in the streets selling or braiding, the more money they earn is very stressful for them. The lack of time and private space influences their religious life in many different ways. Praying is confined to mornings and evenings; they pray twice in the morning and three times when they return home from work in the middle of the night. As nobody seems to know what kind of Spanish food they can eat to avoid the risk of pork or derivates of pork, they mostly avoid food other than their own. This means that they spend most of the day without eating. During Ramadan, the month of fasting, everybody tries to go home to Senegal. Those who cannot because of lack of money and valid papers have to break their fast at night, while working out in the streets. This is difficult for those who refuse to eat Spanish food. They often end up with just a cup of coffee at McDonald's, close to the main street where they sell and braid.

All work carried out and all money earned and given away as *addiyya* (donations of money for religious purposes such as covering the costs of a visiting *marabout*, repairing the mosque or constructing a hospital in Touba) is regarded as a substitute for prayers or as a religious act. Each night one or two young men walk around the central streets of Playa de las Américas to collect *addiyya*. Some gifts are voluntary and vary according to each person's will and ability. Other fees, such as the monthly fee to the *daira* in Santa Cruz (also called *addiyya*), are fixed. Each year before the *magal* in Touba and in Porokhane, people are free to give as much as they want. The sum is noted in a list and receipts for the money are sent to Touba and to Porokhane.

It is an obligation for a Mourid to give donations to the association. As social control is strong, payment is also a prerequisite for feeling comfortable with others. This situation certainly creates stress and anguish for many Mourids in the diaspora and is sometimes a real burden for those who have failed economically. For a time they get financial help from their compatriots, but they sometimes end up marginalized in the Mourid diasporic community.

Some women who migrate to Tenerife are not Mourid but come as members of other religious orders. Still, as the Mourids are such a strong and dominant group in Tenerife, the others also pay the monthly *addiyya* to the Mourid association. In Senegal, the daily and varied collections of money that are found in Tenerife do not exist. In the homeland, access to cash is scarce and people are more scattered and hard to locate.

Mourid women in Tenerife have a direct and close relationship with Mam Diarra Bousso. For instance, the female migrants count on her help and protection; the money they pay to her and to Porokhane is a sign of the conservation and activation of this tie. One woman in Puerto de la Cruz, Tenerife, showed her pliable cardboard poster, on which she had attached different sorts of wraps for sale. She put it in front of her on the sidewalk and quite spontaneously said: 'I have given my cardboard the name of Mam Diarra Bousso. Each day I tell her to come with me and give me luck in my work. Without her I can do nothing.'

Mourid women in Mbacké, Senegal

Most women who live in the town of Mbacké, 180 kms from Dakar and 8 kms from Touba, belong to the biggest ethnic group in Senegal, the Wolof. The great majority of them are Mourid. Female urban associations flourish in Mbacké, dominating women's social, economic and religious daily life. Apart from the *dairas*, the women see each other in self-help and rotating savings associations. Their economic means are small and, from their perspective, every coin that they have to pay for religious purposes deprives their fund of money for family food, medicines and school fees. They prefer to work in the fields of the *marabouts* and the *khalif général* whenever they get the chance, in order to be good Mourids. The *marabouts* use the local radio to call for people's help with the harvest of millet or groundnuts and Mourid urban women hurry to present themselves as soon as they get the message. They can thereby compensate for their lack of money for religious purposes and fulfil the Mourid ideal of work as prayer.

Many women in Mbacké have also paid small annual extra fees to Porokhane, money that was not given as *addiyya* to the *marabout* family in Porokhane. The women have bought special cards from the Mourid *marabouts* to finance the construction of what was said to be a Women's Pilgrims' House in Porokhane. On my visit there in spring 2001 I found to my surprise that the new buildings were meant for the male Mourid establishment, mainly for the *khalif général* and his sons and grand-sons with their families. The women's house was not yet ready and not designated for 'ordinary' female pilgrims but for the religious and political elite. No signs of disappointment, however, were noticeable among the women. They expressed pride over the large buildings that had actually been constructed with the help of their physical work and money. At the 2003 *magal* a special department for *sokhna Mai* (Mam Diarra Bousso's representative in Porokhane) was ready and in use for eminent Mourid women and *sokhna Mai*'s guests.

The women's piety and their willingness to endure bodily pain and fatigue contributes to the glory of Mouridism and generates female moral and religious credit (cf. Tapper 1990: 234). Physical effort for the good of Mouridism could be interpreted as both a religious strategy and a search for ways to increase their scarce economic resources through different forms of petty trade. They invest their available time for work and financial resources in the name of Shaykh Amadou Bamba and his mother. The majority of women whom I met in the association described below talked about Mam Diarra Bousso, the generous mother, as a source of concrete hope for them. That was why going to her tomb in Porokhane on pilgrimage was so important for them.

The *daira* of Mam Diarra Bousso in Mbacké

In Mbacké, I studied one of the *dairas* dedicated to Mam Diarra Bousso that has only female members (cf. Evers Rosander 1998). Besides the collection of money (*addiyya*), the members inform each other about various current religious events in the neighbourhood and invite *marabouts*, who call themselves 'religious experts', to their meetings. The 'experts' tell already well-known legends about Mam Diarra and answer religious questions.

The main ambition of the Mam Diarra Bousso *daira* is to go to Porokhane each year. The trip is a major undertaking, demanding organization and planning. Usually the members of the *daira* stay away from home for two days and one night. A vehicle has to be hired and the food for the trip has to be prepared. All this requires time, money and initiative. There is also a moral component, which must be taken into account. The women are not expected to travel without male protection far from home with all the money collected by the *daira*. The members of the *daira* said that they travelled respectably as a group and with an acknowledged, religious purpose. Their president also had a good reputation for piety. Even so, a police officer, who hired a room in her compound, accompanied the group on the trip I undertook with the *daira* in 1995, to guarantee that the trip was conducted in an honourable and respectful manner.

The women of the association in Mbacké go to Porokhane to ask Mam Diarra for help with cases of infertility, matrimonial difficulties and economic problems. As I have already mentioned, the visit to the tomb of Mam Diarra is by far the most important part of the pilgrimage. No promises are given that, if a woman's request should be fulfilled, she would make a return gift. Mam Diarra gives and helps unconditionally.

For the members of the Mam Diarra Bousso association, the expenses connected with the pilgrimage can be a heavy economic burden or can even prevent them from going. In addition to the total sum of the monthly *addiyya*, which they have paid to the Mam Diarra association during the whole year, they must add the necessary money to enable the association to afford to hire a vehicle and buy food for the trip. In return for the effort of going to Porokhane and performing the *ziyara* – the walk with thousands and thousands of pilgrims in the overcrowded and hot shrine – the women gain access to Mam Diarra's mystical powers of healing and help. They have shown their capacity to make a physical effort (Wolof: *jëf*) because of their strong desire to go to Porokhane. For these women, a sense of physical co-presence such as walking, seeing, touching, hearing and smelling the pilgrimage is of the greatest importance (cf. Urry 2002: 261). Besides the *barke* (Wolof: blessing) they receive from the *marabout* (or, in the case of the women, from *sokhna Mai*), they also gain *tiyaba* (Wolof: religious merit) from God directly.[2]

To get religious merit the women do not need the *marabout*'s mediation. Religious merit is something that God offers both men and women as a 'payment' for the good acts that they carry out for him. On Doomsday, the women say, God will state how much *tiyaba* each person has accumulated during his/her lifetime. It is true that both women and men can collect it; there are no gender constraints. However, *tiyaba* may be more important for women, as their access to *barke* or blessing is more limited compared with the men (cf. Buitelaar 1993). *Barke* is mainly inherited patrilineally and women, daughters and wives of *marabouts* transfer less *barke* than male family members.

The *daira* of Mam Diarra Bousso in Tenerife

The Mam Diarra Bousso *daira* in Tenerife is not at all as active as the one in Mbacké, if it could be said to exist at all. In Tenerife, the association for both men and women is called the Tenerife-Touba *daira* and it is totally dominated by the men. The men refer to the women members of the Tenerife-Touba association as a Mam Diarra *daira*. However, the women say that ever since the president of the female *daira* went to Mallorca nobody has been in charge. Very few women gather in Santa Cruz for the monthly meetings of all the members across Tenerife. Those few women who do attend sit in the terrace or in a room separate from the men. The women make food for the men, who eat apart from the women once the formal monthly meeting has finished.

The women also exchange news from Senegal and, above all, tell each other about merchandise and its prices. The men pray and sing the religious songs called *khasaids*, after which they start planning for the arrival of the *marabouts* from Senegal as well as discussing the coming religious events and *magals* and the financial situation of the association. Sometimes they have no time for anything but the financial discussions. In 2001 the high cost of looking after the visiting *marabouts* was a hot topic at these monthly meetings.

Since women are not asked to participate in the financial discussions or decision-making of any other kind, they find it a waste of time and money to attend *daira* meetings in Santa Cruz. Consequently, their *daira* activities are minimal compared to Senegal. The women who do not live in Santa Cruz prefer to use the time for wrap making or selling clothes and tree sculptures in the streets and marketplaces. Each hour not dedicated to selling T-shirts or making braids seems to cause irritation. Most women do not stay at home for any other reason than sleeping for a few hours from late at night until morning. The rest of the day they work.

Women compensate for their absence by paying their monthly fees to the Tenerife-Touba association, which are 5,000 pesetas a month (in 2001) – a little more than 30 euros. Moreover, they give money to visiting *marabouts* and to other collectors of money for special Mourid purposes (see pp. 73 and 76). According to the women, the *marabouts* 'sell' prayers and the women 'buy' them with the money they get from wrap making, petty-trading and wholesale commerce. One of the visiting *marabouts* explained that he 'sold' prayers to the Mourid, just as, he argued, God 'sells' Paradise to the faithful. The money 'works' for the Mourid believer who gives *addiyya*. It is by studying the practice of *addiyas*, and by investigating what 'selling' and 'buying' means in religious terms, that one begins to understand how religious activity actually is constituted in this particular Islamic setting. It definitely leads to understanding how intensely Mourid women in Tenerife experience their own participation in religious life by earning their own money and giving *addiyya*.

The women in Tenerife who claim not to have the time, the money nor, in many cases, the visa for attending to the *magals* in Senegal stay in Spain. They prefer to earn more money as street peddlers, market vendors and, particularly during the busy season of spring and summer 2000, making braids in a 'rasta' hairstyle for the tourists. The height of the tourist season in the Canary Isles coincided with the *magal* in Touba between 1996 and 2000. The *magal* in Porokhane is generally celebrated some months before the *magal* in Touba, and the women would have liked to go to both but could not be away for so long.

All these factors contribute to the women's decision to stay in Tenerife. The women said to me in summer 2001 that they would have liked to go to Porokhane in spring 2001 and that they had the *intention* (Wolof: *yéene*) to go. The intention counts as a religious act as well as the money they give to the Bousso and Mbacké *marabouts* in Porokhane for the pilgrimage. The more money one can give, the more prayer and blessing one will get. This may not literally be the case, of course. However, the general idea is that the money will work for the donor so that the *marabout*'s prayer will be more effective if the sum offered is big. The money, given to the *marabout* in Porokhane, is also perceived as a gift to Mam Diarra. The act of giving and the intention to go to Porokhane work to create a notion of participation at a distance in the *magal* and encourage imaginative travel. A representative of the religious Mourid association of Tenerife goes to Porokhane, sometimes together with other Tenerife Mourids, to hand over the money on behalf of the members of the Tenerife-Touba association. Some women talk about the *magal* in Porokhane as if they had really participated in the *magal*, thereby including the site of Porokhane in their imagined diasporic sacred space. Their gifts of money are travelling for them, like pilgrims.

When I talked to some of the women who were going to Senegal from Playa de las Américas to attend the *magal* in Porokhane in 1997, they made it clear that they were going as members of the Tenerife-Touba religious association. They had chosen not to go with family members nor with the former Senegalese *daira* in their hometowns. As members of a rich diasporic *daira*, they expected to be treated by the members of the Bousso *marabout* family in Porokhane with much more respect and attention than ordinary Senegalese people. This meant that the association's representatives were offered a very prestigious place near the dwellings of the famous *marabouts* in Porokhane. They were served food by Mourid disciples. Futhermore, the *daira* did not usually have to wait long for an audience with the *marabout*, a grandson of Shaykh Amadou Bamba, when the *addiyya* was handed over together with the list of the names of the donors in Tenerife. Each of the attending pilgrims from Tenerife was introduced by his or her name to the *marabout*. He gave them an individual as well as a collective blessing, promising to pray for them and for the migrants in Tenerife who had contributed to the *addiyya*, so that their wishes would be fulfilled.

The Bousso establishment's respectful behaviour towards the *daira* female and male members increased their social status and added to their social capital among the other pilgrims. Rumours about the treatment of the Tenerife *daira* members in Porokhane rapidly spread along the channels of the family network and the Tenerife pilgrims were received as eminent persons in their Senegalese homes. They were looked upon as some sort of 'stars', giving receptions in their homes and receiving demands for economic support from relatives and friends. The religious image added to their fame and respectability. The fact that the size of their financial contribution to the Bousso *marabout* was considerable and increasing annually facilitated the transformation of the *addiyya* into social capital, visible in the Bousso family's way of receiving them in Porokhane. These deeds of merit of pilgrims/donors meant an increasing moral capital, which affected their standing in relation to relatives, neighbours and other people in Senegal.

Religious experts in Tenerife

When the *marabouts* come to Tenerife on their regular visits, they call themselves 'religious experts'. They are put up at expensive hotels at the cost of the Mourid community members in Tenerife. Food is prepared by a few women and carried to the hotel suite of the *marabout*, where he receives the male disciples for prayer, economic and political discussions and planning of future Mourid activities in Senegal and abroad. He also presides at the collection of *addiyya* from the Mourid community members in Tenerife.

Women generally take time off from their work to go and see the visiting religious leader at night, when he has finished his religio-political discussions with the Mourid men. This is a unique occasion for the women because they are in the presence of and in close, almost physical, contact with the holiest and most prestigious leaders of the Mourid establishment. In Senegal, female Mourids would never get a chance like this, being low status women from families with modest incomes. Their religious associations at home usually lack any financial significance, especially compared with what the diasporic *daira* can offer the Mourid *marabout*.

One by one the women approach the *marabout*, sitting in an armchair in front of the kneeling or prostrating disciples. The women are not supposed to look at the *marabout*. They cannot touch any part of his body, not even his hands. The women are introduced by their names to the *marabout* and the men in his entourage learn them by heart for future visits. The *marabout* first receives an envelope containing money, which is handed over to a young Mourid male assistant, and then listens to the woman's preoccupations. Questions and pleas for help concerning the Spanish police and difficulties with visa or labour permits dominate the conversations. The religious leader promises to pray for the woman and blesses her. She thinks the *marabout* has magical powers and that his blessing will actively influence the outcome of her commercial activities so that her living conditions in Tenerife will be improved (cf. Evers Rosander 2000). His physical presence radiates *barke*, which to some extent is transferred to the woman's body.

The *marabouts*' visits to Mourid *dairas* all over the world are dedicated to building and maintaining religious networks. The travelling *marabouts* exchange information with male *daira* members in the diaspora about other Mourids, about national and international politics and about financial matters. The Mourid establishment in Touba constitutes the centre of the overlapping networks of the travelling *marabouts*, whose approach is characterized by a mix of formal and 'personal, fluid and informal forms of social linking' (Putnam 2003: 647). There are good contemporary examples of interpersonal networks whose spread and increasing size is very much dependent on aeroplanes and mobile telephones. Because of illiteracy, virtual networks and contacts through e-mails do not work efficiently.

The reciprocal character of the visiting *marabouts*' relations with their disciples is, quite naturally, more accentuated than with Mam Diarra Bousso, who died 150 years ago. Encounters with the great Mourid *marabouts* abroad contribute to the migrants' social capital. Thus, through money and through presence, women get access to the blessing of the *marabouts* in a direct and personal manner, something not available to 'ordinary' Senegalese women in the homeland. The money is transformed into social and moral capital, as status and prestige, resulting from the blessing and the prayers of the *marabout*, accumulate (cf. Bourdieu 1977). Outside the migrants' Mourid network in Senegal and in Tenerife, money spent on Mourid *marabouts* is devoid of meaning. In Spain it gives status and prestige among other Mourids only in relation to the size of the *addiyya*. In Senegal, such donations may even be regarded by non-Mourids as a waste of money, spent by uneducated people who do not know better.

Among the Mourids in Senegal the migrant woman needs the status that the co-presence and proximity to the great *marabout* in Tenerife have given her. This helps her not to be looked down upon in Senegal for being a woman trader who works among unbelievers and lives in Spain, a non-Muslim space. Earning money outside a religious framework may even do more harm than good to a woman trader or hair braider in

Tenerife, since it could give rise to hate and envy back home. The female migrant runs the risk of being regarded as an immoral woman, thereby spoiling her chances of becoming a reputable wife and a respectable mother in Senegal. She may even be accused of having earned her money through witchcraft, at the expense of other women in Tenerife whose luck will decline. Consequently, the *marabout*'s visits and the blessing he gives make her strong and powerful. Her economic success will be interpreted in religious terms – as a sign of God's benevolence towards her, because of the *marabout*'s prayers.

Mouridism and money

The importance attached to the collection of money within the *daira* and for other religious purposes demands some further explanation. Money in Senegal is to a very high degree considered to be a part of oneself. The relationship established by monetary transactions is seen as loaded with significance. Money spent on the *marabout* is really money with agency, acting for the giver, and money with a spiritual dimension. It can also be said to act as a metonymical representative of the women with a mediating mission.[3] At the same time, giving *addiyya* to a Mourid *marabout* or to the *khalif général* provides a kind of strengthened identity both as a *daira* member and as a Mourid, since one is behaving in a moral and correct manner. Through intense communication by mobile telephones and travel, the women's social and moral reputations are rapidly spread through the channels of the social networks.

The money that a woman does not invest in Mouridism at different levels goes to her own family in Senegal, to the husband and his family and into her own purchase of cars, houses, jewellery, children's education, and so on. Family and religion are certainly areas of strategic investment for the women, who, even as rich and devoted Mourids, have to consider their moral vulnerability as females. Morality and respectability are key words in the negotiation of a woman's social reputation, especially for a successful female trader. Even if economic change affects Mourid women's room for manoeuvre in new ways, the underlying religious ideas and the symbolic and social structure seem firmly established (cf. Parry and Bloch 1989). As mentioned, the gendered religious ideology, asserting men's superiority over women, is only slowly affected by these new economic opportunities for women.

Mam Diarra Bousso: images, rituals, realities

The general idea of the Mourid women seems to be that Mam Diarra Bousso as a sacred mother is a generous and loving person, who gives away unconditionally and quickly what the pilgrim asks for by using her mystical power. The plea is particularly successful when enacted at her tomb in Porokhane. Her son, who was buried in Touba, also gives what the pilgrim asks for, even if, according to some women, his gifts are more restricted. According to Mourid tradition, the Mourid founder once said: 'If you give me a sum, you will get back ten times as much.' However, Mam Diarra doesn't put any limit on her generosity, the women in Tenerife declared.

The women's opinion about Mam Diarra's generosity reflects ideas about female religiosity as the unconditioned care taking of others (cf. Sered 1992). Mourid women see Mam Diarra as the ideal mother, whose qualities distinguish her from other women. She uses her mystical ability according to the prevalent gender ideology: as a self-sacrificing mother and submissive wife she sees to it that her children at Porokhane get the help they want.

The notion that Mam Diarra Bousso gives the pilgrims what they ask for could be interpreted in a way similar to, although not identical with, what Parry calls a 'pure gift', which he defines as 'altruistic, moral and loaded with emotion' (Parry 1986: 466). The other extreme, as he sees it, is associated with the self-interest of market exchange. These two extreme ideologies of reciprocity define each other (Tapper 1990: 251). Mam Diarra's 'gift' is, to some extent, interpreted by the pilgrims as reciprocal – as a result of their going to Porokhane, of visiting her tomb and of asking for her help. In the case of the women who stay in Tenerife, their *addiyya* for the *magal* confers agency. If Mam Diarra fulfils their wishes and demands, she has responded in a reciprocal way to women's sending of *addiyya*. So Mam Diarra gives back by responding to Mourid women's financial contributions and physical efforts. At the same time Mam Diarra 'binds' the receivers of her mystical powers and resources to herself with other kinds of reciprocal links. Her venerators do not stop telling others and talking among themselves about all the good things they have received from her. They become closely attached to her and to Porokhane as fervent witnesses of her ability to help and to give generously. No promises to Mam Diarra or to her son about sacrifices or other counter-prestations are pronounced.

Some Mourid women in Playa de las Américas expressed their feelings for Mam Diarra Bousso, the mother of Shaykh Amadou Bamba, in the following way:

> Mam Diarra is in the centre of our hearts. She is the best woman in the world. Women do all that is good and well done and Mam Diarra is number one among them all.
>
> I owe everything in my life to her.
>
> Everything you ask for, she will give you.
>
> There are three, only three: God, his prophet Mohammed and Mam Diarra.

The sons of Shakyh Amadou Bamba have all contributed to making Mouridism a successful and expanding *tariqa* in Senegal. One of the sons developed Porokhane as a pilgrim centre during the 1950s. Today, visiting Porokhane has also taken on political dimensions: Senegalese government representatives and ministers cannot afford to be absent from the *magal*, which is shown on the TV news and in a special annual TV programme about the most recent *magal* in Porokhane. In that programme, VIPs from the political establishment are shown as being devoted Mourids.

The *magal* in Touba and its counterpart in Porokhane have different characteristics. In Touba, hierarchy, segregation of the sexes, distance and silent participation by the women are the dominant features. In Porokhane, it is easy to be impressed by the sensual and embodied rituals that are performed by the great majority of the people present. Men, as well as women, playfully enact the rituals, imitating drying laundry on the branches of the trees, pounding millet, like Mam Diarra, and creeping in the sand, like her son. Imitation is more than just play, since it provides all the pilgrims with blessing – the mystical and the healing power of the great Mourid 'saints'. The typically female household chores of Mam Diarra achieve a holy dimension. The men, who smilingly carry out tasks in Porokhane that they would never dream of doing at home, do so with a sacred motive. The ambition is to be 'like her'. And she, a model for men and women, is a woman! In this sense, Porokhane is unique among the Mourid pilgrimage settings.

So, the annual pilgrimage event in Porokhane makes women more visible in religious life than anywhere else in the Mourids' Senegal. Men and women stand in long queues – even if the queues are segregated by gender – to enter Mam Diarra's tomb and pray there. Both men and women visit the mosque. Men and women go together to the well, the trees, the place for the preparation of the millet, to the sandy spot where the pilgrims crawl around, imitating Serigne Touba as a child – everywhere men and women mix, performing the same movements, the same actions. During the entire pilgrimage it is the *mother* image and personality which is the centre of everybody's attention; the mother, who has given birth to her son not only through the grace of God or the holy spirit, but also because of the mother's self-sacrificing behaviour and outstanding moral character.

The sense of joy among the pilgrims is really remarkable. The women express their satisfaction at being 'with Mam Diarra', as they say. Also the male pilgrims in Porokhane seem relaxed and pleased. There is a strong feeling of communality, of shared experience, resulting from the enactment of the rituals. The female pilgrims want everybody to be there, together, close to Mam Diarra, even if they also want to have their own individual links directly to her through prayers, acts and gifts of money. This kind of female religiosity has similarities with what Sered calls 'the domestication of religion'. She defines it in the following way: 'a process in which the people who confess their allegiance to a wider religious tradition *personalize* the rituals, institutions, symbols and theology of that wider system in order to safeguard the health, happiness and security of particular people, with whom they are linked in relationships of caring and interdependence' (1992: 10).

At the same time although the image of *communitas* dominates the women's discourse, individuals strive for access to Mam Diarra's blessing as a kind of competition for a limited good. A feeling of unease exists, albeit more or less hidden behind a screen of family love and equal sharing. I cite from an interview with a Mourid woman, who tells about her experiences in Porokhane:

> Not all women can participate in the things we do when we venerate Mam Diarra. In Porokhane we find it, for example, very difficult to reach the well. One could actually say that almost everybody in the whole world is gathered around that well. It is nothing other than an ordinary well, but the waters of the well are very special. Serigne Touba and Sokhna Diarra will fulfil every wish that you make while washing yourself, and drinking the water. It is just the same when one goes out into the wood, where she performed most of her domestic tasks. All the Mourids who put their feet in that wood think that they, alone, belong to Mam Diarra. Sometimes each of us thinks of herself as her owner and that she is a personal, very private and

special guard against the perils. That is at least how I myself imagine the relation. I think that Mam Diarra exists for me, all alone, that I do not share her with anyone.

I simply cannot believe that there could be anyone who loves her more than I do.[4]

Conclusions

In this chapter I have compared Mourid women's religious practices in Senegal and Tenerife in the context of changing financial resources and social status. As well as presenting some ethnographic data about female Mourids in a popular tourist centre, I have also focused on women's adaptation to diasporic living and working conditions and the influence of these conditions upon their religious ideology and practice.

For Mourid women in Senegal, religious devotion and contemplation, time dedicated to *daira* meetings and hard physical work in the *marabouts'* fields in order to fulfil the moral obligations connected with Mourid ideals constitute the core of their religious practice. The physical efforts of the women in a sacred context bring them religious merit, which helps them cope with fatigue and physical strain. Hard work replaces the generous sums of money sent by the women in Tenerife to the *marabouts*.

Pilgrimage to Porokhane means for Mourid women in Senegal the possibility of renewing their 'contract' based on unlimited love and generosity with the Mourid 'saint' Mam Diarra Bousso. It also confirms them as active Mourids. Scarce economic resources do not seem to hamper their energy or the force needed to overcome the practical and financial constraints involved in going to Porokhane on the annual pilgrimage. Corporeal travel and co-presence, where the body is subjected to the direct encounter of 'facing the place' (Urry 2002: 262), are vital ingredients for the female pilgrims living in Senegal. These pilgrims derive both social and moral capital from their travelling to and co-presence in Porokhane.

In Tenerife the Mourid women's access to fairly large financial resources has clearly influenced their religious practice and changed their position in relation to Mourids and non-Mourids in Tenerife and, above all, in Senegal. The accumulation of social and moral capital through women's financial and religious engagements (*addiyya*), their access to the blessing of the visiting *marabouts* and their economic success have provided them with new possibilities in life. Women traders have bought houses and cars for themselves and their families and could certainly, by doing so, have influenced family politics. The religious framing and the status and prestige derived from economic resources have contributed to a change in the women's respectability. The boundaries for women's agency have been extended and some women know very well how to take advantage of this situation through investing money in new ways, with the consent of their husbands. However, the gendered religious ideology has not permitted any drastic changes to achieve gender equality.

Women have less time for ritual and associational activities in Tenerife than in their home country. The lack of time for religious activities is compensated by the generous gifts of money for religious purposes. Money has become the substitute for work in the *marabouts'* fields and for visiting pilgrimage sites. Corporeal travel has been exchanged for imaginative travel and the physical movement of objects (*addiyya*). Occasional co-presence, characterized by the generation and maintenance of social networks, has been exchanged for imagined co-presence. Money has travelled instead of the women, thereby representing them and increasing their social and moral status despite the geographical distance. Mourid women in Tenerife have the intention of going to Porokhane but they remain in Spain for a variety of reasons. Access to financial resources has changed the women's religious practices with the result that, in many cases, women can enjoy the effects of corporeal co-presence in Porokhane without actually going there.

The tourist setting in Tenerife, which has served as a stage for the women's financial activities, does not seem to attract them very much. Outside the tourist space, the women maintain as much as possible a Senegalese lifestyle. It was not in Tenerife in the first place that women manifested their improved economic status and religious image but in Senegal among family and kin, neighbours, friends and old patrons.

Travel is evidently a core issue in Mouridism. Ever since Shaykh Amadou Bamba, the founder of Mouridism, was exiled from Senegal by the French during the colonial period, coerced travel has been a popular theme in Mourid cosmology. Even if going to Porokhane is not associated with exile but with Mam Diara Bousso, it is an important event in Mouridism, and involves travel. In this chapter a great deal of attention has been paid to the issue of going and not going to Porokhane. Current changes in religious practice and travelling patterns have been noted and analysed. These changes are mainly due to new economic conditions for women, combined with strong female religiosity in a transnational setting.[5]

Notes

1 Fieldwork in Senegal was carried out during short periods of time in 1993–8, and financed by the Danish Centre for Development Research, Copenhagen, and the Nordic Africa Institute, Uppsala, Sweden. Fieldwork in Tenerife and Madrid, Spain, was carried out in September 1996 and during the summers of 1998, 2000 and 2001, and was financed by Sida (Stockholm), within the framework of the research project 'Translocal Islam: Mourid women in Senegal and Spain'. I was assisted in Tenerife by Salimata Thiam, Cheikh Anta Diop University, Fann/Dakar, Senegal.
2 Tapper reports a similar idea from Turkey: 'Respectful behaviour in all contexts is associated with religious merit (*sevab*), and reward for piety and meritorious action' (1990: 238).
3 Written communication with Birgitta Percivall (Stockholm University).
4 Interview by Salimata Thiam, who worked as my research assistent in Senegal in 1996. Translated by her from Wolof to French. My own translation into English.
5 This chapter has been presented in different versions during 1999–2001. I am grateful for useful comments on this version from the editors Simon Coleman and John Eade and also from Bente Nikolaisen (Oslo University), Birgitta Percivall (Stockholm University) and Benjamin Soares (Leiden University).

Chapter 5

Embedded motion

Sacred travel among Mevlevi dervishes

Bente Nikolaisen

Introduction

Travel inland and abroad has been a significant practice among the Mevlevi dervishes in Turkey since the 1950s. One of the first journeys abroad to perform *sema*, the whirling ritual, was made in the 1970s to Paris. Since then various groups within the Mevlevi environment have travelled to places such as Sicily, Jerusalem, Granada, Cairo, Karlsruhe, Bavaria, Helsinki and Stockholm as well as several places in the USA. These travels have in common one main activity, namely performing the *sema* in public.

Travel is not a new phenomenon in the history of dervishes – rather it can be understood as a continuing practice where movement in itself is central. Sufi thought is embedded in the idea of movement – the idea of being on your way towards the Deity – expressed through practices of various kinds. Sufi thought conjures up images of the early wandering dervish, visits by dervishes to other lodges or mystics, as well as journeys to holy places such as tombs. Situated at the heart of Mevlevi theology is not only travel through geography, i.e. travelling *to*, but also travel of the mind – travelling *through*. The journey of the mind or the soul to reach God is intimately linked to bodily movement through ritual. Therefore, movement through geography, the soul's journey through bodily movement, as well as the process of passing the various stages of your training as a dervish all contribute to the higher goal of seeking knowledge.

Mevlevi travel has been profoundly affected by the political situation in Turkey. By 1925, two years after the foundation of the secular Republic of Turkey, the lodges had been closed, financial support denied and specific clothes showing order affiliation forbidden. Kafadar (1992: 310) notes that this did not necessarily mean that the order's activities ceased but that they no longer appeared in public. Displays of religious difference were forced into the private realm and an official presentation of mystical belonging only appeared again in 1953 during a memorial service for Mevlana in Konya (Halman and And 1992: 103).

I intend to explore transnational Mevlevi travel, focusing on the performance of the *sema* and revealing the connections between travel, local knowledge and culture. Specific conditions within Turkey and abroad have been crucial in shaping the travelling practice, which emerged after the 1970s, together with the dervishes' desires for new arenas in which to enact their Mevlevism.[1] During the early republican era no old lodges functioned where *sema* could be performed, parts of the political climate were still anti-religious, and few people were interested in attending the mystics' rituals. However, interest abroad in mystical thought and practice partly provided the dervishes with the financial means to travel as well as an interested audience.

My contention is that these travels can be understood as a form of contemporary sacred travel, and not merely tourism or performative or theatrical activity. Sacred travel has two main objectives, travelling *to* and travelling *through* – namely, movement to a place abroad and the enactment of the *sema*, seeking spiritual transformation. These objectives are intimately linked and are dedicated to a religious purpose. The dervishes' journey can be understood as creative and constructive processes where the dervishes shape and present their religiosity and reconstruct their identity as Mevlevi male mystics. Sacred travel by the dervishes is closely linked to global networks and flows, partly effected by the Turkish diaspora in Europe and the USA and shaped by the wish to visit religious and spiritual places such as the Alhambra in Granada or the old Mevlevi lodge in Jerusalem.

In order to develop a fruitful understanding of contemporary sacred travel among the Mevlevi, it is necessary to understand it as a social practice. This approach opens up a field of complexities and practices, which are intimately linked to other forms of social phenomena besides travel. The Mevlevi dervishes (re)construct religiosity through travel and the travels are seen by them as an opportunity to enact the *sema*. It is linked to webs of consumerism where spirituality is one field, in the sense that the dervishes present a religious ritual, which is often adapted to an audience within the discourse of cultural heritage. The audience buys, consumes and enjoys the ritual. The dervishes also obtain larger degrees of visibility through their travelling, thereby spreading knowledge about mysticism. Movement and place interrelate, therefore, in significant ways through the dervishes' travelling and perceptions.

Pilgrimage and sacred travel have often been studied within universalizing models. This tendency has partly been a consequence of Victor and Edith Turner's work on Christian pilgrimage in *Image and Pilgrimage in Christian Culture* (1978). Concepts such as *communitas* and anti-structure have also been applied to analyse a variety of ritual processes in non-Christian contexts. If not used directly, they have provided points of departure for arguments within the same framework (see Werbner and Basu 1998). Eade and Sallnow (2000), on the other hand, have approached pilgrimage as a contested arena. They also argue that within a frame of contested sacredness a universal definition of pilgrimage, which they saw as part of the Turners' agenda, cannot be regarded as fruitful. The attempt to uncover structural elements in pilgrimage may function to restrict the understanding of it rather than opening it up. Paying attention to the complex social relations in which contemporary pilgrimage takes place and, at the same time, focusing on various travellers and how they experience and interpret pilgrimage will enable us to shed more light upon issues related to sacred travel.

Prescribed forms of pilgrimage in Islam and travels to shrines and holy places have been a large part of both social activity and discourse. The pilgrimage to Mecca and the emigration from Mecca have functioned as metaphors at many levels. Eickelman and Piscatori (1990a: 5) suggest that the migration of the Prophet and his followers from Mecca to Medina became a political theme in Islamic political thought in the same way as did the story of the Exodus in Western political thought. Furthermore, religiously inspired travel has always combined concerns about finance and spirituality (Eickelman and Piscatori 1990a: 5; Faroqhi 1994: 2; and see Rosander, Chapter 4 this volume). Sacred travel among the dervishes can, therefore, be understood as a complex of economic, social and political relations.

Mevlevi dervishes in Istanbul

The Mevlevi dervishes in Istanbul are part of a Sufi tradition that traces its genealogy to the mystic Celaleddin Rumi, later named Mevlana, born in 1207. During the thirteenth century Mevlevi dervish life came to centre around the lodge (*tekke*) and this tradition was sustained in Turkey until the ban on the lodges in 1925.[2] During the Ottoman period there were 105 lodges throughout the empire. A sheikh would typically live with his family in rooms separated within the larger *tekke* structure for this purpose. Each lodge contained a *semahane*, a space designed for performing the *sema*. It would often house libraries in addition to the rooms appropriated for lodge functions such as training, cooking, praying and reception of the sheikh's followers, who came seeking his guidance and blessings (Lifchez: 1992: 76; Holbrook 1999: 105).

Rumi's thoughts are expressed in the many philosophical and spiritual works he wrote, among which the *Mesnevi* is the most famous.[3] The major theological theme of his teaching is the notion of love for God and the possibility of being one with the Deity. Turning movements are central to the whirling ritual, the *sema*, through which dervishes seek unity with God. This is an activity and a spiritual state most cherished by the Mevlevi dervishes.[4]

The Mevlevi groups with whom I worked consisted of men from diverse social backgrounds. Among the men between the ages of 30 and 70, there were academics, musicians from the national radio, bureaucrats, journalists, small business owners and some living on income from land and buildings. Some of the musicians had been educated in the Academy of Arts. It has often been noted that the Mevlevi order was an elite phenomenon during Ottoman times, but Holbrook (1999: 107) has challenged this view. The social background of the dervishes varied, but I would say it was mostly middle class. The elders, leaders and sheikhs were inclined to have higher education but they varied in their social background.

Preparation and the recollections of *sema* to be performed abroad: dwelling intersected by movement

Many have described and noted the increasing interest in movement and mobility. Urry (2000) focuses on mobilities of people and material objects, as well as of images and information. In describing an increasingly globalized world, Appadurai (1993) has noted the shifting worlds of tourists, immigrants, refugees, exiles, guestworkers and other transient groups and persons. Relatively stable communities and networks of kinship, of friendship, of work and of leisure, as well as of birth, residence and other filial forms still exist in this world but they are shot through with human motion, as more persons and groups deal with the realities of having to move, or the fantasies of wanting to move (Appadurai 1993: 297). It is from the location of the 'home' and the dwelling of the Mevlevi dervishes that I will move into the more specific and diverse experiences of their travel. My own encounters with travel among the dervishes in Istanbul were through their preparations and recollections at home of international travel. Fantasies of wanting to move motivate and inform the dervishes in their preparation and recollections of their travels as well as in their actual travelling. The fantasy is twofold in the sense of being both a desire for movement through geography and a desire for spiritual travelling through the *sema* performed once arrived.

Preparing for travel

Preparation for travel involved a whole range of tasks as well as much debate among the dervishes about the conditions of travel. An important part of the preparation process concerned the possibility of performing *sema*, and the envisaging of the space that had been designated for the *sema* abroad. Different initiatives could come from organizers of festivals and seminars, persons in the Turkish diaspora with connections to the dervishes or those directly linked to the dervishes through the same or different mystical organizations through invitations to perform *sema* outside a larger organization. Thus a journey to Cairo entailed the inauguration of a newly restored lodge. Ties would cut across each other so that an individual belonging to the Mevlevi environment in one city would invite dervishes from Istanbul to enact the *sema* at a concert or festival.

Very often dervishes who engaged most actively in the debate on the suitability of travelling would express gratitude for the possibility (*imkan*) of being able to whirl, to seek God through *sema*. However, there was a danger that some of the travelling was too commercialized and, as one man put it, functioned merely as theatre. Travelling was, therefore, in no way part of a harmonious field. It was debated and contested by individuals, and internal hierarchies were expressed through these debates. Invitations to ethno-music, world music, New Age festivals and seminars would frequently trigger discussions as to which of them were worthy of attending, in contrast with those that were directly initiated by fellow mystics or other persons known to the dervishes. These debates were informed, as I see it, by the diverse and often intertwined motivations of wanting to travel and perform *sema*. As I have already pointed out, Sufism contains the inherent idea of mobility and movement, and travelling is often understood as a desired activity. This is also linked to the interpretations of the meaning of the *sema* performed abroad, which were expressed through the recollections of the journeys by the dervishes. I will return to this later in the chapter.

Much has been written about the travelogues of famous Muslim voyagers. Netton (1996: 121), in his analysis of Ibn Batutta's writings, finds that four elements can be identified in his text – namely, the search for the shrine and/or a religious landscape, the search for knowledge, the search for recognition and power, and the satisfaction of a 'basic wanderlust'. These categories seem fruitful to me when trying to understand the intentions of the dervishes. The overall justification given by the dervishes for travelling was *sema etmek* (to perform *sema*). This can be likened to the search for a religious landscape in two ways: the inner landscape of the person to be achieved through *sema*, and travel to religiously meaningful places such as Alhambra and the Mevlevi lodges in Jerusalem and Cairo. The search for knowledge was revealed by their desire to see and experience new places, as well as to perform the *sema* and thereby obtain closer knowledge of God. This desire cannot be clearly distinguished from the urge to travel since these intentions are intertwined in the male mystic's life in Istanbul.

The third element involving the desire for recognition/power could be frequently seen in descriptions of the political situation in Turkey. The leading dervishes would often express their frustration over the lack of interest and knowledge of the Mevlevi path and religion, in general, across Turkey. They were cultural heritage 'workers' whose views about political and social issues differed from orthodox Islam, the secular authorities and the Kemalists. The opportunity to perform the *sema* abroad, especially with large audiences, as in Stockholm where 2,000 people watched the ceremony, could function as a statement and recognition of themselves. They were seen as actors in a transnational context, not just a leftover symbol of Ottoman times. They saw themselves as having a legitimate right to act and speak. The dervishes' visibility, their performance of the *sema* and textual presentations placed them as one of many political actors (in its wider meaning) conveying meanings about Turkey, religion and politics. The fact that they performed *sema* abroad both strengthened their identity and recognition as Mevlevi dervishes and commented on the problem of finding room for public performances within Turkey. They formed a new place transnationally for the ritual, which was less dependent on a *particular* place. Rather, it came to depend more on their bodily knowledge and the performance of the ritual.

When it comes to the rather romantic term 'wanderlust', I think that it cannot be detached from other categories. Wanting to travel and imagining travel are also shaped within a world where images of other places are exhibited through the media. In that sense the desire to travel is a socially constructed category. On one occasion a prominent dervish expressed the view that it would be nice and relaxing for the younger dervishes to get away from the worries of daily life in Istanbul. It is also quite clear that some of the younger dervishes would not have been able to travel abroad for financial reasons. Belonging to the Mevlevi order, therefore, offered not only spiritual commonality but also opportunities to experience other physical worlds. The imagining of and the desire for travel intersects with patterns of tourism. They are shaped not only by Sufi paradigms of movement and travel but also by the wider social setting.

Preparing for travel the dervishes had to sort out the financial and administrative aspects of the journey. They discussed the organization of the ritual and such related issues as the concerts before or after the *sema* and the production of the texts or other material presented at seminars. Generally, the inviting institution would pay for the tickets and provide accommodation but this phase of the preparations could take a long time. Sometimes a passport had to be renewed while there would be complaints about the tedious and never-ending task of obtaining visas or booking flights. Everybody needed to sort out their ritual clothing and many had to obtain leave from their employers. Another financial issue concerned the number of dervishes and *semazen* (whirling dervishes) who could attend, given the amount of money raised by the organizers abroad. This was often a matter of negotiation because organizers frequently suggested reducing the number of participants.

An important aspect of preparing for the journeys involved the writing and preparing of the texts, which might be used in the performances. Often the festival organizer would ask the group to join a conference or seminar after the performance of the ritual. These seminars were, in most cases, directed towards mysticism in general or Mevlevi teaching in particular. The texts would often contain brief information about the Mevlevi dervishes, who they were, how they defined their belonging to Sufism and Mevlevism, as well as how they interpreted the ritual clothing and the various stages in the ritual and the purpose of the *sema*. They would often attach an account of the musical instruments used in the *sema*. There would sometimes be general theological information, which related mysticism to orthodox interpretations of Islam. These texts had to be translated, either by one of the dervishes or by others.

Sometimes, the organizers would request a concert in addition to the *sema*. If so, they would discuss the repertoire. Depending on the time available and the expected audience, they would play *tassavuf müzigi* (mystical music) and/or *türk klasik müzigi* (turkish classical music). The spaces offered to them abroad, except for the Cairo Mevlevi lodge, were most often secular structures such as city halls, concert houses and theatre stages. The problem of solving the internal organization of these spaces frequently became an urgent issue. However, discussion was limited by the fact that the dervishes received little information before they travelled about the spaces and how they functioned, apart from certain technical details. Although they acted on this sparse information using memories of earlier travels and *sema*, their embodied memories would only find expression when they actually reached their destination.

Performed space

Debates about space, place, location and identity have increasingly focused upon flows and movements. Morley and Robbins (1993: 5) argue that due to increased migration around the world, faster information flows and economic globalization, identity is no longer supported by place. Clifford (1997: 3) claims that within anthropological theory 'roots always precede routes' but suggests that movement is just as much involved in human location as what he terms 'stasis'. In the case of the Mevlevi dervishes it is clear that their travels within Turkey and abroad weave together a multitude of places, landscapes and relations, thereby supporting the processes of identity formation in which they are engaged. Coleman and Crang (2002a) propose that places can be seen as performed. Spaces are created through tourism and this is the desired effect. Coleman and Crang want to open up the possibilities of understanding tourism as an event that is about mobilizing and reconfiguring spaces and places, bringing them into new constellations and therefore transforming them.

This is true not only of tourism but of other forms of travel as well. When debating pilgrimage and sacred travel, theories of tourism can expand our view of the complexities that exist within and between diverse forms of travel. It seems clear that the Mevlevi dervishes engage in a travel practice that is also crosscut by tourism in the sense of the shifting roles they are a part of when travelling. They can be seen as performers when presenting the *sema* abroad, while those hosting the event become tourists in their own city. In turn, the dervishes become tourists or guests as they move about the foreign city.

Place is about doing as much as it is about being and bodily memories played an important part in the performance of the *sema*. Certain spatial problems had to be engaged with in the most effective way. Many of the spaces utilized for performances abroad were secular structures, most often in the form of a stage. I will discuss the problems linked to performing *sema* that the dervishes encountered in such places and argue that, through the performance of the *sema*, they actually transformed secular space into acceptable ritual rooms, sacralizing the secular structure but also secularizing the ritual. The boundaries between sacred and profane contexts did not appear fixed and rigid anymore, because the dervishes collapsed these distinctions by 'disciplining' the audience and the space. Embodied knowledge obtained through long training also informed the dervishes about how to move in non-ritual spaces. The ideal space for performing *sema*, namely a *semahane*, functioned as a model into which new experiences could be moulded and enabled the dervishes to transform the new spaces offered them abroad. Sacred travel as a travel practice in line with tourism reconfigures and transforms space. It debates the role of space related to *sema* within the Mevlevi environment as well, since it offers the audiences possibilities to reflect upon their views about concert halls and stages used for religious rituals.

I will now describe the *semahane* of the Galata Mevlevihanesi, now the Divan Edebiyat Müzesi, a museum, before proceeding to a short description of the ritual. Then I will discuss how the dervishes dealt with spatial practices abroad.

The Galata Mevlevi lodge contains a traditional well-preserved *semahane*, which is one of the most desired places for many Mevlevi dervishes to whirl in Istanbul. It was of utmost importance for the various groups to whirl there on special occasions and thereby express their belonging to the place. This was partly due to what they often conceptualized as the 'impact of architectural solutions on the experience of the ritual'. The Galata Mevlevihane became a symbol of what they thought to be their lost past as much as a symbol of the coming of a new age. It played a vital role as a key metaphor in a number of discussions. Dervishes wanted to regain and repossess the lodge, both physically and symbolically, not only from the state but from each other as well, because this was a struggle for establishing their legitimacy. The lodge served as a place of reference when they had to transform new spaces, and experiences of it formed part of the dervishes' embodied knowledge and memory of whirling.

The structure is aesthetically spectacular. The lodge, along with art deco buildings, Byzantine structures, Genoese buildings and seventeenth- and eighteenth-century buildings, constitutes part of the historical mosaic of the area. The Rum Orthodox Church, the Italian Catholic Church and the Assyrian Church, among other historic sites,

are situated along the Istiklal Caddesi, Galata's main street. The largest
and the most frequented synagogue is also situated in the area.

   The Galata Mevlevi lodge consists of many buildings but the museum
is located in the *semahane*. Every architectural structure in this building
is centred around the platform which constitutes the *semahane*. The
ritual space occupies two floors. The ground floor is arranged with the
octagonal space in the middle, surrounded by beautiful low ornamented
wooden fences. The *mihrab*, a richly decorated wooden piece in dark
brown indicating the direction of Mecca, is placed opposite the entrance
to the ritual space. The ceiling is shaped like a cupola and has detailed
ornamented wooden panelling. Balustrades support the cupola. Seats
for the audience are placed around the ritual space at ground floor
level. Mevlevi dresses – both ritual costumes and the more daily costumes
used in the seventeenth and eighteenth century – are displayed on
the walls. Musical instruments, books, Korans, richly decorated versions
of Mevlana's large poetic work, the *Mesnevi*, and various examples of
calligraphic work are displayed in glass cases. Crystal chandeliers provide
the light on the ground floor. Several doors open up to stairs leading to
the upper storey. Quite a few small chambers and galleries are situated
around the ritual space on the second floor. Examples of Islamic marbled
art forms and examples of various forms of embroidery, prayer beads and
typical headdresses are on display in this room. Dark wooden walls
pierced by tiny holes separate some of the chambers. The *mutriphane* (the
chamber where the musicians sit) is located on the first floor with an open
view to the *semahane* underneath. The architectural organization of the
semahane, with the cupola-shaped ceiling, offers excellent acoustics.

Remembering spatial problems

In the dervishes' recollections of travel and *semas* performed abroad,
some key themes recurred while memories of travels were often set off
by videos or recordings of music. They functioned as efficient mnemonic
devices.

   One spatial problem they frequently encountered was where the
dervishes would enter. There had been occasions when they entered
through a corridor among the audience, or from the middle of a stage
or from above. These were all problematic in the sense that they altered
the relations between the whirling dervishes and the audience. According
to the dervishes, these space issues lessened the heightened experience
of the ritual and, furthermore, altered the formality of the ritual. When
watching a video of one of the *sema* they pointed this out to me. The

desired effect of the dervishes' sudden entrance before they enter a
semahane, as in the Galata Mevlevi lodge, could not be created. At some
places the dervishes had to walk a long way in their ritual clothes before
entering the designated space.

Another aspect of organizing secular space and transforming it into
an acceptable ritual place was the problem of how to honour the sheikh
on those occasions when he took part in the travel and the *sema*. The
sheikh is supposed to sit on a sheepskin in front of the *mihrab* and the
semazens should enter the ritual space in front of him. On one occasion
there had also been a problem of how to address the *Hat-i-Istihva* – the
invisible line dividing the floor and the world into a material and a
spiritual realm. When crossing this line the dervishes bow their head in
salutation to God and the sheikh. The audience in this case could not
see the faces of the dervishes when they were bowing to the sheikh.
The dervishes later discussed this and when they watched a video of
this particular *sema* they noticed that one should also pay respect to the
audience by letting them see the dervishes clearly. When they watched
videos or photographs of dervishes turning, they remarked upon the
facial expressions of the whirling dervishes.

All these various elements, such as the entrance of the sheikh,
the honouring of him, the beginning of the whirling, as well as the
various musical elements, create a certain rhythm. One of the ritual
masters emphasized that the rhythm of the ritual changes when the
sheikh is not present. The *sema* can vary, therefore, as performers adapt
the rigid structure of rules and staging to local conditions. The dervishes
approached the performance of the *sema* abroad or in secular structures
at home with flexibility in order to solve spatial challenges. The dervishes
moulded old experiences onto new and established ritual spaces in which
to perform *sema* through their use of embodied knowledge in the ritual.
Although, as I mentioned earlier, the Galata Mevlevi lodge functioned
as a model for the dervishes, it was their own activity and creativity based
on new and old experiences, and not replicas and copying, that played
an important role and shaped the visual unity, experience and meaning
of the *sema*.

Another issue, which might have altered the meaning of the *sema* for
the dervishes, or at least some of them, was the possibility of performing
ablutions. This required water facilities, which could not always be
found. Some of the dervishes refused to perform *sema* if they could
not perform their ablutions. The event would become 'solely a *gösteri*
[performance] not a *sema*'. However, people were not agreed about this
interpretation within the Mevlevi order.

Large spaces provided abroad could also produce a lack of intimacy between the *semazen* and the audience during the performance. In the Galata Mevlevihane, one of the Mevlevi lodges, one could hear the long white dresses touch the floor. At some *semas* performed abroad there was a much wider distance between the audience and the dervishes. This was an issue intimately linked to the question of how the audience were to be integrated within the ritual itself. A successful *sema* is not only one where the central dervishes have a spiritual experience but also an occasion where the audience is able to *bizimle sema etmek* – 'make or experience the *sema* with us'. It seems that this problem was not solved in larger spaces, such as the City Hall in Stockholm. Even though they tried to alter the relations between the audience and themselves and redefine it, they did not always succeed. On one occasion they had asked parts of the audience in a larger space to move closer to the stage. The ritual master noted laconically on this occasion: 'We did not have any success on this. Nobody moved and anyway it did not turn out to be a successful *sema*.' On some occasions they told the audience not to applaud or leave the room during the ritual. I see this as a way of informing the audience that it was not involved in an ordinary performance but a ritual. Disciplining the space and the audience were the means by which the dervishes sacralized the secular spaces they performed in.

The placement of the musicians (*mutrip*) was a further significant issue. As I noted in my description of the Galata Mevlevi lodge, musicians sit in a chamber located on a balcony, set apart from the whirlers. In larger spaces abroad this never happened, except at the Mevlevihane in Cairo. Before the *sema* was to be performed the dervishes would, therefore, try various solutions in order to create the best possible sound and obtain the desired distance between the *semazens*. Since the dervishes need a specific number of square metres in which to whirl, they pointed out that being too close can cause them to bump into each other, while being too far apart would destroy the visual unity of the ritual.

Many practical matters were always present with non-*semahane* performances. One issue was the floor. It is important that the floor is totally level or else the whirling can be unsuccessful. On one occasion during a domestic performance, there was wall-to-wall carpeting, which could not be removed. According to the dervishes, they whirled but under a lot of difficulty. In this case, the dervishes interpreted the absence of information as a lack of respect and knowledge on the part of the organizers, who 'were supposed to be religious people'.

Concluding remarks

I have in this chapter described how the Mevlevi dervishes engage in travel in order to enact the *sema*. I have argued that this travel could be understood as sacred because it entailed the desire for spiritual transformation through the *sema*. Dervishes transformed spaces through performing the *sema*. At the same time sacralizing the space also led to a secularization of the ritual. By reaching a wider and different audience and performing the *sema* within the framework of festivals and concerts, as well as orchestrating the *sema* in, sometimes, unfortunate spaces, secularization seems to have been the result. Secularization and sacralizing appear, therefore, to be parts of the same process, and the distinctions between them have been collapsed as the dervishes have acted with their embodied knowledge.

In spite of the dervishes' authoritative architectural and spatial tradition, the use of secular spaces reflects the fact that traditions are to be seen as lived experiences and that they are continuously changing. The increasing influence of identity politics and the arenas where the issues of identity can be enacted can be said to increase. The meaning of the ritual is altered, in the sense that different audiences interpret it, and it has been turned into an occasion for consumerism. New audiences emerge as well – audiences who attend not only once but several times. Furthermore, in 2002 I even noticed that three various groups of diverse national origin had been performing the whirling ritual in Europe.

Transnational travel, sacred in its nature, has given the dervishes possibilities to redefine the space for ritual action, providing them with the opportunity to (re)define themselves, to debate the place of space in their tradition and to communicate this to others and themselves. Pilgrimage tied into global networks and mass mobility emerges. The objectives of reframing pilgrimage should be directed towards how mobility is constitutive of social practices and how embodiment serves to shape new experiences, so that pilgrimage is recreated.

Notes

1 Victoria Holbrook translates the title of Gölpınarlı's book *Mevlana'dan sonra Mevlevilik* (1983) as Mevlevism after Mevlana in her article 'Diverse tastes in the spiritual life: textual play in the diffusion of Rumi's order' in *The Heritage of Sufism: the legacy of medieval Persian Sufism (1150–1500)* (1999). I will follow her translation of the word Mevlevism taking it to mean a variety of practices and activities of the Mevlevi order.

2 The word *tekke* is most often translated as 'lodge' although some scholars

such as Holbrook (1999: 105) prefer to use 'dervish house'. It must be noted that in Turkish Islamic sources, in addition to *tekke*, the words *hanekah*, *asitane*, *zaviye* and *dergah* are used. These words used for buildings of the Mevlevi order had slightly different meanings according to Lifchez (1992: 76). *Tekke* and *hanekah* were used for dervish facilities, *asitane* for a grander lodge, *zaviye* for a dervish hostel without any special belonging and *dergah* for a dervish facility with a tomb. I will use lodge when I don't use the emic term *tekke*.

3 *Mesnevi-i-Manevi* is the Turkish title of Rumi's most known work. I use the Turkish spelling throughout the chapter, both for this title and for other Turkish words originated within other languages.

4 I note that the term Mevlevi dervish(es) refers to men initiated and attached to a sheikh or a leader in a larger web of spiritual and religiously concerned persons. Historically there are no female dervishes in the Mevlevi *tarikat*.

Chapter 6

'Heartland of America'

Memory, motion and the (re)construction of history on a motorcycle pilgrimage

Jill Dubisch

Introduction

On a cool day in mid-May, 1996, I found myself standing in the parking lot of the American Legion Hall in Flagstaff, Arizona, surrounded by a group of rather wild looking bikers, about to embark on a remarkable journey. Although my partner Ray and I were not newcomers to motor-cycle riding, these men and women were very different from the riders we were used to from our Honda Gold Wing motorcycle club.[1] These were 'real bikers', many mounted on Harleys, and most dressed in the Harley 'outlaw' style with leather boots, black leather jackets, head scarves and silver chains. And although we had ridden our motorcycle on several cross-country trips before, this journey promised to be very different from any we had previously undertaken, for most of the men we would be riding with were veterans of America's war in Vietnam. Along with spouses, supporters and other interested riders, they were embarked on a motorcycle pilgrimage from California to the Vietnam Veterans Memorial in Washington, DC, an annual journey known as the Run for the Wall (or simply 'the Run'). We were planning to join them, a prospect both exciting and intimidating.

As the riders helped themselves to coffee, juice and pastries at a table set outside the Legion Hall, courtesy of the Flagstaff chapter of the ABATE[2] motorcycle club, I struck up a conversation with a local woman. Although she was not travelling with the group that year, she had been on the Run for the Wall before and she spoke encouragingly of the experience. 'You'll be amazed at the reception you receive,' she told me. 'In California, and once you get to DC, no one cares, but in between, in the heartland of America, you'll be greeted with open arms.'

How right she proved to be. And yet even her encouraging words gave me no hint of the ways in which the journey itself would create a new

American landscape for both the riders and those who welcomed them along the way – a landscape that is part of the healing process that is one of the goals of what I came to see as a motorcycle pilgrimage.[3] Nor did I yet appreciate the ways in which both the journey and the landscape it traversed played a role in constructing, and reconstructing, a period in American history that continues to be troubling, contentious and painful for many Vietnam veterans (and for many non-veterans as well).

For the veterans making this pilgrimage, what unfolds during the journey is, in part, a landscape of memory, as recollections of the Vietnam war – often long buried – resurface in the course of the cross-country ride. At the same time, however, these memories are confronted in a particular context, in a landscape of 'home', peopled by those who turn out to honour all veterans, both those making the pilgrimage and those who never returned. 'Welcome home, brother' is the greeting that the pilgrims receive, both from fellow veterans and from others who host them in communities along the way. The landscape thus constructed is a contrast to another landscape, the historical landscape of big cities, hostile war protestors and an indifferent society that many veterans remember as their reception when they returned from Vietnam. Their pilgrimage through the 'heartland' thus offers veterans a chance for 'the parade they never had' and for the reshaping of personal memory, and of history itself, as a new narrative of the Vietnam War is created through the medium of pilgrimage. At the same time, the Run's political focus on the POW/MIA issue (see p. 107) offers veterans a sense that, rather than simply riding for their own benefit, they also are still fighting on others' behalf.

That this journey is made on motorcycles is a significant element in the reconstruction of history and memory. Motorcycles are seen by many who ride them as symbolizing important American values of freedom, self-reliance and individualism. They are also associated with the American idea of the 'open road': the wide-open spaces and the beauty of the landscape that characterize the American heartland, and the infinite possibilities symbolized by the unfolding of winding highways. The sense of solidarity and 'brotherhood' that exists among bikers also comes into play during the pilgrimage, and echoes the cama-raderie of warriors in combat (see Wolf 1991). In addition, the visceral dimension of motorcycle riding – the noise, the motion, the riding in formation with several hundred other motorcycles, the hazards of the road – as I will argue, combine to create a psychological receptivity to the ritual messages imparted along the journey's route.

The idea of 'home' plays an important role in this journey. As Rapport and Dawson have observed, the concept of 'home' 'brings together memory and longing, the ideational, the affective and the physical, the spatial and the temporal, the local and the global, the positively evaluated and the negatively' (1998b: 8). And if 'home' is the place 'in which one best knows oneself, where one's self-identity is best grounded' (Rapport and Dawson 1998c: 21), then the lack of a sense of 'homecoming' that many Vietnam veterans experienced when they returned from the war left them feeling displaced and contributed to their difficulties in postwar adjustment. Through its journey across the country, the Run for the Wall serves to define a 'home' to which veterans cannot only safely return, but in which they can also realize a new, empowering identity. In this sense, it is through movement that participants both create and experience a sense of place and of 'coming home'.

Thus the Run for the Wall is a pilgrimage of connection – connecting the country coast to coast, veterans with each other and with other Americans along the way, and those who returned from a foreign war with their homeland. But it is also in some sense, at least, a journey of disconnection in that it defines a particular identity, that of the United States of America, in relation to the outside world. In this particular foreign war, the Vietnam War, the United States government is viewed as having failed in its duty to its citizens in not accounting for all those who are missing, those who have not yet 'come home', whether missing in action (MIAs) or still live prisoners of war (POWs). Insofar as a theme of the Run for the Wall is 'bringing home' those who are still missing in a foreign war so that they can be 'buried on American soil', it defines a relationship between a national entity and the soldiers it sends to fight in foreign lands. As various messages delivered in rituals and speeches performed along the journey's route attest, such accounting is felt to be a responsibility the US government owes both to those it sends to fight abroad and to the families these soldiers leave behind. In this sense, the Run for the Wall might be seen to carry a message of isolationism. At the same time, however, this isolationism is breached by ties among warriors, and to some extent, among bikers. Canadian, Australian and other non-American Vietnam biker veterans participate in and are honoured by the Run.

I suggest, then, that the Run for the Wall can be seen as a pilgrimage, one that not only has a sacred destination ('the Wall') but also combines the individual search for healing and identity with the creation of a collective narrative, a narrative that unfolds as the Run moves across the United States. It thus serves as what Nancy Wood (1990) has termed a 'vector of memory', a ritual performance that constructs a collective view of the past as well as contributing to the construction of a common identity. But this narrative and this collective memory are not developed in the context of the pilgrimage alone. Although the riders are the ones who are making the journey, the ones who are moving across the 'heartland', this heartland itself is created by the many individuals and groups along the way who host the Run, who honour the veterans, and who utter the words that have become part of the ritual of the Run: 'Welcome home, brother'.

History and purpose of the Run for the Wall

The Run for the Wall began in 1989 when a group of Vietnam veterans decided to ride their motorcycles across the United States, from California to Washington, DC, to visit the recently inaugurated Vietnam Veterans Memorial ('the Wall'). The riders also planned to join Rolling Thunder, a large motorcycle rally and parade, which was taking place (and which continues to take place) in Washington on Memorial Day weekend (the last weekend in May). First established as an event for the support and recognition of veterans, Rolling Thunder takes its name from the 'carpet bombing' of Cambodia during the Vietnam War. It has now become a large biker gathering that draws 200,000 to 250,000 participants every year.

Originally intended as a one-time event, a chance 'to say good-bye' to comrades whose names are engraved on the Wall, the Run was greeted so enthusiastically by the communities where it stopped along the journey's route that, as one of the original organizers told me, 'we knew we had to do it again'. Thus the Run for the Wall has become an annual pilgrimage with a national organization and a website, drawing hundreds of riders each year. (And it has become so large that an additional, more southern route has been added to the main route across the centre of the United States.) In the beginning, the Run was loosely organized through personal networks among veterans that developed and expanded out of the original Run for the Wall. In the last few years, however, the Run has become more formalized, with a board that chooses the Run leader every year and makes decisions regarding routes and stops for the journey. The Run for the Wall is not an organization to which one 'belongs', however, and there are no dues. Nor is there a fee for joining the Run; one simply shows up at one of the Run's stops, signs in, and travels as long as desired with the group. Money for chase vehicles and other collective expenses along the way is raised through raffles, the sale of T-shirts and donations. Participants in the Run include not only Vietnam veterans, but also veterans of other wars, family and friends of veterans, supporters of the cause and those riders who, at first 'just coming along for the ride', are ultimately drawn into the issues that the Run represents.[4]

What are these issues? As various rituals and speeches that take place in the course of the pilgrimage emphasize, the Run's goals are twofold. One goal is the personal healing of veterans who are still suffering from the psychological, emotional and spiritual effects of their Vietnam War experience, whether these are manifested in the now officially recognized form of post-traumatic stress disorder (PTSD)[5] or are the no less painful 'invisible wounds' that still afflict many of those who participated in this conflict, the psychic legacy of their combat experience. Healing is not confined to veterans, however. An important additional category of participants consists of those who lost a loved one in the conflict, whether brother, father, son, fiancé or some other individual who figured importantly in their lives. And in a larger sense, the pilgrimage might be said to have as one of its goals to 'heal a nation', a phrase that has been applied to the Run's ultimate destination: the Vietnam Veterans Memorial (Scruggs and Swerdlow 1985).

The Run's second purpose is political: to demand a full accounting by the United States government of those who are missing in action or prisoners of war from the Vietnam War. ('Bring them home or send us back!' was a slogan we saw several times on our first Run for the Wall.) While the issue of MIAs and the question of whether there might still be living prisoners of war from the Vietnam conflict are controversial,[6] this political agenda provides an integrating focus for the Run for the Wall, a 'mission' with important symbolic dimensions. It also offers participants a sense of riding for something beyond themselves. They are not simply 'whiney Vietnam vets' who cannot leave the war behind and get on with their lives. Rather, they are warriors on a mission, 'riding for those who can't'. At the same time, as has been stated explicitly on several occasions on the Run, the concept of the POW/MIA is metaphorical as well. There are many veterans who, because of their continued sufferings, are still in their own minds prisoners of the Vietnam War, or who can be said to be still 'missing in action' (or 'Missing in America') psychologically, as they have never come back to 'normal' life since their return from Vietnam. To free both kinds of prisoners is the major goal of the Run for the Wall.

One of the symbolic messages of the focus on the POW/MIA issue is that the Vietnam War in some sense is not really over. Although it officially ended over 25 years ago, unresolved conflicts over the meaning of the war, and the fact that it is a war that the United States cannot be said to have 'won', have created what Kristen Hass has termed 'a restless memory that continues to haunt the American imagination' (1998: 1). Many of the young men who served in Vietnam had their faith in themselves, and in the values of their culture, shaken by the experience (Shay 1994). And when these veterans returned home, their belief that those who risked their lives in defence of their country would be honoured was undermined by the indifference, and sometimes outright hostility, with which a number of homecoming veterans were received. Rapport and Dawson suggest that the traditional conception of 'home' has been 'the stable physical centre of one's universe – a safe and still place to leave and return to' (1998b: 6). But for many of the veterans we have spoken to, the country that they believed they had been fighting for was not the country to which they returned. It was a land of war protesters, 'hippies' and, perhaps worst of all, those who simply cared little about what these combat veterans had just experienced.[7] We have heard stories of veterans' sense of unreality when they returned from the combat zone to the everyday life being carried out by their families and friends back home, a 'home' that they now did not recognize. The response of a number of veterans to this encounter with a world into which they no longer fitted was to re-enlist.

Not all Vietnam veterans have such experiences, but the feeling of not belonging, or of outright rejection, is a common one. Even veterans' organizations such as the American Legion and the Veterans of Foreign Wars (VFW) rejected the returning Vietnam veterans, feeling that they had not been in a 'real war'. (It is only relatively recently that such organizations have been making overtures to the veterans of the Vietnam conflict, and at a number of the stops made by the Run, American Legion and VFW halls are hosts for the various events.) Because of the reception many veterans received when they returned home, they were often reluctant to speak of their experiences. Many were also reluctant to connect or identify themselves with other veterans. As a consequence, wives and children of Vietnam veterans, while suspecting that their husbands and fathers were suffering the consequences of their combat experience, could not comprehend what that experience had been. And the veterans themselves saw their post-combat symptoms as signs of their own craziness, rather than the consequences of a collective experience. Suffering was individual, not social (see Kleinman *et al.* 1997). Veterans who ended up in therapy groups in veterans' hospitals might have had some opportunity to speak of their experiences and to realize their shared nature, but many, if not most, Vietnam veterans bore their emotional burdens alone.

The situation of these veterans is encapsulated in the title of a recent publication of the North Carolina Humanities Council: 'Breaking the silence: the unspoken brotherhood of Vietnam veterans'. The author, Sharon Raynor, was inspired by her own father's reticence about his experiences in Vietnam and undertook an oral history of veterans. The following quote from her father, Louis Raynor, about why he had not talked about his combat experiences expresses the feelings of many:

> There are many reasons why Vietnam veterans decided not to talk about our war experiences when we arrived home. For me, no one seemed to care about my time in Vietnam, especially people who had not themselves been vets. Everyone either looked at me like I had done something bad or they didn't believe what I had to say about my tour of duty. Usually people would ask questions like, 'How many people did you kill?' I never would answer that question. People have mothers, fathers, brothers, and sisters, and I did not want to think about having taken that life from someone, so I just kept quiet.
>
> (Raynor 2002: 7)

It is from the need to address both the long term and the delayed consequences of the war, both for themselves and for others, that many of the participants came to be involved in the Run for the Wall.

A note on methodology

As the Introduction to this volume points out, the study of pilgrimage offers a challenge to the traditional anthropological method of participant observation. Pilgrimage usually involves the conjunction of a moving body or bodies of individuals with a specific geographic location, or locations, which will have their own cast of characters involved in various ways in the pilgrimage. In addition, a specific pilgrimage is an ephemeral phenomenon (though much the same could be said for any social activity) and certain pilgrimages (such as the Run for the Wall) may take place only once a year, or in some cases even less frequently. At the same time, the study of pilgrimage fits well into changing anthropological conceptualizations of 'the field' and of the objects of the anthropological gaze. As Malkki (1997) points out, while one of the strengths of anthropology has been its concern with the quotidian, with the details of ordinary life as elucidated through long-term face-to-face fieldwork, this has led to a neglect of the extraordinary and exceptional events that may radically shape individual and collective lives. Pilgrimages can be one such category of events.

Our own participation in the Run for the Wall was complicated by the nature of our initial involvement, and by our own historical relationship to the Vietnam War. While our analysis might be considered a case of fieldwork 'at home', it has led, to use Gupta and Ferguson's words, to 'the acquisition of new perspectives on things we thought we already understood. Fieldwork, in this light, may be understood as a form of motivated and stylized *dislocation*', and location itself becomes 'an on-going project' (1997: 37; emphasis added). In our case this dislocation was the product not simply of the act of leaving home and traversing the country on motorcycles but also one that is perhaps intrinsic to the nature of pilgrimage itself as well as to the narrative construction and reconstruction of a particularly painful period of our own personal and national history.

Before our involvement in the Run for the Wall, motorcycle riding was for my partner Ray and myself simply a hobby. At the same time, in our excursions to various motorcycle rallies, I began to develop an anthropological interest in the phenomenon I encountered: thousands of motorcycle riders gathering at ritual events, many on elaborately decorated bikes, pumping thousands, even millions, of dollars into the economies of the local communities that hosted these gatherings. (I even discerned elements of pilgrimage in these ritual events, as for some bikers they constituted almost a kind of 'tribal gathering'.) It was not, however, out of anthropological interest that we first became involved in the Run for the Wall. Rather, like many pilgrims, we were 'called'.

The summer of 1996, the summer of our first Run for the Wall, we had been intending to ride across the country, attending various motorcycle rallies. Knowing of our plans, a friend handed us a flyer about the Run for the Wall. As soon as we read it, we somehow felt that 'we had to go'. As we learned later, our response was shared with a number of people on the Run. 'A friend told me about it, and I just knew I had to go'; 'I saw a flyer in the Harley shop and felt I had to go' were typical responses when we asked people how they came to be involved. In our case, this strong feeling was not due to either of us being veterans. We were not, and in fact both of us had been opposed to the war. And yet the Vietnam War, and the domestic turmoil that accompanied it, were major, even defining, events of our generation, and had shaped our own coming of age in the late 1960s. And so it came about that we were

drawn into this cross-country journey of memory, mourning and reconciliation, a journey that changed our lives.

It was only later that we came to analyse the journey from our
perspectives as social scientists and to develop the desire to write about
it.[8] Because we did not set out to study the Run, because we have
been personally involved in this event, and because we did not employ
any systematic data collection in assembling the material for our writing,
we have termed our method 'observant participation' (rather than
'participant observation'; see Michalowski and Dubisch 2001: 20–1). We
have ridden all or part way with the Run for the Wall every year since
1996 (three times making the journey all the way across the United
States to Washington, DC), taken part in annual reunions of Run
participants, followed the Run for the Wall website and newsletter,
and become close friends with some of the Run participants. We have
engaged in numerous conversations during and after the Run, observed
countless rituals along the route, shared meals, laughter and tears, held
and comforted others along the route and been held and comforted
ourselves. Thus we are as fully pilgrims as the others who take part in this
journey.

At the same time, as someone who had spent considerable time
studying pilgrimage in another culture (see Dubisch 1995), I found
myself on the Run for the Wall experiencing in a vivid emotional, and
even physical, way some of the concepts I had only observed and written
about previously: liminality, *communitas*, the power of ritual, suffering
and transformation. In this sense, the analytical and experiential merged
in the course of the journey, providing me with an understanding of
pilgrimage I am not certain I would otherwise have had.

Transforming meaning and history: the Run for the Wall as pilgrimage

'We're not tourists. We're pilgrims'.

Thus spoke our companion Rich as he surveyed the crowds at the
tables around us in the crowded café in Rock Springs, Arizona, where we
had stopped for lunch on our way to join the 1998 10th anniversary
Run for the Wall. Rich's words were a recognition of the seriousness of
our endeavour, for the Run is not mere travel, but a journey with a
mission, contrasting with trips taken for novelty or pleasure. Nor was his
use of the term 'pilgrim' an idiosyncratic one. Indeed the term 'pilgrimage' is used repeatedly by participants on this cross-country journey.

What is it that makes this journey – undertaken on motorcycles, travelling interstate highways and back country roads, to a purely secular memorial and with an explicit political purpose – a pilgrimage? Part of the answer lies in our friend Rich's comment. The participants in the Run for the Wall are on a mission; they are serious travellers, not mere tourists or sightseers. This is not to suggest that seriousness is always a defining characteristic of pilgrimage, nor that there is no time for fun and socializing during the course of the Run. Rather, what is important here is the participants' own view of what distinguishes their journey from other mundane trips, and particularly from purely recreational motorcycle rides. The political goal of the Run for the Wall (increasing awareness of the POW/MIA issue and 'bringing them home') is certainly a serious one. But in addition, the Run is a painful journey for many of the veterans as they confront memories of their combat experience, the death of comrades, feelings of 'survivor guilt', and their own struggles and suffering since their return from the war.

But it is more than the seriousness of the journey's goals, or the pain and suffering experienced by many of the participants, that defines the Run for the Wall as a pilgrimage, and more than the length and difficulty of the long ride across the United States. The Run is also transformative: transforming meaning, transforming history, transforming the emotional state of those participating.

I have already mentioned that in the course of the Run for the Wall, I have experienced personally some of the concepts I had until that point only read or written about. Certainly liminality and *communitas* – those much critiqued characterizations of pilgrimage developed by Turner and Turner (1978) – were present on the Run for the Wall, in varying form and degrees. Many of the participants in the Run for the Wall inhabit a doubly liminal status: as Vietnam veterans and as bikers. Motorcycle riding and biker culture have long had a particular attraction for veterans, from the returning veterans of World Wars I and II (Lavigne 1987; Pierson 1997) to Vietnam veterans to veterans of the Gulf War.[9] There are several reasons for this. The sense of marginality that some veterans feel upon their return to civilian life, and the difficulty they may experience in adapting to that life, resonate with the marginality of at least some segments of motorcycle culture, especially that of the outlaw biker culture and the 'saloon' biker culture modelled on it. The hardship and danger of motorcycle riding also provide the 'edge' and the adrenalin high that some combat veterans find themselves missing after their return, as well as the intense sense of camaraderie and of 'brotherhood' that they have experienced in wartime conditions.[10] The patriotic symbolism and ideology that are part of many biker sub-cultures are also an attraction for some veterans. In addition, as we have heard from a number of the veterans on the Run for the Wall, motorcycle riding can have important therapeutic effects, providing a space in which veterans feel that they can 'clear their heads' and find some peace from the emotional demons haunting them. As one veteran put it:

> When I wasn't working, I was out riding my bike at 100 miles an hour in the dead of night. It was all that kept me together. It was the only place I could escape the pressure. When I couldn't take the stress, I'd go out and ride.
>
> (Michalowski and Dubisch 2001: 127)

Motorcycle riding is more than a symbolic or social activity. It is also a visceral experience, one that transcends the power of mere words to describe. Movement itself becomes a form of therapy, taking the veteran away from the memories that haunt him, and toward an open and undefined horizon. At the same time, riding combines the individual and the collective. As the Run speeds down the highway, each rider is enclosed in his own space of noise and movement while simultaneously being part of the larger formation that visually (and audibly) represents the collective endeavour that is the Run for the Wall.[11]

By riding motorcycles, the participants in the Run for the Wall set themselves apart from those making a cross-country journey by ordinary means.[12] The parade of motorcycles (at points numbering from 200 to 250 bikes) riding side by side in formation down the highway presents an impressive sight which is part of the strategy employed by the Run in its political agenda – calling attention to the POW/MIA issue. At the same time, riding motorcycles represents a more conventional element of pilgrimage – the role that hardship and suffering often play in the pilgrim's journey. And while the speed with which motorcycles traverse the countryside contrasts to what one often thinks of as the deliberately slower, more difficult pace of pilgrimage (for example, going on foot or one's knees; see Dubisch 1995; Frey 1998), riding a motorcycle can provide an often gruelling, sometimes dangerous and always absorbing means of travel. There is also a psychological – some would say a spiritual – state induced by riding. The very landscape through which one rides, however familiar it might be from other journeys, suddenly becomes new and unfamiliar. This altered state – which on the Run is height-ened by the deafening roar of a hundred or so motorcycles hurtling down the highway together at speeds of 65–75 miles an hour – increases receptiveness to the experiences, impressions and messages encountered in the course of the journey.[13]

Hardship and suffering are not only physical, however. More difficult than the physical danger and obstacles that the riders face may be the emotional and psychological pain. As Reader points out (1993: 225): 'Grief-centred pilgrimages have their share of pain and suffering, and such emotional pain is often a vital element in the development of a pilgrimage.' It is the unhealed emotional wounds of war that bring most veteran participants to the Run. At the same time, it is the pain of such wounds, and not the physical hardships and dangers of the journey, that has kept some of the veterans we have encountered from completing, or even attempting, this pilgrimage.

Malkki speaks of 'accidental communities of memory', individuals joined by the accidental sharing of transitory (but often powerful) experiences (1997: 91–2). Vietnam veterans could certainly be considered such an 'accidental community', sharing a common experience of combat in a harrowing and controversial war. Drawing upon such a community, the Run for the Wall transforms it into something more. Through the shared journey and the hardships of the road, the presumed common goals of the pilgrimage, the common bonds of biker culture and of veterans' experience, a sense of *communitas* may be created. That is, insofar as to participate in the Run is to show one's dedication to veterans, to their problems and to the cause, regardless of one's own veteran status, bonds are created that transcend other differences that might exist outside the Run. When we first considered joining the Run for the Wall, we were concerned about whether or not we would be welcome in what we saw as a mainly Vietnam veterans' event. But when Ray telephoned John Anderson, the 1996 Run organizer, he was assured that all were welcome as long as they supported the cause. The only rule, John told him, was 'no attitudes'. And what we discovered in the course of our journey was that, although not veterans, we too were part of a larger 'accidental community of memory', composed of those who as young adults had experienced the turbulence, the pain, the fear and the anger of America's Vietnam War years.

The intensity of the trip, and the emotions it evokes, as well as the experience of living together in another reality for the duration of the 10-day trip, also help to bond together those who make the journey. This bonding is particularly strong among those who go 'all the way' together, making the entire journey from California to Washington, and is reinforced for those who repeat the trip on an annual basis. And while it is a common assumption nowadays that the only people who can afford motorcycles are doctors and lawyers (the Rich Urban Bikers, or RUBs), the range of individuals drawn together by the Run for the Wall is wide. Among those we have encountered on the journey are career military personnel, a lawyer, a college professor, the owner of a tattoo parlour, business people, firemen, police officers,[14] civil servants and ministers and missionaries, as well as a number of veterans who are just managing to survive on disability pensions. We ourselves have formed close relationships and strong emotional bonds with individuals with whom we would otherwise have had little in common and would never have met, let alone come to view as friends, had we not been involved in the Run for the Wall.[15]

This does not mean that there are not tensions and divisions, both structural and personal, on the Run. Long-buried memories and emotions can resurface during the pilgrimage, and interpersonal conflicts can erupt. Organizing such a large cadre of motorcyclists and taking them safely across the country can require that the Run's leaders enforce a certain degree of order, which may be resented by some participants. ('When I left the army, I swore I'd never stand at attention again', one rider remarked as we were called to order for the daily morning meeting.) In addition, there are social divisions that may manifest themselves in the course of the Run: between veterans and non-veterans, between combat and non-combat veterans, between 'old timers' and those who are new to the Run. Sometimes groups of friends ride and socialize together. While occasionally these may reflect relationships that existed in Vietnam, more often they are the consequence of friendships made on the Run itself, of common membership in a local biker or veterans' organization, or other non-military affiliation.[16] Yet whatever conflicts or divisions arise, participants remind each other not to forget 'why we ride': for the cause and for the healing of individual wounds of war. And while the Run may honour those who go 'all the way' from California to Washington, DC, for their commitment, anyone who has participated in the Run for the Wall, whether by riding with the group or by greeting and hosting it along the way, is considered part of the Run for the Wall 'family' (see Michalowski and Dubisch 2001).

Ritual, narrative and healing

I mentioned that the physical state induced by the long motor-cycle journey creates a receptivity to the ritual messages presented along the way. These in turn are part of the transformation wrought by

the pilgrimage upon its participants. But what, exactly, are these ritual messages, and what transformations do they produce?

One of the goals of the Run for the Wall is to overcome the liminality I have discussed above. To draw a veteran into the Run, to encourage him to join with other veterans and to ride with them to the Wall, is to bring that individual out of the isolation imposed by his stigmatized status as a veteran and by his own psychic wounds and to reintegrate him into society, both the society of other veterans and the larger American society. An image often employed in discussing this goal is the veteran who 'lives in the woods', that is, alone and isolated. While in a few cases this image can be applied literally, it is also metaphoric, referring to the individual hiding in the forest of his own memories and pain. To draw this person into the Run, to demonstrate to him that he is not alone, is one of the goals of the Run for the Wall and the first step in reintegrating such individuals into society. At the same time, the Run itself represents a liminal and stigmatized social group, that is, 'bikers',[17] and one of its additional goals is to portray bikers in a positive light, as veterans and patriotic Americans.

While the riders set themselves apart by their mode of transportation, they also seek a connection that is established in the many stops that the Run makes in its cross-country journey. At small communities in the 'heartland of America', at veterans' hospitals, town centres and parish halls, truck stops, schools and war memorials across the United States, the Run for the Wall is greeted and hosted by a variety of local organizations and individuals: veterans' groups, motorcycle clubs, motorcycle dealers, churches, schoolchildren, community officials and local supporters. Participants seldom pay for a meal in this 10-day cross-country journey, and in many places camping for the riders is free. In the mountainous town of Cimarron, New Mexico, for example, dinner and breakfast are provided by the local Catholic parish. At a highway rest area in Kansas, lunch is served to the group courtesy of the Kansas chapter of ABATE, which also pays the group's highway tolls. In the impoverished mining town of Reinell, West Virginia, hundreds of riders are fed at the local Moose Lodge Hall.

It is these groups and individuals who organize many of the rituals that greet the riders in the course of the Run. At the same time, these rituals are experienced by the Run for the Wall participants in the context of the totality of their journey, with all its physical hardships, its emotional intensity and its collective sense of mission. Some examples of events along the route will give a sense of this experience.

For the last four years, the Run's first overnight stop after leaving

California has been Williams, a small town in northwestern Arizona. Here at the campground where many of the riders stay, Dick Darnell, a veteran from Phoenix, Arizona, brings an entire crew to cook dinner and breakfast for the riders. The dinner is preceded by a ceremony in which the symbolic 'remembrance table' plays a central role, a table set for the various branches of American military service. Each branch has an empty place with plate, silverware and overturned glass, and each military service is honoured in turn with the playing of its anthem. The empty places remind us of the dead and of the fact that they will not return home to drink and dine with us again.

The next day's journey is from Williams to Gallup, New Mexico. New Mexico, with its large, mostly poor, Hispanic and Native American population,[18] gives the Run for the Wall one of the warmest receptions of its entire cross-country journey. Several years ago, the Navajo reservation was added to the Run's landscape when the riders were invited to attend ceremonies at the then almost completed Navajo Vietnam Veterans Memorial. This has given a new dimension to the Run and, especially for those of us who were present on that first occasion, created an indelible memory. That particular year, the Run had endured snow on its way through the mountains of northern Arizona and temperatures hovering around 40 degrees Fahrenheit as we crossed the high desert toward Gallup. Just before we crossed the border from Arizona to New Mexico, we turned off the highway to be met by a contingent of Navajo police at the small town of Lupton. Expecting to be escorted directly to the reservation's administrative capital of Window Rock, we were surprised when our escort instead led us into the Lupton schoolyard. There a large crowd of Navajo awaited us, bursting into applause as we pulled in and circled our bikes. As the riders parked and dismounted, Navajo moved forward shaking hands, hugging us and thanking us for coming. We were ushered toward the schoolhouse and a receiving line of Navajo elders waiting for us on the porch. They greeted and hugged us and thanked us again for coming. We were overwhelmed. Why were they so glad to see us? Why were they thanking *us*?

Inside the schoolhouse we were served coffee and hot 'fry bread', a welcome offering to people on the edge of hypothermia. Before we departed, an elderly Navajo woman blessed us with a long prayer in her native tongue. Then we mounted up, and behind our police escort, sped deeper into the reservation. All along the route, groups of Navajo were standing next to cars and pick-up trucks waving and applauding as we rode by. We had been told that this was the first time the Navajo Nation had formally invited outsiders to participate in its Memorial Day ceremonies. Moreover, they were holding these ceremonies a week before Memorial Day in order to coordinate with our arrival. As we rolled to a stop, the waiting crowd burst into enthusiastic applause. In response the bikers gunned their engines in a collective roar. From the podium at one end of the parking lot, a Navajo leader said: 'Look around you, white men – you're surrounded by Indians. We'll take your bikes. You can have our horses.' With that comment he acknowledged both the differences that separated his people from this predominantly Anglo group of bikers and the shared history, particularly military history, that bound them together. The long history of the Navajo as warriors was also emphasized in the ceremonies that followed. Navajo leaders gave the Run a Navajo Nation flag to carry to the Wall, a Navajo folk singer performed a song he wrote in memory of a brother who died in Vietnam, Navajo children took our pictures while balancing precariously on the rocks above. Then Navajo and non-Navajo saluted while a bugler played taps as the light dimmed around the mystical symbol of Window Rock in a final tribute to all the warriors who had died in defence of their country.

The following day, the Run reaches another dramatic place in New Mexico that has also become part of the sacred landscape of this pilgrimage: the Vietnam veterans' memorial at Angel Fire, high in the mountains above Taos. Although Angel Fire is known chiefly as a ski area and resort, for many of the participants in the Run for the Wall it is forever a sacred place associated with their pilgrimage. The power of the site, a wind-swept valley surrounded by snow-capped peaks, is breathtaking. And the memorial itself, with its chapel shaped like a giant white wing, stands upon a hill high above the road. We have heard many stories from veterans that it was here, at Angel Fire, with its war museum, its chapel, its incredible natural setting, that their own memories and wounds of Vietnam were opened and their journey toward healing began.[19]

The next day at Limon, Colorado, a campground becomes the site of a ceremony organized by Task Force Omega, an organization of families of POWs and MIAs. Here every year the names of the Colorado Missing in Action are read in a candlelight ritual that begins at dusk. One year the audience intoned, 'Missing but not forgotten', as each name was called. Another year, we formed into couples, and the woman read the name of one of the missing men while the man called out: 'Still on patrol, sir!' Afterwards we all join hands in a 'healing circle'.

The healing circle is repeated in the town park in Salina, Kansas, the next day's stop. Here, after being fed and entertained by the townspeople, one of the organizers of the event calls upon us to form 'The largest friendship circle we ever had.' As we sing 'Amazing Grace', the circle moves in and out. The line from the song, 'I once was lost but now I'm found', resonates with the feeling many veterans on the Run for the Wall experience as they are 'welcomed home' in communities such as this. A truck stop is the unlikely location of another roadside ceremony at Mt. Vernon, Illinois. Here the group is fed and ceremonies are held. The first year we participated in the Run for the Wall, the names of soldiers from Illinois who died in Vietnam were read and an artificial rose placed in a basket for each name, the basket to be carried to the Wall. On other occasions, the remembrance table has been repeated here. Included in the Run's itinerary are also stops at various Vietnam War memorials along the route, each honouring the dead of that particular state. Among the many such memorials dotting the landscape, the memorial at Lexington, Kentucky, stands out. It is in the shape of a large sundial, with the names of the Kentucky Vietnam dead engraved seemingly at random on granite blocks all around it.

The Run's last stop before Washington, DC, is the tiny, impoverished coal mining town of Reinell, West Virginia. Screaming, pom-pom waving children line the street as the bikers ride in and then crowd around to collect autographs as the riders dismount. There are ceremonies in the schoolyard, in which most of the town population participates, and which include the singing of patriotic songs, flag ceremonies by local scout troops and speeches honouring the veterans. Then the entire crowd, now numbering several hundred, is fed at the local Moose Lodge.

Within the context of the rituals and other events that take place along the pilgrimage route, both being a veteran and being a biker are legitimized. Neither status is problematic in this context; rather both are celebrated. The veteran thus learns to accept his status *as* a veteran as the rituals of reintegration that were lacking to him after the war are enacted in the course of the Run. As one veteran said to me after his reception in Reinell, 'This is the welcome home I never had.'

Yet the Run for the Wall is painful as well. During the course of the pilgrimage, memories of the war which may have been long buried begin to surface. Indeed, some veterans who join the Run feeling they really had 'nothing to get over' from their wartime experiences learn otherwise once they are confronted with reminders of these experiences. As one veteran repeated tearfully as he joined hands in the 'healing circle' that is part of the ritual at the Run's stop in Limon, 'I thought I was just going for a ride. *I thought I was just going for a ride!*' And the most painful – and intimidating – part of the journey is the destination, the Vietnam Veterans Memorial – the Wall. 'I'm terrified of getting to the Wall', one veteran confided to me at the start of our last day out. And for some veterans, the thought of confronting the Wall is so painful that they are unable to complete, or even to begin, the journey, despite the encouragement and support of fellow veterans and of others who have been on the Run.[20]

It is the Vietnam Veterans Memorial, 'the Wall', that is both the destination and the emotional climax of the pilgrimage. On the last day of its journey, the Run for the Wall enters the nation's capital, Washington, DC. After stopping for group photographs at the World War II Iwo Jima Memorial, the Run rides to the Vietnam Memorial. Parking the bikes in a field across the street, the riders collect themselves and then move singly and in groups to confront the Wall. There, face to face with the black granite surface in which the over 58,000 names of American dead are inscribed, one weeps, one looks for names of departed comrades and relatives, one leaves offerings, one offers a shoulder to those who grieve. Although communal support is available to those who need it, here the rituals performed are individual ones, which, while often involving conventional objects and forms (flags, flowers, letters, etc.), are shaped by each participant's own experience of grief and loss. Some lay wreaths beneath significant names, others kneel in prayer, some speak to the dead while others make rubbings of the engraved names. For some, it is the first time they have confronted the Wall, and more experienced pilgrims are close by to offer help if needed. Others have private rituals they repeat year after year. Some veterans are so emotionally over-whelmed they must move away, seeking nearby benches to nurse their grief in solitude. Then, individually or in groups, their rituals completed, the riders return to their bikes and make their way to the motel where Run participants will spend the night.

Other ceremonies follow the next day, Saturday, including laying a wreath at the Tomb of the Unknown Soldier, and most of the riders will join the giant Rolling Thunder parade on Sunday as it roars through Washington, DC. But it is here at the Wall, on the day of the pilgrims' arrival, that the pilgrimage itself culminates. That evening, partici-pants celebrate together at a local restaurant, enjoying their sense of accomplishment at having completed their pilgrimage as thanks and awards are handed out to various individuals who helped to organize and support the journey. Some, however, remain in a sober mood, as the effects of their visit to the Wall still linger. At the end of the week-end, the pilgrims will make their way home, some in the company of others, some stopping to visit friends or relatives along the way, others making a quick and solo journey back. There is no group ritual for the return.

The Vietnam Veterans Memorial has been described as 'America's greatest national shrine'. Why this should be so is beyond the scope of this chapter, but one dimension of the Wall that is particularly important to mention here is the spiritual quality of this ostensibly secular monument. For many veterans, it is the Wall, not the individual grave sites scattered across the country, where their dead comrades reside. 'When you touch a name on the Wall, it brings back that person's soul', one veteran said to me. Another veteran recounted that during the 'night patrol', the midnight vigil that some of the veterans hold at the memorial the evening of their arrival to be alone without the presence of crowds of tourists, he was suddenly overwhelmed by a cacophony of voices seemingly coming from the Wall. A friend gently pulled him away, saying that he, too, had experienced the same phenomenon, as if all the men whose names were there were speaking to him at once. The concept of 'Wall magic' is one that we have heard articulated at various times in the course of our journeys. It is a quality that causes miraculous things to happen, that creates connections among people.

The leaving of offerings at the Wall is a practice that any student or practitioner of pilgrimage will recognize.[21] Since its inauguration in 1982, the Vietnam Veterans Memorial has attracted such objects by the thousands (see Hass 1998). Some are generic, such as wreaths, flowers or American flags. Others are individualized, such as letters and photographs or personal items. One year I watched a veteran from the Run place a newsletter from an Arizona biker club and a pack of cigarettes beneath the name of a fallen comrade. 'He loved to ride his motorcycle', the man explained to an onlooker. Another time I myself placed beneath the name of someone from New Mexico a pair of miniature moccasins given to me by a girl on the Navajo reservation. On one Run for the Wall (before we ourselves began participating), a brand new Harley Davidson motorcycle was taken to the memorial and left as an offering. And on the 1998 Run, the ashes of a deceased Vietnam veteran were carried in an ammunition box on the back of a motorcycle across the country, to be left at the Wall.

The carrying of objects on others' behalf connects communities across the country to both the Run for the Wall and to the Wall itself. Similarly, objects may be taken to the Wall and then back across the country, thus connecting the Wall to those back home. (One may also take rubbings of names of individuals on the Wall.)[22] Thus a long thread of ritual and offerings runs through the 'heartland of America', connecting coast to coast, entwining with local Vietnam memorials in various states along the way and finally arriving at the Wall. The fact that the Run stops at a number of local memorials, each commemorating the Vietnam War dead of that particular state, and then arrives at the Vietnam Veterans Memorial ties the local to the national, and the individual dead to the collective sacrifice. At the same time, as Berdahl points out (1994: 96), the leaving of offerings has established the Wall as a place where *individual* suffering and loss are commemorated and *individual* stories are told.

Healing, identity and memory

For some veterans, the Run for the Wall has become a psychological necessity. 'I live for the Run each year', we have heard people say. These individuals will repeat all or part of the journey every year. Others will participate once or twice and then will not be involved again (though they may keep in touch with friends they have made in the course of the journey). However, the power of the Run for the Wall lies not only in the support and understanding individuals receive from other participants and from those they encounter along the way, but also in the Run's ability to transform meaning and identity.

One of the paradoxes of individualism in American culture is that it is often through joining a community that the individual may most fully realize his or her identity.[23] Out of their experience in the Run for the Wall, many of the veterans who participate find themselves developing new identities *as* veterans. On the Run, veterans can share their experiences with others who understand what they have been through, and in a context in which it is not only acceptable to be a veteran but even a matter of pride. The Run has also introduced veterans to others in their city or state who are not only Vietnam veterans but also bikers. Such relationships can become the basis for a new social world, and a new identity, once these individuals return home. Helping to sustain these effects are various forms of contact among participants that may take place between Runs. There is a Run for the Wall website that provides information on each year's Run, events of interest to Run members and news of individuals involved. Local reunions are held between Runs, and there are gatherings of participants for events such as weddings or birthdays. Such occasions may also be the means of recruiting new participants and are often attended by those who wish to join the Run and are seeking information or support. For those for whom the

Run becomes an annual event, these contacts serve to maintain and strengthen the changes the Run for the Wall has brought about and to provide some of the 'corporeal co-presence' (Urry 2002) that is so much a part of the intensity of the Run for the Wall itself. In these ways, then, the Run for the Wall carries effects that extend beyond the duration of the pilgrimage.

Through the Run for the Wall, and the activities that sustain and support it, the suffering that veterans have undergone both during and after the war is not so much given *new* meaning as given *meaning*. This transformation does not necessarily happen immediately, but is often part of a process that participation in the Run for the Wall has initiated. It is in the process of transformation that the particular power of the Run for the Wall is most striking, for it also seeks to transform the meaning of history. Or perhaps more accurately, it seeks to establish a meaning for a period and events in American history for which meaning is at best, contested, and at worst, simply lacking.

Recent discussions have suggested that there cannot even *be* 'experience' in any meaningful way unless we can construct a narrative. This narrative, however, is constructed in a cultural context. If there are past experiences that are difficult or impossible to talk about, it may be not so much that language is inadequate, or that memory is too painful, but rather that 'sometimes there are situations or events . . . that are the occasions of "experiences" that cannot be expressed in the terms that language (or, more broadly, the symbolic order) offers *at that moment*' (Van Alphen 1999: 26). This has also been a problem for Vietnam veterans. Part of the reason for this is that the Vietnam War itself 'had no conventional narrative structure – a war without a clear beginning or end, without well-articulated goals, fought sometimes with scant regard for geographic boundaries, and indeed, remaining undeclared, technically not a war at all' (Allen 1995: 94). The Run for the Wall thus offers veterans a 'symbolic order' in which a narrative can be constructed, one that reframes the veteran's own history and identity.

This is not to say that no other narratives have been available. While for many veterans, one of the problems of constructing a coherent and meaningful narrative of the war was the public silence during the immediate postwar period, there were popular culture accounts of the war (particularly movies) that began to emerge in the decades after the Vietnam War ended. However, such representations, for the most part, have not offered an account of the war experience with which most Vietnam veterans could identify themselves. Indeed I have heard more than one veteran blame pre-Vietnam movies for their own naïve images of war. As one veteran so eloquently stated: 'When I went to Vietnam, I was John Wayne. When I returned I was a turd.'

Part of the postwar trauma, at least for some veterans, was the controversy over, and opposition to, the war on the home front. Part of the therapy of the Run for the Wall, then, lies in the ritual 'welcome home' that is received on the Run, both from fellow veterans and from non-combatants and communities along the way. Individual suffering becomes transformed into meaningful shared experience. The veteran is not just a wounded, suffering individual who feels inadequate because he has not been able to adapt or cope after his experience (or because after leading a 'normal' life he finds himself in mid-life reliving his trauma) and not just someone experiencing a personal problem or defeat. Rather he is a returned warrior who, with self-sacrificing patriotism, fought for freedom and who, betrayed by the government that sent him to fight and the citizens he fought to protect, is finally receiving some of the recognition he deserves.

A slogan seen on banners and T-shirts sums up this construction of a new narrative of the war: 'Forget the War, Remember the Warrior'. This slogan demands that we put the controversial politics of the Vietnam War behind us and instead focus on those who fought the war and are still suffering its consequences, thus making the shaping of memory a process of both remembering and forgetting. In addition, this refocusing seeks to overcome one of the difficulties many veterans have experienced in their attempts to make sense of their wartime experience: the discrepancy between official statements during the war (in which the light was always visible 'at the end of the tunnel') and their own combat experiences in which they saw little in the way of victory but much in the way of confusion, death and loss. In the case of the Vietnam War, the suffering achieved no satisfying end, accomplished no goal and left its participants with no satisfying narrative into which to insert their own part in the conflict. While some veterans we have met are bitter because they feel that the war *could* have been won if the United States government had not bowed to political pressure, others feel that the war was a mistake and that there was never any question of 'winning'.

There is another way in which the narrative of the Vietnam War is reframed in the context of the Run. For veterans who saw themselves as failures for not being able to adjust after their wartime experience, the only alternative to self-blame has been a medical model. The diagnosis of post-traumatic stress disorder (only established after some struggle and controversy; see Young 1995) has enabled veterans to see their emotional problems (sleep disorders, nightmares, flashbacks, irritability, persistent mobilization for danger, etc.) not as individual failings but as symptoms of an illness that is the consequence of their combat experience. At the same time, the concept of PTSD has medicalized and individualized the veterans' suffering. In their own way, then, both the Run for the Wall and the POW/MIA movement have sought to re-politicize the issue of the Vietnam War by calling for government accountability for all the consequences of the war.

At the same time, this message carries a potential contradiction. Many of the veterans on the Run for the Wall would regard themselves as patriots, warriors who fought for their country and for freedom. The Run is filled with patriotic symbolism in the form of flags, songs, slogans and speeches. How, then, to reconcile this with the criticisms of the United States' treatment of veterans and with the deep ambivalence that many veterans feel about the war itself? One way of addressing this contradiction is summed up in the slogan, 'I love my country, but I don't trust the government'. By separating nation from state, the veteran can present himself as a patriot while at the same time engaging in political protest. Thus the Run for the Wall can be seen as a social movement that challenges the government at the same time as it reaffirms what many participants see as the values that characterize the American 'heartland'.[24] (There is a tremendous irony here, of course, as the cry 'don't trust the government' was the mantra of anti-war protesters in the Vietnam era, who were branded as unpatriotic for their criticism of government policies.)

As Alex King and others have suggested, forgetting may be an essential element in war memorials, conferring upon such monuments their sacred quality and their ability to achieve consensus (King 1999: 163). Sellers and Walter note that the Vietnam Veterans Memorial, while it refuses to shape a heroic and moralizing narrative about the war, 'allows, yet does not force, repentance for our part in the war as well as honour for those who died' (1993: 189). Like other Vietnam memorials, the Wall 'has created a dominant memory of Vietnam that focusses on *individual* experiences and tragedies of the war' (Berdahl 1994: 117; emphasis added), thus separating both the living and the dead from the pain and shame that accompanied the conflict in Vietnam. This focus also separates the American dead from any larger social or global context. As Rowlands points out, the Vietnam Veterans Memorial makes 'no mention of the thousands of Vietnamese who died or the social inequalities hidden in the representation of the American dead' (Rowlands 1999: 142–3). Moreover, in its representation of sacrifice, the memorial says nothing about the United States' foreign policies which were ultimately responsible for so much death and suffering.

Conclusions: from biker to pilgrim

Hastrup and Olwig have noted (1997: 12):

> the central importance of place as a source of life and a reference point which people may identify with from their particular position in the more global network of human relations. By viewing place as a cultural construction that is part of the process of human life, and not as a fixed entity, we shall be able to examine critically the historical context within which these cultural constructions take place.

In the Run for the Wall we see pilgrimage used as a means for constructing a particular place, a particular landscape, the 'heartland of America'. This landscape, in turn, becomes part of a process that seeks to heal both history and the individual veteran by providing a 'welcome home' that transforms the veteran's own identity as well as the meaning of the Vietnam War.

At the same time, the Run for the Wall, like most rituals, also offers itself to many meanings and interpretations. That two individuals who opposed the Vietnam War, and who find some of the kinds of patriotic sentiments celebrated on the Run distasteful, can nonetheless find their participation in the Run for the Wall one of the most moving and powerful experiences of their lives, is testimony to this. It also became clearer to me through my own participation in the Run that pilgrimage can be many, even contradictory, things at once: a political movement and a personal journey of healing, a celebration of the warrior and a memorial to the tragedy of war, an experience of liminality by the marginal and a mode of integration and the overcoming of marginality, a place of *communitas* but also riven with divisions and conflict, a journey and a coming home.

Unlike other pilgrimages described in this volume, the Run for the Wall is not linked to global diasporas, international travel or other processes grouped under the currently popular rubric of 'globalization'. Indeed, in contrast to many other pilgrimages, the Run can be seen as isolationist, even chauvinistic, in its politics, its messages emphasizing the consequences of sending America's sons and daughters to die on 'foreign soil'.[25] At the same time, however, the Run for the Wall is a direct consequence of global events, a reflection of the long-lasting domestic repercussions of United States imperialism and interventionist foreign policy. In that sense, while uniquely American in many of its elements, the Run, in its own way, is as much enmeshed in the global as any other pilgrimage.

In addition, in recent years, the Run for the Wall has sought to broaden its message by calling attention to the missing from *all* of the United States' foreign wars, and by emphasizing the brotherhood of warrior veterans, whatever their nationality. Even the Wall, which is usually viewed as a quintessentially American monument, has been subject to some degree of internationalization. Not only is there a Canadian 'Wall' honouring Canadians who died in the Vietnam conflict, but a 250 foot replica of the Vietnam Veterans Memorial was taken to Ireland in 1999, brought there through the efforts of an Irishman named Declan Hughes who had participated in the 1999 Run for the Wall 'in remembrance of at least 21 Irish-born citizens who died in Vietnam'.[26] Declan Hughes is also involved in the Irish Veterans Memorial project, which held its 2nd annual Memorial Day Service in Athlone, Ireland on 26 May 2002.[27] Among those attending the 2002 Memorial Day service were veterans of the Gulf War, Vietnam, Korea, World War II and Cyprus. In this fashion, then, the Run for the Wall serves to provide inspiration for, and to create connections with, other groups and events relating to veterans.

But the Run for the Wall is more than a political movement or a celebration of veterans. While it can be termed a 'secular pilgrimage' in that it is not specifically religious in its organization or its destination and has overtly political purposes, it is nonetheless a profoundly spiritual journey. Insofar as it is a journey with and for the dead, it bridges the mundane and the invisible worlds. (One of the early slogans of the Run was 'We Ride for Those Who Died'.) Every day begins with a prayer by a Run chaplain who asks for 'travelling mercies'. While for the most part the prayers are Christian, there are also elements of Native American spirituality invoked by some participants. The Run is also a journey of profound transformations, a journey toward healing and away from pain and grief, a journey in which veterans and their supporters, in the course of their 3,000 mile trip, find themselves transformed from bikers to pilgrims. The Run for the Wall thus reveals pilgrimage as a creative invention that combines personal healing, political protest and the reconstruction of history and memory. In this ritual journey we see, to use the words of Coleman and Eade in their Introduction, how 'practices of displacement are not incidental to, but actually constitutive of, cultural meanings in a world that is constantly "en route"'.

Nancy Wood, in her discussion of collective memory, sees such memory as performative, 'as only coming into existence at a given time and place through specific kinds of memorial activity', and she sees such performativity as situating 'representation of the past within recognizable temporal and spatial structures and sensibilities' (1999: 2–3). The participants in the Run for the Wall, by using the culturally familiar ritual pattern of a pilgrimage, have shaped this ritual into a 'vector of memory', not merely to reflect but to shape culture, memory, history and concepts of 'home' for both individual and collective ends. In this sense, the Run does not merely traverse the 'heartland of America'; it constitutes it as well.

Notes

1 Honda Gold Wings are large motorcycles, particularly suited for touring by couples. Gold Wing riders tend to be middle-aged and do not normally dress for riding in the black leather 'outlaw' biker style.
2 ABATE stands for 'American Brotherhood Aimed Toward Education', a national organization whose goals include political activism on behalf of motorcycle riders.
3 The term 'pilgrimage' is one used by the participants themselves to refer to this journey.
4 For examples of the latter categories, see Michalowski and Dubisch (2001).
5 On post-traumatic stress disorder, see Dean (1997); Picquet and Best (1986); Shay (1994); Young (1995).
6 For a discussion of the POW/MIA issue as a social movement (one that extends beyond the Run for the Wall), see Michalowski and Dubisch (2001). For two different views of the POW/MIA controversy, see Franklin (1993) and Jensen-Stevenson and Stevenson (1990).
7 There is some controversy about the extent to which returning veterans actually experienced a hostile homecoming (see, for example, Lembcke 1998). However, what is important here is that there is a strong feeling among veterans on the Run that, whatever their personal experiences might have been, returning veterans in general were not welcomed when they came home.
8 I am an anthropologist; my partner Raymond Michalowski is a sociologist. Our collaborative effort has resulted in a book, *Run for the Wall: Remembering Vietnam on a Motorcycle Pilgrimage* (Michalowski and Dubisch 2001).
9 It remains to be seen whether the Run will eventually draw veterans of Afghanistan and of the American invasion of Iraq. These veterans are already being acknowledged in the Run's events, including Lori Piestewa, a Hopi Indian, who was honoured as the first Native American woman to die in combat.

10 As Coleman has pointed out, one of Victor Turner's own inspirations for the concept of *communitas* was his experience as part of a bomb disposal unit during World War II (Coleman 2002: 364). On the concept of 'brotherhood' among outlaw bikers, see Wolf (1991).

11 I am indebted to 'Snake Byte' for this observation.

12 Some participants make the journey in more ordinary, four-wheeled vehicles ('cages' in biker jargon) but they ride at the back of the 'pack'.

13 See Winkelman (forthcoming). On the physiology of ritual, see Davis-Floyd (1992); D'Aquili *et al.* (1979).

14 A remarkable number of veterans we have met are, or were, policemen or firemen, perhaps seeking to continue the 'adrenaline high', as well as the sense of service, that characterized their Vietnam experience.

15 For some vets, the fact that non-veterans would ride with them was moving and impressive. Both of us (but especially Ray) had veterans confide their stories. In other situations we experienced the dividing line between veterans and non-veterans.

16 The organization of the Run for the Wall in no way reflects or attempts to recreate military divisions from the Vietnam War. Many veterans have not kept in touch with their military units and may even meet former comrades from Vietnam on the Run for the first time since their return from the war.

17 The other side of the coin of such stigma is the romanticizing of the 'outlaw biker' in American popular culture. The Hell's Angels, for example, enjoy a certain contemporary cachet despite their many criminal activities.

18 Poorer states such as New Mexico, Kentucky and West Virginia provide a disproportionate number of soldiers to the United States military. During the Vietnam War, when the military draft was active, fewer young men from these areas could obtain educational or other deferments than could those from more affluent areas.

19 For more on the power of Angel Fire, see Michalowski and Dubisch (2001).

20 This might be seen as a reversal of Urry's observation regarding 'obligatory, appropriate or desirable' proximity to places or events as motivating travel (2002: 258). In this case, the idea of proximity is what prevents the journey from being made.

21 However, objects left at the Wall differ from the votive offerings left at religious shrines, as the latter are usually left as part of a request to a sacred figure or as thanks for requests that have been granted. Objects at the Vietnam Veterans Memorial are similar to those left at other sites of death or tragedy, such as the site of the World Trade Center or the Oklahoma City bombing.

22 There are also several 'travelling Walls', replicas of the Vietnam Veterans Memorial, that tour the United States, allowing those nearby who may not be able to visit the memorial itself to experience some of the Wall's power.

23 On this topic, see Ginsberg (1989) and Varenne (1978); on individualism and group identity in the outlaw biker world, see Wolf (1991).

24 This is not to imply that everyone on the Run shares these values equally. Rather here I am speaking of the ideas and symbols seen in the public rituals, performances and displays visible during the pilgrimage.

25 Throughout the chapter I have referred to veterans as male. Women did

serve in Vietnam, particularly as nurses, and they have suffered some of the same long-lasting consequences of their experiences as men who were in combat (see, for example, Van Devanter 1983). However, we encountered no women veterans on the Run for the Wall and the stories of such veterans have generally been ignored in accounts of the Vietnam War.

26 RFTW.org, Summer 2002 Newsletter on line. Declan Hughes kept a diary of his 1999 pilgrimage, which was posted on the RFTW website.

27 Ibid.

Chapter 7

Coming home to the Motherland

Pilgrimage tourism in Ghana

Katharina Schramm

Introduction

Cape Coast is a town in Southern Ghana, at the shore of the Atlantic Ocean. The former commercial and administrative centre of the colonial Gold Coast, it is now famous for its excellent secondary schools (a remnant of extensive missionary activity in the region) as well as for the impressive Cape Coast Castle and Dungeons.[1] The recently renovated structure with its high, imposingly hostile walls is one of over 30 castles, forts and smaller European trade-posts dotting Ghana's coastline.[2] Such a dense concentration of fortifications is to be found nowhere else in the whole of Africa. It gives an impression of the fierce competition amongst different European powers along this narrow strip of coast from the 1500s onwards. Portuguese, Dutch, English, Swedes, Danes, Prussians, French – all of them left their traces here, in their insatiable quest for gold and slaves. Today, most of those structures are in ruins, while others are used as lodges (Gross-Friedrichsburg), prisons (until recently, Ussher Fort) or administrative centres (Christiansbourg Castle, the seat of Ghana's government).

Some, however, especially Cape Coast and Elmina castles, have been designated as World Heritage Sites by UNESCO (as far back as 1972) and are increasingly gaining importance as Ghana's most significant tourist attractions. Within the country's growing tourism industry, 'heritage tourism' with its emphasis on culture and history features prominently. Particular attention is paid to people from the African diaspora,[3] who are invited to 'come home' to Ghana and re-establish their linkage with 'Mother Africa'. In principle, the rhetoric of home-coming applies to all African descendants in the diaspora, but the African American market is the most significant. This is mainly due to the availability of financial resources necessary for the expensive journey – many more African Americans can afford the trip than, say, Jamaicans.

In advertising brochures and videos as well as in public forums,[4] Ghana appeals to this group of travellers as 'brothers and sisters' – long-lost relatives who are welcomed back to the family. Their journey to the Motherland, and more specifically to stations on the slave route, is referred to as a pilgrimage which is nevertheless incorporated into a tourism infrastructure and itinerary.[5]

Those who come frequently share the assumptions of 'family' and have high expectations of the experience of homecoming. Some of them truly feel themselves to be pilgrims – Africa, and Ghana more specifically, is regarded simultaneously as a promised land and as the place where the horrors of the slave trade began and ought to be remembered.[6] The representation of the slave trade and the 'sites of memory' (Nora 1989) within the conventions of the tourism industry may turn into a source of serious offence to them, expressed in the repeated formula: 'They sold us once, and now they are selling us again!' This struggle over meaning (Bruner 1996) will provide the background for my analysis of homecoming. Before I turn to the concrete encounter of African Americans with the Motherland, however, I want to briefly discuss the connections that have been drawn between pilgrimage and tourism and develop my concept of 'pilgrimage tourism' from there.

Pilgrims and tourists in theoretical perspective

The recent literature on pilgrimage has shown that the framing of pilgrimage within the discourse and practice of the tourism industry is far from unusual. Rigid distinctions between (serious) pilgrims – always on a journey to a sacred site – and (playful) tourists – always on a trip to places of secular pleasure – have become blurred. Centres of religious pilgrimage such as Lourdes in France have virtually grown into tourist attractions. As Eade (1992) has demonstrated, the commercial refashioning of religious zeal has become a marked feature of this (and other) sacred sites. The strict dichotomy of sacred and secular, where a fixed pattern of appropriate behaviour would be regarded as a distinguishing feature of a sacred site (Hubert 1994), is thereby thoroughly called into question. The pilgrims themselves may behave like tourists when they purchase religious souvenirs, or they may turn again into 'proper tourists' immediately after their visit to the shrine when they continue their holidays in the region or beyond.

Apart from such analysis of the close correspondence between pilgrims and tourists at an empirical level, the two concepts have also been brought together within wider theories of travel and identity. In a cultural critique of the postmodern condition, Bauman (1996) regards pilgrims and tourists as opposing metaphors, each standing for a distinct conception of identity. To Bauman, man (sic!) as pilgrim is the ultimate metaphor for the modern subject, constantly preoccupied with the building and sustenance of an identity through which he can give meaning to the confusing world surrounding him. For modern 'man', life is determined by the point of arrival (whether real or imaginary) always gleaming in the future. And the past, one may want to add, is represented in the form of grand narratives. For the postmodern subject, however, the future seems to have lost its magnitude and allure – it has collapsed into a present that has established its permanent rule. Now, fixation needs to be avoided and identities must be prevented from 'sticking'. Bauman singles out the stroller, the vagabond, the player, and finally the tourist as the inherent states of being in today's world. Out of those four, the tourist, quite in contrast to the player or the vagabond, seems to be devoid of any creative potential – 'the strange is tame, domesticated, and no longer frightens' (Bauman 1996: 29); it is presented in a package which he buys without questioning. He is gazing (Urry 1990) at a product, not engaging in a world.

One question, however, continues to disturb this picture. Who precisely are those 'postmodern subjects', who want to (or, perhaps, have to) 'keep the options open' (Bauman 1996: 18)? Massey (1992), in close correspondence with bell hooks, has reminded us that the discourse of dislocation reflects the perspective of an elite – Western, white and male. The experiences of this rather small group differ sharply from those of other people 'on the move' – migrants, refugees, etc. (cf. Kaur and Hutnyk 1999). While the identities of those people, too, are certainly fragmented and shifting, this is not only the result of arbitrary choice but also determined by political contexts and power hierarchies. Bauman acknowledges that identity has always had the 'ontological status of a project and a postulate' (1996: 19). A fixed sense of location has therefore never really existed. In order to grasp his perspective properly, one would rather have to speak of 'disorientation' than 'dislocation'. Yet this qualification does not solve the problem that I have briefly sketched, namely who is affected by this epochal shift and in what ways?

When Bauman states that the modern 'problem of identity' – its construction and maintenance (associated with the pilgrim metaphor) – is no longer relevant, one also wonders how to fit movements which propagate a cultural or 'racial' essentialism, such as Afrocentrism, or the growing preoccupation with heritage and personal as well as collective roots (Lowenthal 1994), into this picture. Longing for a 'stable identity' (or be/longing) is not all that outmoded, it seems. That does not mean, however, that an individual's notion of the meaning of such a proclaimed collective identity (as, for example, that of an 'African family') would have to correspond with that of others who relate to the same ideal. Neither does it indicate that this aim could ever be reached. Yet, as I would like to demonstrate in my discussion of homecoming, the promise of fulfilment and arrival lingers in the notion of return to Africa – even though such expectations may be unfulfilled and the journey towards an 'African identity' may have to continue.

In order to understand that particular movement it will prove useful to broaden Bauman's perspective and to introduce a more differentiated perspective on pilgrims and tourists. The African Americans who are coming to Ghana share much with both types, in terms of their politics of identity (and identity formation) as well as their actual behaviour. Their journey may show that the pilgrim's wandering in search of a spiritual centre 'out there' has not simply been replaced with the (efficiently planned and thoroughly organized) movement of a growing number of tourists to places 'elsewhere'.

'The pilgrim' is not a fixed or one-dimensional state of being (cf. Eade and Sallnow 1991b). Neither is 'the tourist'. Both categories are open to transformation and inclined to internal diversification and hierarchy. It is, therefore, necessary to distinguish between different motivations for, as well as different forms of, travel that are all classed under a general term such as tourism. More than 20 years ago Cohen (1979) introduced his 'phenomenology of tourist experiences', which may still serve as a useful tool to grasp the continuum of travel (Smith 1992) and the floating subject positions involved in it. Cohen draws analogies between pilgrimage and tourism that go beyond the recognition of movement as characteristic for both. At the same time he avoids a mere equating or replacement of one term with the other, as Graburn (1977) has attempted in his analysis of tourism as 'the sacred journey'. Cohen detects five different tourist objectives or modes of experience: recreational, diversionary, experiential, experimental and existential. For my discussion of homecoming, the categories of experiential and existential tourism are the most significant. The former resembles a quest for authentic experiences, a search for 'meaning' (Cohen 1979: 186) at another place that nevertheless always remains remote and 'strange'. The latter is 'characteristic of the traveller who is fully committed to an "elective" spiritual centre . . . external to the mainstream of his native society and culture' (1979: 190).

The notion of 'centre' is important here. According to Cohen, the pilgrim is seeking to reach the centre of his own world, no matter how far away it might be in place. A special case in point is the so-called 'archaic pilgrimage'. Here, the distance from the centre is not a matter of place but of time. This archaic centre is associated with a pristine existence and is mythically constructed as a paradise forever lost – never to be fully restored, yet always longed for. The imagination of Africa as the Motherland, at once bucolically peaceful, almost innocent and at the same time superior for the greatness and power of its ancient civilizations, comes close to this notion of 'archaic pilgrimage'.

For the tourist, on the other hand, the centre that he is striving for is located outside of his world. Once 'there', he may look at it with curiosity, awe or even some understanding, yet as a conscious outsider – this is characteristic of the experiential tourist. Or the centre may become the place of an elected 'home', where the existential tourist wants to restore energies for sustaining his ordinary, everyday life, which is perceived as one of 'exile'. The only meaningful life then is projected onto the centre to which the existential tourist may eventually convert. For Cohen, this notion of an 'elective centre' also includes that of a 'historical home' to which a person could trace her spiritual roots. In that particular case, the centre becomes laden with the desire for true (and due) belonging. However, the journey, the 'homecoming' itself, does not guarantee fulfilment of this desire. The 'real life' at the centre may thus turn out to be incommensurable with the high hopes and expectations of the traveller.

Homecoming as pilgrimage tourism

How do the concepts outlined above relate to the process of homecoming by African Americans? One could assume that their experience would make a perfect match with Cohen's category of existential tourists. Nevertheless, it is a matter of a complex conglomeration of different motives and aspirations, and the people who are coming cannot easily be grouped under a singular heading. The spectrum of travel reaches from a one-time visit on a package tour to physical repatriation; it oscillates between strangeness and familiarity. Even though the people who are coming could be said to have a similar class background (middle class with a comparatively high level of educational capital), they differ in political as well as ideological orientation and consequently in their attitude towards issues such as 'race', tradition or belonging. This heterogeneity is mirrored in varying understandings of the meaning of homecoming as well as the perceptions of the actual process.

A further complication arises from the fact that their homecoming is not just to an ancestral land but also to sites of traumatic memory: the slave dungeons. For many African Americans, no matter what their ideological divisions might be, these places resemble shrines and are attributed a strong potential for cathartic healing. Here, what is referred to is not the healing of a bodily ailment, but rather a healing of the soul suffering from the psychological wounds of slavery. Such healing may equal a 'totally spiritual experience' and can take the form of an 'emotional possession' inside the dungeons, where 'the spirits and the souls of those [ancestors] . . . almost the voices [are] still there'.[7] To some people even, the dungeons are too meaning-laden and potent to be visited – their ascribed power to change an individual may thus lead to anxiety. A woman, who had recently repatriated with some of her children and grandchildren to Ghana because she felt a strong need for connectivity with the Motherland, told me that she did not want to go there and confront herself with that experience.[8] Such sentiments cannot be confined within a category such as existential tourism – they have to be analysed in a pilgrimage framework.

However, as noted above, that sense of pilgrimage is taken up by the Ghanaian tourism industry and turned into a commercial enterprise. On the one hand, it is the growing tourism sector (addressing all kinds of potential visitors) that first of all provides the opportunity for African Americans to come to and experience Ghana. This is important not just in terms of infrastructure (access to the places of interest, accommodation, etc.) but also in terms of what Coleman and Crang have called the 'dissemination of place' (2002b: 11). It is the tourism industry, in close cooperation with the media, that spreads knowledge about Ghana as a destination and about its attractions, including the forts and castles. Furthermore, and perhaps even more so, images of places circulate through the 'travellers' tales' (Robertson *et al.* 1994) of those who have already 'been there'. Hence, a visit to the slave dungeons may turn into an obligation (Kugelmass 1996) for those who have not yet experienced it, while the place and its aura are continually re/produced through such visits.

Yet, on the other hand, the open discussion of slavery and the slave trade in a tourism framework is highly contested. Within the discourse on homecoming, the terms 'tourist' and 'pilgrim' are represented as diametrically opposed. While in feasibility studies and the internal discussions of tourism professionals, African Americans with their spiritual quest are portrayed as an important market segment, such assessments are carefully avoided in public. Nevertheless, the inconsistency between rhetoric and praxis exists and is consequently sensed and criticized by African American 'homecomers' and Ghanaian intellectuals alike, who seek a different approach to the history of slavery. It is true that there is no such thing as an 'adequate representation' of history. For that matter, one cannot speak of a single 'critical voice' as against an equally homogeneous 'commercial voice'. Positions within either faction are multifarious and overlapping. Even so, the conflict over representation (and meaning) manifests itself in the discursive opposition between 'tourists' and 'pilgrims', strangers and family members. This is apparent not merely in public discourse and in opposing subject positions. The ambiguity is virtually embodied in the travellers themselves, as their roles are continually changing and their identities are perpetually re/created throughout the journey. I have therefore decided to speak of pilgrimage tourism in my interpretation of homecoming. Such a term captures both the sacred and the secular dimensions of the phenomenon without giving analytical preference to just one of these poles.

What follows is the discussion of an event where the ambivalent character of pilgrimage tourism becomes particularly clear. It is all the more interesting since it represents an attempt (involving both Ghanaian and diasporic actors) to resolve the above-described conflicts and to institutionalize and better control the movement of the pilgrim/tourists. Yet, despite rigid planning and organization, 'Emancipation Day' developed its own dynamic, which produced new antagonisms as well as the creative forging and appropriation of 'sacred space'.

Staging the sacred: the celebration of Emancipation Day in Ghana

In July and August 1998, Ghana for the first time invited the 'dispersed children of Africa' to participate in the celebration of Emancipation Day and thereby to 'embark on a pilgrimage perceived as one of rediscovery of your roots' (Emancipation Day Programme 1999). They were encouraged to 'discover the kith and kin and [to] satisfy all those ancestral yearnings too deep to be expressed, in the rejuvenating fountains in the land of our birth' (ibid.). Until that appeal, 1 August had been observed mainly in the Caribbean – to remember the victims of the transatlantic slave trade, as well as the 'peculiar institution' (chattel slavery), and to celebrate its final abolition in the British colonies during 1834–8. Throughout the African diaspora, similar dates (e.g.

'Juneteenth' in the USA) have over the years become part and parcel of the collective commemorations of African descendants. But never before had the abolition of chattel slavery been a topic of public concern in Africa itself.

The 1998 celebrations in Ghana attracted a large body of visitors from all over the diaspora to participate in the week-long festivities. The agenda included not only a one-day conference on Emancipation but also a beach party, a fashion show and a craft market – clearly features of a tourism framework. Yet those festive activities were marginal in comparison with the incontestable highlight of the programme: the re-interment of the remains of two former slaves from the USA and Jamaica, who were said to have stemmed originally from Ghanaian soil. This return of the bones of the enslaved was intended to symbolize the final reversal of the original movement of dispersal, which had created the African diaspora under such painful and destructive circumstances.

Following a carefully mapped choreography, the participants were led to accompany the remains of Samuel Carson (USA) and Crystal (Jamaica) through different stations of the 'slave route'. On that journey, the level of participation and involvement of those who had come to take part in Emancipation Day was continually raised. From being a mere (though attentive) audience of a staged performance, the pilgrim/tourists slowly turned into the main producers of the event. One could argue that this was a calculated effect on part of the Ghanaian planning committee – an example of 'staged authenticity' (MacCannell 1973) where the difference between front and back regions was no longer detectable.[9] However, it needs to be pointed out that the choreography of Emancipation Day was planned, at least in part, by the very people who were later affected by it in a very powerful way. Even though the event was not spontaneous, the reactions of the people who participated in it were. Thus, for example, during the re-interment ceremony, Sonny Carson, a direct descendant of one of the slave ancestors, proclaimed: 'I'm a warrior and I'm not supposed to cry. But I'm so moved . . . *because I never thought it would become like this.* I'm so proud of being an African and being here that I cannot even describe it! I'm really overwhelmed!' (*The Great Homecoming* 1999; my emphasis).

Throughout the week, several re-enactments of the slave trade took place. During the official opening ceremony at the International Conference Centre, the National Dance Company performed an abridged version of its dance drama 'Musu: The Saga of the Slave'. In it there were scenes of shackled slaves being guarded and maltreated by European soldiers. Later that day, a totally different performance took place, the so-called 'Slave March'. Dozens of members of the Ghana Actors Guild proceeded through the streets of Accra in metal chains. On their way, they were whipped and shouted at by fierce-looking slave-raiders who represented African middle-men and wore straw-hats, calabashes and raw-fibre overalls – resembling Northern Ghanaian styles. It is interesting to note that in those two performances any allusion to the involvement of African chiefs in the slave trade was scrupulously avoided. This could be attributed to the fact that within the Ghanaian cultural politics, (Southern) Ghanaian chieftaincy, with its splendid and colourful durbars, stands for cultural wealth and national pride. Moreover, symbols associated with Akan royalty, such as *kente*-cloth, have long been appropriated by African Americans as part of their heritage – not the heritage of slavery but the heritage of perseverance. Their appearance in the re-enactments might have disturbed the celebratory outlook that was inherent in the motto of 'emancipation: our heritage – our strength'.

Another aspect is crucial as well – the contrasting effects of the two performances on the audience and the actors. A member of the National Dance Company who was involved in both plays described his feelings during the Slave March as follows: 'I am an artist, so for me it was a role that I played. You know, in "Musu" I am the traitor, so during the march I was also playing this role, hindering the slaves from escaping.'[10] To him, it didn't make any difference – he was 'on stage' in both settings. For the audience, however, the Slave March had far greater efficacy than the dance drama. In the safe, air-conditioned environs of the Conference Centre, the boundaries between stage and auditorium, show and reality, remained stable. In contrast, watching the slaves march along the streets produced an overwhelming sense of immediacy for some of the on-lookers. The scenery that unfolded before their eyes gave way to deep emotions of compassion, grief and anger. A woman was reported to have bought water for the slaves who were crying out for it. When she gave it to the guard, he simply knocked it out of her hand and she started weeping. Other incidents involved white people who happened to pass by and were vehemently confronted by African American participants, who accused them of being the descendants of the perpetrators. One of the organizers of the Slave March, who had told me of those events, admitted:

> I was scared myself because I realised that if you don't take care the focus will be lost. The thing is not to intimidate anyone, it is just to tell a story . . . But . . . there can be an announcement to that effect

that this is just a performance, it is not a real thing and that emotions must not go out of control.[11]

His statement indicates the tensions that are implicit in the embedding of Emancipation Day within the wider context of the Ghanaian tourism industry. Whilst the organizers rely on the emotional appeal of such an enactment and the resulting influx of people who would feel addressed by it, they have legitimate fears that it could lead to a conflict with other tourists, namely whites, who still constitute the largest group of foreigners (and investors) coming to Ghana. It also proves that the reactions of different people to such a performance cannot be entirely predicted or even controlled. No announcement could possibly prevent the participants from being 'moved' by it in their own, dynamic ways. Movement here, as throughout the whole event, needs to be understood in a twofold manner. On the one hand, it refers to the physical movement of the slaves, together with the audience, along the streets and more generally on the slave route. On the other hand, it denotes the emotional stir that occurred in many of the pilgrim/tourists as they engaged in that physical motion. Participants from the diaspora who expressed their feelings in ways described above can be said to have fitted the (staged) Slave March into the framework of their collective (and still painful) memory of slavery and thereby turned it into a unique experience. Through such a process of transformation, a sense of 'being there' is being created, which goes beyond the mere physical proximity achieved through travelling and mobility in general (Urry 2002).

A still further degree of involvement was approached when the remains were eventually taken on their final journey. Friday, 31 July 1998, was assigned as 'Martyr's Day' in the official programme (Emancipation Day Programme 1998). Early in the morning, several buses (provided by the Ministry of Tourism together with the individual tour operators who had been commissioned to see to the needs of the foreign participants) left Accra for Kormantin, a small fishing village on the road to Cape Coast. Here, the coffins were transferred to a canoe to be taken to Cape Coast Castle by sea. Thus, the former slaves would triumphantly return on the Atlantic, the very ocean that had been the scene of the dreadful Middle Passage and traumatic dispersal of African people.

Inside Cape Coast Castle, the most significant place for many Africans from the diaspora (next to the slave dungeons) is the so-called 'Door of No Return', the final exit point for the slaves leaving Africa. When the boat carrying the remains arrived at the shore of Cape Coast Castle, the space outside the gate as well as on the castle balustrades was crowded with people anxiously awaiting its landing. The remains were then received in 'a solemn ritual and atonement ceremony by chiefs of Oguaa Traditional Area and the Diasporan community in Ghana' (Emancipation Day Programme 1998). This atonement was of great symbolic value, as it complemented an official apology for the profitable involvement by some African chiefs in the slave trade. When asked about the motivation for the performance of the ceremony on part of the chiefs, the then president of the National House of Chiefs answered that it was mainly due to the interest of African Americans in such a gesture.[12] Again, one could speak here of 'staged authenticity' and denounce the ceremony as a 'shallow' tourist performance. Yet, in the particular situation it also provided the space for the emergence of a sense of harmony – even *communitas* – among the diverse participants by discursively erasing the historical (and present-day) differences and conflicts among African Americans and Ghanaians and proclaiming a unified 'family identity' instead.

After the pouring of libation, the 'Door of No Return', which had been decorated with a new plaque reading 'Door of Return', was opened. A long procession of people filed through, past the female slave dungeons, into the castle. Singing Ghanaian youths, members of the organizing committees from Ghana and the diaspora, African Americans living in Ghana as well some of the pilgrim/tourists who had come especially for the occasion – all escorted the coffins to the castle courtyard, where the rest of the participants were anticipating them. The fact that not all of the participants entered the castle through the 'Door of Return' was probably due to organizational problems as well as safety considerations. However, it also indicates a hierarchy among participants (from VIP to 'ordinary') that contrasts with the notion of *communitas*. In the staging of Emancipation Day, different degrees of involvement were not only manifested in the succession of events, but also at each single station.

For those diasporic participants who passed through the gate, however, the emotional appeal was immense. Many of them were in tears and some even broke down. Again, I would like to point out the connections between physical and spiritual movement. In their entering of the castle through the 'Door of Return', the African descendants took symbolic possession of the castle and turned it into a 'space of their own'. Pressed against other bodies; pushed forward by the advancing crowd of people; from time to time touching against the outer walls of the slave dungeons; perchance catching a glimpse of the coffins while stepping on the very ground that may once have been the last piece of African soil trod upon by a departing ancestor – all these sensual impressions only lasted for a short moment but nevertheless created a sense of what I would like to term 'arrival in motion'.

Cape Coast Castle was not to be the last station of the pilgrimage. After a short interlude of prayers, the whole congregation moved on to Assin Manso, half an hour's drive from Cape Coast into the interior. Here, the bodies would find their final resting place. Assin Manso was chosen because it has been identified as one of the important slave markets on the slave route from the north down to the coast and to Cape Coast and Elmina castles in particular. In the choreography of Emancipation Day, the village was furthermore staged as the place where the slaves had their 'last bath' on African soil. The Nnonkonsuo or 'Slave River' runs through a sacred grove,[13] which is said to be a mass grave for slaves who died on their way to the coast. On their arrival at Assin Manso, the participants were first led to the Nnonkonsuo, following a narrow path through the sacred grove. When they stepped down to the river, many washed their faces with the water that mixed with their tears of simultaneous loss and relief. Some filled small containers with river water to take along with them.

At this stage of immediate contact, the participants had finally turned into pilgrims. They were now at the heart of the event, no more watching a performance but going through a unique experience, physically engaged with their environment (the river) and mentally as well as spiritually absorbed by the confrontation with a collective past. Along with the remains of the two slave ancestors they had moved to reach this special place – even though their journey took place in air-conditioned buses and not on foot. Connerton (1989) has pointed out the close connection between social (collective) memory and ritual performance and ceremonies, enacted through the body. While in his analysis, the element of repetition and habitual behaviour is of central importance, this cannot be said for Emancipation Day 1998, since it was the first of its kind and gained its power precisely from its uniqueness. Still, there were allusions to well-known cultural motives and practices – the baptismal resonances of the 'last bath' may be considered as a case in point.

The re-interment itself was enacted as a royal burial. The 'ordinary participants' were again shifting positions on the tourist–pilgrim continuum and turned into an audience, while the community of Assin Manso together with the VIPs from both Ghana and the diaspora took over as the major actors. A ceremonial exchange of greetings followed by some speeches took place, as is customary for any durbar of chiefs in Southern Ghana. Wailing women were mourning not only the death of the two ancestors but also, symbolically, all those who had died during the slave trade and in slavery. The paramount chief of the Assin Traditional Area, Barima Kwame Nkyi XII, entered the durbar ground in a palanquin, which was dressed with black *chedda*-cloth. The chief himself was clad in his 'war costume' (Emancipation Day Programme 1998) and had a small bunch of pepper between his lips, 'a symbol of emergency, of urgency, of life' (*The Great Homecoming* 1999).

He was introduced as the chief mourner. This is significant, because it demonstrates the shifting of subject positions during the event and its resulting ambivalence. Barima Kwame Nkyi XII had been instrumental in bringing the remains to Assin Manso. He was a member of both the Central Region Tourism Development Committee and the Planning Committee for Emancipation Day. Interested in (and held responsible for) the advancement and development of his community, he had (and still has) a clear interest in making Assin Manso a further 'tourist attraction' in Ghana.[14] The chief could thus be regarded as a representative of the Ghanaian tourism industry. His full participation in the funeral rites, however, challenges any opposition between a Ghanaian interest in commercialization and African Americans' desire for commemoration. Just like the pilgrim/tourists from the diaspora, he and the other local participants 'made' the event through their active involvement. The funeral was distinct from cultural performances staged for tourists.[15] It entailed the application of powerful symbols and a genuine engagement by the Assin Manso traditional authorities and community.

The journey for Samuel Carson and Crystal had at last come to an end. They were buried at the edge of the sacred grove. The comment on the video covering Emancipation Day 1998 interprets this as a 'circle [being] completed, never to be broken again' (*The Great Homecoming* 1999). Nevertheless, I would argue that the physical repatriation of the bones of the enslaved did not result in the definite arrival of the diaspora 'back home'. On the contrary, it has, in a way, further complicated relations between Ghanaians and African Americans, because the promise that lay in the opening of the 'Door of Return' was not matched by day-to-day realities. Furthermore, the subsequent stagings of Emancipation Day neither attracted an equally large group of people nor reached the same emotional appeal as the 1998 event. Participants whom I spoke to in 1999 complained of the overt presence of commercial interests as well as the poor organization of the event. The latter was attributed to a serious lack of financial resources by the organizers.

The attempted institutionalization of pilgrimage tourism thus leads to a major and irresolvable conflict. On the one hand, there is a need to generate revenue from the events so that they can be performed on a regular and sustainable basis; on the other, the visibility of commercial considerations leads to a decline in their attraction, because people (especially those participants coming from the diaspora) feel that they are not 'real'. The incorporation of Emancipation Day as part of the Ghanaian tourism calendar, 'so [that] at least every year there will be a major cultural programme . . . to get a lot of tourists to come',[16] can be said to have failed, even though it is still carried out on an annual basis. Nevertheless, the re-interment of the slave ancestors has given rise to further movement, since it has produced a new place on the map of worship for pilgrim/tourists seeking a connection to the Motherland.

Conclusions: homecoming to where?

Before Emancipation Day 1998, Assin Manso was not 'known' among African descendants in the diaspora. Today, however, there are more than 100 entries on the village to be found on the internet, 50 of which refer directly to the existence of the slave river. Equalling the slave dungeons, the Nnonkonsuo has become a site of memory for African descendants in the diaspora. Probably, many more people have already heard about it than have actually visited. The image of Assin Manso as a pilgrimage or sacred site has travelled (not least because of the impressive staging of the first Emancipation Day) and has created a desire in people to go there and experience it for themselves through a 'direct encounter' (Urry 2002). The village has thus turned into a destination – in a spiritual as well as a physical sense. In 1999 I met an African American professor, Gary L.H., who described his experience at the Nnonkonsuo. The local guide had encouraged him to bend down and drink some of the water. At first, he did not want to do that – having in mind all the warnings about unwholesome water and terrible diseases associated with it. But then he gave it a second thought:

> and what I thought about was: maybe my great-great grandmother or . . . grandfather took their last bath on African soil in that river. Maybe they came through there. And here I was, standing there, so I reached down and got the water and drank it, so that always a part of me would be the last bath of my ancestors before they were

taken away from Africa. So it's just kind of a ceremonial thing, that water of the last bath will always be a part of me. And that . . . is something I could tell my children, that I drank the water of the last bath of my ancestors and let them know where it is, so if they would ever visit, they could do the same.[17]

From one moment to the other his position had changed from that of an American tourist, unaccustomed to (and suspicious of) the local water, to that of a worshipper – bending down literally to the river and paying tribute to his ancestors. Through that small gesture, he had turned the Nnonkonsuo into a place of his own. It had become sacred to him. Following Eade and Sallnow (1991b) it has to be pointed out that the river (just like the slave dungeons) does not carry the property of sacredness as an inherent quality. Rather, sacredness is produced by the application of meaning to a shrine, which derives its power precisely from 'its character almost as a religious void, a ritual space capable of accommodating diverse meanings and practices' (1991b: 15).

The experience described by Gary L.H. is important in an additional respect. It points to the fact that a true sense of homecoming and healing can only be achieved when the pilgrim/tourist reaches the centre of his/her own world (Cohen 1979). As I have demonstrated in my discussion of Emancipation Day, for African Americans coming to Ghana in search of their 'roots'[18] the slave sites are of particular concern. They represent the history of slavery and dispersal, which is to a large extent the history of the African diaspora. I want to argue that it is not an African identity *per se* that is reinforced through the experience of the slave sites, but rather a specific diasporic identity. It is in that sense that their homecoming can be understood as a pilgrimage; not as a pilgrimage to a lost homeland but rather as a pilgrimage that provides a linkage to a history of survival, endurance and uplift.

Notes

1 During a conference addressing a heated controversy over the adequate preservation of Cape Coast and Elmina castles a proposal was made to rename those monuments and to call them Cape Coast and Elmina Castles and Dungeons (cf. Report of the proceedings . . . 1994). In practice, however, this policy has not been enforced.
2 Numbers vary. Van Dantzig (1980), in his comprehensive study, lists 50 castles, forts and lodges, some of which left no tangible traces. Anquandah (1999) estimates an average of one fort per every 15 kilometres (p. 20). On

its website, the Ghana Tourist Board (GTB) mentions 32 (visible) forts as places of attraction; see Ghana Tourist Board (2002).

3 Larson defines the African diaspora as 'including both source and destination societies for slaves within [its] scope . . . transformed as both types of communities were by economies of enslavement and their accompanying displacements' (1999: 338). This is a compelling argument, which has also been advanced by Patterson and Kelley (2000). In the context of the Ghanaian tourism industry, however, the term refers exclusively to non-continental Africans. In this chapter I am going to use the term in that rather narrow sense.

4 Panafest '99 (1999) *The Great Homecoming* (1999), Ghana Tourist Board (n.d.); cf. Kwarkeng (1999).

5 See Ebron (1999) for similar observations in Senegal and Gambia. Her discussion of 'tourists as pilgrims' focuses on the commercial aspects of that encounter. In my chapter I am going to concentrate more on the linkages between travel and identity that manifest in pilgrimage tourism.

6 Drawing a comparison with the Jewish diaspora after the Holocaust, one could argue that Africa/Ghana is symbolically understood as *both* Israel *and* Poland/the death camps by African (American) descendants. Both locations are sites of pilgrimage for Jews today, yet with totally different memories (and expectations) attached to them. For difficulties involved in the Jewish encounter with Poland, see Kugelmass (1992); with Israel, see Rapport (1998).

7 Rabbi K., interview, 02.09.99, p. 15. Rabbi K. repatriated to Ghana from the USA around 1993. He is the spiritual head of a community of African Hebrew Israelites (see Markowitz 1996) in Ghana.

8 Empress B., fieldnote 12.09.99, TB VII/1159. She was born in the USA, but spent more than 20 years of her life in Jamaica before she went back to the United States and later decided to move to Ghana.

9 Drawing on Goffman's division of social establishments into 'front' and 'back' regions, MacCannell has developed his scheme of the tourist experience. Front and back regions thereby constitute two opposing poles of a continuum on which a variet of tourist settings are arranged. The front region signifies the 'meeting place between hosts and guests' whereas the back 'is the place where members of the home team retire between performances to relax and to prepare' (MacCannell 1973: 590).

10 Sebastian A., fieldnote 17.08.99, TB VII/1078.

11 Efo K.M., interview 21.12.98, p. 11.

12 Odefuo B.A., interview 03.09.99, p. 6.

13 Sacred groves are an important feature of the Ghanaian landscape. Nobody is supposed to cut any of the plants or otherwise disturb the grove. Often, these sites are associated with royal burials. See Chouin (1998).

14 A feasibility study on Assin Manso mentions the building of a two-star hotel, the development of a reception area 'with ticket sales, small shop for sales of souvenirs, crafts, literature, film etc., snack bar and interpretative exhibition' (Wells *et al.* 1996: 16) as parts of the 'village tourism project' associated with the Nnonkonsuo and the gravesite. When I visited Assin Manso in May 2002, none of these proposals had been realized.

15 It should be noted that there is probably no such thing as a 'pure' tourism

sphere as opposed to a real and/or sacred sphere. See Nikolaisen, Chapter 5 this volume, who demonstrates that even in a stage-setting a sacred space can emerge.

16 Statement by the former director of the Ghana Tourist Board, Doreen O.-F. (interview, 16.09.99, p. 6). In that passage, she was connecting Emancipation Day to PANAFEST, another cultural festival which makes references to Pan-African solidarity and takes place biannually under the motto: 'The re-emergence of African civilization'.

17 Gary L.H., interview 09.08.99, p. 6. He also told me of his plans to retire to Ghana and to build a hotel near Cape Coast.

18 This popular phrase goes back to Alex Haley's book *Roots* (1991 [1976]) and the resulting heritage boom among African Americans. It simplifies the complex motivations behind the homecoming process. Nana O., who had repatriated to Ghana in the early 1990s and said that he had returned 'home to [his] home', refused the application of the term 'roots' altogether. He said that 'we are not coming home to find our roots, we are coming . . . to claim our inheritance. Because when I was taken from here, I must have had something, I had a family, I had a village, I had land – you understand what I'm saying? So this is an inheritance here that we have come to claim' (interview, 05.09.99, p. 3).

Chapter 8

Route metaphors of 'roots-tourism' in the Scottish Highland diaspora

Paul Basu

> I am not opposed to metaphor here. Rather, I am saying that one must
> pick one's root metaphors carefully, for appropriateness and potential
> fruitfulness.
>
> Victor Turner, *Dramas, Fields, and Metaphors*

It was while pursuing another project, exploring the mnemonic role
of ruins in the Scottish Highland landscape (Basu 1997, 2000a), that
I became aware of the profundity of the journeys to the research to which
I would devote the next few years. While conducting fieldwork in the
Northern Highlands, I was fortunate to meet a middle-aged couple from
Arizona. They had come in search of his Ross ancestors who, in the
eighteenth century, were recorded as being millers at Milton, a small
'mill town' on the banks of the Dunbeath Water in Caithness. I was
invited to join them as they were taken around the ruins of this long-
deserted settlement by a number of local people. The Arizonans were
regaled with stories of the place and details of its history – *their* history
– before standing to have their photograph taken beside a large broken
millstone that had been built into a nineteenth-century wall. Finally, the
couple were shown the old, overgrown well that had once served the
township's community. With tears in their eyes, they knelt first to cup
the still-clear water in their hands to drink, and then to fill their emptied
flasks so that they could carry the spring water back to Arizona with
them. I was immediately struck by the symbolism of what I observed and
the powerful emotions it seemed to engender. The significance of this
site . . . this source . . . this shrine . . . became unequivocal, and I realized
then that there was manifestly nothing 'ordinary' about their journey.

Since the publication of Alex Haley's seminal family saga, *Roots*
(1976), genealogical research has become an almost global pastime

and, aided by the internet and relatively cheap air travel, genealogy-related tourism has become an important revenue-earner for numerous 'old countries' throughout the world. Diasporas, as David Lowenthal observes, 'are notably heritage-hungry. Five out of six ancestry searches in Italy are made by Italian-Americans. Dublin is deluged with inquiries from Sons of Erin abroad . . . [and] so many Jews today seek memories of *shtetl* forebears that East Europeans call them "roots people"' (1998: 9–10). This phenomenon is certainly evident in Scotland, particularly in the rural Highlands and Islands, where there are few 'bed & breakfast' operators who don't have stories to tell of their North American and Australasian guests' quests to locate the remains of abandoned family crofts or moss-covered gravestones in forgotten cemeteries or ancestral names inscribed in old parochial records. Indeed, so significant has 'roots-tourism' become in the region that the Scottish Executive has identified it as a key 'niche market' deserving of capital investment to encourage its development (Scottish Executive 2000). But, if state agencies such as VisitScotland (previously the Scottish Tourist Board) have few qualms approaching such genealogical journeys as touristic products to be marketed, many participants in these journeys have a very different opinion and are keen to distance themselves from what they perceive as the superficial consumerism of tourism (Basu 2000b). 'I am not, and never will be a tourist in Scotland', asserts an informant from Canada. 'To me it was a pilgrimage, a searching for roots', recalls a New Zealander of her journey. 'It was a life-changing experience', 'a journey of discovery', 'the closing of the great circle of life', a 'mystical homecoming', 'a very special quest', report others from elsewhere in this Scottish diaspora.

According to VisitScotland statistics, the overwhelming majority of these travellers are middle-aged and middle class: characterized, for example, as 'US Seniors' ('travellers, aged 55–75, with an income over £35,000 a year') and 'Australian White Collar Affluents' ('sophisticated "baby boomers" aged between 45 and 70 from urban, East Coast or Western Australia . . . "empty nesters", travelling in couples, whose children have left home') (www.scotexchange.net). Dispersed across the continents, though often networked via genealogy and Scottish-interest email lists, all claim a common Scottish heritage and have at least one Scottish emigrant among their forebears. Quite often their enthusiastic identification with Scotland is an intentional act, a tacitly chosen heritage selected from a number of émigré 'ethnic options' in their family histories, reflecting value judgements regarding what is considered good and not good to be (Waters 1990). Their journeys are typically extensions of internet- and documentary-based genealogical research conducted in the diaspora and, indeed, this research is often described as the 'first step' along a path that will eventually culminate in the ancestral homeland itself. 'You've explored your Scottish heritage', exhorts a VisitScotland advertisement, 'Now explore your ancestral homeland' (*Scotland Magazine* 2002: 92).

Such journeys have many forms. I have written elsewhere, for instance, about the remarkable gatherings organized by international clan societies, in which otherwise dispersed clansfolk are drawn together in their respective 'clanlands' to participate in a series of commemorative ceremonies, at once reaffirming their collective identity as a clan and their clan's association with its traditional territories (Basu forthcoming [a]). I have also discussed other packaged events such as the 'Orkney Homecoming' of 1999 in which over 150 Canadians of Orcadian descent travelled together to their ancestral islands to celebrate a shared heritage with their old country 'cousins' (Basu 2004). Such collective practices appear to have much in common with those described by Kugelmass (1996), concerning North American Jewish 'missions' to Poland, and Schramm, concerning African-American 'pilgrimage tourism' in Ghana (Chapter 7 this volume), although the nature of the 'foundational trauma' which dispersed the Highland Scots from their old country is certainly more controvertible and the differences between these contexts should clearly not be underestimated either (Basu forthcoming [b]). The majority of these journeys are, however, much more personal affairs undertaken by individuals or small family groups and, in addition to those iconic sites of Highland or clan history, have as their destinations more intimate sites associated with their particular family histories (Basu forthcoming [c]).

Rather than presenting a more thickly descriptive essay, my objective in this chapter is to explore the dominant 'root metaphors' – which are, inevitably, also '*route* metaphors' – through which roots-tourists in the Scottish Highlands and Islands typically characterize and understand their journeys.[1] In a volume concerned with reframing pilgrimage in a broader context of social processes and spatial flows, such 'emic' metaphors – 'homecoming', 'quest' and 'pilgrimage' – also provide a heuristic framework for the 'etic' interpretation of these contemporary travel practices. Metaphor, as Lakoff and Johnson (1980) have observed, is not merely an aesthetic embellishment of language, but is a faculty of cognition through which we perceive and experience the world. Metaphor is a 'carrying over' of meaning, a translation, an understanding of one thing in terms of another (1980: 55). In the words of Robert A.

Nisbet, 'metaphor is our means of effecting instantaneous fusion of two separated realms of experience into one illuminating, iconic, encapsulating image' (quoted in Turner 1974c: 25). In this respect, whilst agreeing with Morinis that it is important for anthropologists to continue to 'plot the boundaries and analyse the meanings' that different cultures assign to pilgrimage (1992b: 3), my interest here is not to argue either for or against the accommodation of roots-tourism within the rubric of pilgrimage (or quest or homecoming): these journeys are, after all, simply what they are. Instead, my purpose is to investigate the 'appropriateness and potential fruitfulness' (Turner 1974c: 25) of these alternative genres of travel as metaphorical referents for roots-tourism, and in so doing seek to discover in what ways they might illuminate and encapsulate these journeys for participant and researcher alike.

At one level – we might call it the denotative level (Barthes 1990) – the use of metaphors such as homecoming, quest and pilgrimage may be seen as a way for roots-tourists to distinguish their earnest endeavours from what are perceived as more trivial, 'pleasure-seeking' touristic practices. Less constrained by academic anxieties regarding misplaced essentialisms, I suggest that for the majority of my informants, pilgrimage (for example) is popularly understood as *representing* a 'sacred other' to the secular practices associated with tourism. As such, pilgrimage may be understood as an 'ideal type', a model or idea of sacred travel which, as the weight of recent anthropological work on the subject has demonstrated, may not exist in practice, but which may nevertheless prove 'good to think' with (Lévi-Strauss 1964; see Eade 2000 for a summary of recent anthropological research on pilgrimage). The same observation holds true for quest and homecoming, although, as I shall argue, these represent alternative, but similarly profound, 'others' to tourism.

Of course, to merely conclude that, through their choice of descriptive metaphors, diasporic heritage-seekers in the Scottish Highlands and Islands consider themselves to be engaged in a kind of sacred (or otherwise profound) practice is not, in itself, particularly enlightening. If this reflects the denotative or primary meaning of pilgrimage, quest or homecoming in this context, then it is necessary to go beyond the 'hearth of denotation' (Barthes 1990: 7) and explore what other meanings these metaphorical referents connote. In what follows, therefore, I consider the connotations of each of these metaphors in turn, before demonstrating how their various 'fields of meaning' converge in the practices of roots-tourism. My contention here is that by making journeys to sites associated with their family histories, roots-tourists are also (metaphorically) enacting these alternative symbolic processes, and through this metaphorical transference their journeys become structured by and infused with qualities associated with these 'other' forms. In short, I contend that homecoming, quest and pilgrimage together provide a more appropriate 'grammar' (including a repertoire of actions and attitudes) for roots-tourism than tourism itself is able to offer: a grammar, furthermore, which has the potential to bear fruit and empower these journeys with the capacity to effect personal transformations, rendering them quite literally 'life-changing' experiences for many participants.

On root metaphors and route metaphors

By choosing Victor Turner rather than any number of other anthropological theorists of metaphor (e.g. Ortner 1973; Fernandez 1986, 1991; Tilley 1999) as my point of departure on this heuristic journey, I acknowledge a continuing debt to his provocative work on symbolic action in human society and express a concern that, in 'contesting the sacred', we should be careful not to throw out the metaphorical baby with the sullied bathwater of dichotomizing theories of structure and *communitas* (cf. Eade and Sallnow 1991b; Coleman 2002). In the preface to his 1971 lecture, 'Social Dramas and Ritual Metaphors', Turner draws on the work of I.A. Richards, Stephen C. Pepper, Max Black and Robert A. Nisbet to consider both the illuminating and the obfuscating potential of metaphor. The phrase 'root metaphor' was coined by Pepper, but was perhaps more succinctly described by Black as 'a systematic repertoire of ideas by means of which a given thinker describes, by *analogical extension*, some domain to which those ideas do not immediately and literally apply' (quoted in Turner 1974c: 26; italics in original). Such metaphors can be so persuasive, their use so conventional, that their analogical nature is obscured and they become, to borrow Simon Schama's phrase, 'more real than their referents' (1995: 61). Indeed, Turner warns that 'the more persuasive the root metaphor . . . the more chance it has of becoming a self-certifying myth, sealed off from empirical disproof' (1974c: 29). For those roots-tourists for whom such myths have ontological valency, homecoming, quest and pilgrimage may legitimately be used interchangeably and unreflectingly to describe their journeys, but for the anthropologist the discrete inferences of each of these domains and the movements of meaning between them are telling in themselves and thus require proper scrutiny.

Turner writes that his own understanding of 'the structure of metaphor' is similar to that articulated by Richards in *The Philosophy of Rhetoric*; that is, 'two thoughts of different things *active* together and supported by a single word, or phrase, whose meaning is a resultant of their *interaction*' (Richards 1936: 93; italics in original). As Turner states, 'this view emphasizes the dynamics inherent in the metaphor, rather than limply comparing the two thoughts in it, or regarding one as "substituting" for the other. The two thoughts are active together, they "engender" thought in their coactivity' (1974c: 29). This thought-engendering 'interaction view' of metaphor is further elaborated by Black in a set of five claims, and it is worth reiterating, in précised form, Turner's summary of these claims, using roots-tourism and pilgrimage as examples:

1   A metaphorical statement has two distinct subjects – a principal subject (e.g. roots-tourism) and a 'subsidiary' one (e.g. pilgrimage).
2   These subjects are best regarded as 'systems of things', rather than things as elements. Thus, both 'roots-tourism' and 'pilgrimage' are themselves multivocal symbols, whole semantic systems, which bring into relation a number of ideas, images, sentiments, values and stereotypes (e.g. roots-tourism as a journey to an ancestral place, pilgrimage as a journey to a sacred shrine). Components of one system enter into dynamic relations with components of the other ('ancestral place' and 'sacred shrine' become dynamically related).
3   The metaphor works by applying to the principal subject a system of 'associated implications' characteristic of the subsidiary subject (e.g. roots-tourism becomes, by implication, a journey to a sacred shrine). The metaphor provokes a rethinking of both the nature of roots-tourism and the nature of pilgrimage.
4   These 'implications' usually consist of commonplaces about the subsidiary subject. You need have only proverbial knowledge to have your metaphor understood, not technical or special knowledge (e.g. the commonplace definition of pilgrimage as a 'journey to a sacred shrine' may not withstand academic scrutiny, but this does not necessarily reduce the effectiveness of such 'proverbial' implications within the metaphor).
5   The metaphor selects, emphasizes, suppresses and organizes features of the principal subject by implying statements about it that normally apply to the subsidiary subject (e.g. the touristic features of roots-tourism are typically suppressed, whereas the implications of roots-tourism as a sacred journey are emphasized and come to shape the experience) (see Turner 1974c: 29–30).

If the illuminating potential of metaphor is made clear in this set of claims, so too is its capacity, through its selective emphases and suppressions, for obfuscation. It is important to be aware, therefore, of the potentially misleading persuasiveness of metaphors. Approached with due caution, however, their 'combination of familiar and unfamiliar features or unfamiliar combination of familiar features provokes us into thought', providing us with new and exciting perspectives (Turner 1974c: 31). As Turner enthuses, 'the implications, suggestions, and supporting values entwined with their literal use enable us to see a new subject matter in a new way' (ibid.).

Whilst Turner provides a starting point for this chapter, by considering homecoming, quest and pilgrimage as 'metaphors for a world on the move' (Turner 1992: viii), I am also involved in a more Cliffordian exercise of unpicking the 'intertwined roots and routes' of identity formation in a modernity of multiple translocal attachments (Clifford 1997). To search for 'roots' is, after all, *already* to engage in a (root) metaphorical process, in which characteristics of the arboreal subsidiary subject (stasis, longevity, being anchored in time and space, receiving nourishment from the land, etc.) are imputed to the 'destination' of the genealogical journey (the principal subject), which has itself no such qualities. For members of diasporic populations who feel uprooted or displaced, the quest for old country roots thus also constitutes a route to this 'other' place, the lost homeland, which, in turn, may be understood as a 'material metaphor' for more abstract senses of lost wholeness, integrity and identity. As Clifford argues, the articulation of such homelands is evident in the *performance* of contemporary culture and identity: in the 'making and remaking of identities', he argues, 'stasis and purity are asserted – creatively and violently – *against* historical forces of movement and contamination' (1997: 7). Such, then, are the rerooting and rerouting metaphors of roots-tourism, and such is the real subject matter I hope, by examining these metaphorical processes, to illuminate in what follows.

Homecoming, quest and pilgrimage may be understood as alternative genres of moving or journeying, but each also implies a different – a differently symbolic – kind of destination. I characterize these, respectively, as 'home', 'the indeterminate' and 'the sacred'. Pursuing the second statement in Black's summary, I suggest that both journeying/route metaphors and destination/root metaphors should be considered as multivocal semantic systems. I make no pretence here of presenting a definitive, all-encompassing account of these systems and, as will become clear, my interest remains with the 'partial-truths' of the 'proverbial'. As Jonathan Schwartz observes of the articulation of genealogical 'roots' in the Balkans: 'the art of deconstruction can be rigorously applied to this [as any other] root metaphor, but those who live by the metaphor will not give it up' (1997: 258). Certainly, this is true among Scottish diasporic roots-tourists, these homecomers, seekers and pilgrims.

Homecoming – the exile's return

Home, homeland, homecoming. These are perhaps the most resonant metaphors associated with diasporic roots-tourism. Home is, of course, a most capacious concept; indeed, as Casey argues, 'part of the very meaning of "home" is that it is able to give rise to quite divergent perceptions and significations' (1993: 294). Much recent academic discourse concerned with modern Western identity has sought to demonstrate that individuals are quite 'at home' in a world in movement, that they are adept at negotiating the flux of multiple and mobile attachments. Quoting Iain Chambers, Rapport and Dawson are, for example, convinced that 'one's identity is "formed on the move": a "migrant's tale" of "stuttering transitions and heterogeneities"' (1998c: 27). In our understanding of the contemporary world, 'metaphors and motifs of movement' have, it is argued, displaced earlier models of stasis and boundedness, and must now be considered 'of the quintessence in the conceptualization of identity' (1998c: 26).

Despite the cosmopolitanism of academia, its championing of a perhaps laudable mission to 'disarm the genealogical rhetoric of blood, property and frontiers' (Carter 1992: 8), there is, however, an alternative view of home, which clings to the commonplaces of dictionary definitions: home as 'a dwelling place'; 'an environment offering security and happiness'; 'a valued place regarded as a refuge or place of origin'; 'a source'; 'the centre or heart of something'; 'an abiding place of the affections'; 'one's native land'; and even 'the native and eternal dwelling place of the soul' (*American Heritage Dictionary* 2000; *Webster's Revised Unabridged Dictionary* 1998). Thus conceived, home remains the physical, social and cognitive place 'in which one best knows oneself, where one's self-identity is best grounded' (Rapport and Dawson 1998c: 21). However, if this proverbial home may be understood as a place where one belongs in some profound sense, to be in a position to make a homecoming suggests that one is not in such a place already: that this home exists elsewhere, somewhere and/or sometime 'other' than the here and now. To contemplate making a homecoming is therefore to recognize that one is living in a state of exile from this longed-for 'place'. Indeed, there is much to justify the view that this seemingly most commonplace of locations has, in an age characterized by movement, also become one of the most elusive. As society becomes increasingly mobile and fragmented, there is thus a corresponding nostalgia for the (imagined) stability and coherence of past times and places. It is precisely in response to this desire of the 'dislocated' self to 'relocate' itself in time and place that roots-tourism is so effective in providing the promise of a route 'back' home.

Perhaps the most detailed exposition of this contemporary nostalgia is provided by Berger, Berger and Kellner in the classic sociological text *The Homeless Mind*. Berger *et al.* argue that the 'correlate of the migratory character of [the modern individual's] experience of society and of self has been what might be called a metaphysical loss of "home"' (1973: 82). As the familiarly Durkheimian argument goes, with modernity comes not only dislocation from a physical home-place (migration to cities or across other borders), but also movement away from the cohesiveness of a social home or milieu represented by 'traditional society' and bound by the normalizing *conscience collective* of shared beliefs, values and experiences. Thus, the experience of 'external mobility' has had an impact 'at the level of consciousness' (1973: 184), with the consequence that 'modern man is afflicted with a *permanent identity crisis*' (1973: 78; italics in original). Alienated from the place and corresponding social structures which hitherto conferred an externally determined and 'given' identity, the individual is forced to search inwardly for some coherent sense of self in a life-world that is increasingly fragmented, plural and shifting. The consequent sense of disorientation – physical, social, psychological – is perplexing and 'engenders its own nostalgias . . . for a condition of "being at home" in society, with oneself and, ultimately, in the universe' (1973: 82).

Of course, it is possible that Berger *et al.*'s analysis of modern identity is itself susceptible to this nostalgia, and this is the crux of Rapport and Dawson's critique of their argument. 'While *The Homeless Mind* remains a challenging thesis', they write, 'it is steeped in a communitarian ideology that can decry modern "ills" (individualism and pluralization, alienation and anomy) only to the extent that it posits an idyllic past of unified tradition, certainty, stasis, and cognitive and behavioral commonality' (1998c: 32). Rapport and Dawson discard such a postu- lated past on the grounds that it is 'mythic', and they believe that the whole theory 'remains ethnographically ungrounded in the present' (ibid.). As I have argued elsewhere (Basu 2001), whilst Rapport and

Dawson may be correct in doubting the *objective* reality of these lost idylls, the evidence of my ethnographic research suggests that they underestimate the significance of the *subjective* reality of such 'myths' for the individuals who live by them and for whom they provide some sense of ontological security in a world often perceived to be moving 'too fast'. The imperative to recover a more 'authentic' sense of home is, I contend, vividly expressed in the contemporary search for roots, and this widespread practice would seem to betray a more pessimistic view of modernity in which the individual evidently does not celebrate his or her liberation from the 'genealogical rhetoric' of blood and territorial attachment, but on the contrary seeks to re-assert it.

The search for identity may thus be equated with a metaphysical search for home. Yet home, that elusive ideal and all it connotes, is also made material in homeland – in this instance, in Scotland. Just as home may be regarded as the 'cradle' of individual identity, so the homeland, as Smith notes, may be regarded the venerated 'cradle' of one's 'people' (1991: 9) and, hence, a source of that 'collective identity' yearned for, according to Berger *et al.*'s thesis, by the homeless minds of modernity. Of course, the homeland may be venerated not only by members of the '*ethnie*' still resident in that land, but arguably even more so by those 'expatriates' who have been physically separated from it and who consider themselves as exiles:

> the sacred centres of the homeland draw the members of the *ethnie* to it, or inspire them from afar, even when their exile is prolonged. Hence, an *ethnie* may persist, even when long divorced from its homeland, through an intense nostalgia and spiritual attachment. This is very much the fate of diaspora communities like the Jews and Armenians.
>
> (Smith 1991: 23)

Whereas Smith here emphasizes the *persistence* of ethnic associations with its homeland, it is evident that such identifications – including self-identifications as exiled and/or diasporic communities – can also emerge at particular times in response to broader social and political trends. There is a tendency in some settler societies for previously assimilated 'groups' (groups, that is, whose 'group identity' has actually been lost over successive generations) to seek to dissimilate themselves and recover a more distinctive ethnic identity: often central to this is the recovery of lost 'historic memories and associations' with lost homelands (Waters 1990).

As Rushdie eloquently articulates, the physical alienation of diasporic populations from their homelands 'almost inevitably means that [they] will not be capable of reclaiming precisely the thing that was lost; that [they] will, in short, create fictions, not actual cities or villages, but invisible ones, imaginary homelands, [homelands] of the mind' (1992: 10). The *symbolic* 'Highland homeland' of the *symbolic* Scottish 'diaspora' is surely one such country that forms in the mind, improvised from the stereotypical representations of *Braveheart* and *Brigadoon*, the literature of Sir Walter Scott, popular histories, websites, postcards, biscuit-tin kitsch and so forth (Womack 1989; Pittock 1991). The paradox is, of course, that whilst this homeland is undoubtedly an imagining of the *mind*, it is also 'rooted' in a particular geographical territory which may be visited by the *body*, touched, photographed, driven across and walked upon (Tilley 1994: 33). Neither does the metaphorical translation end in this interaction between the 'imagined' home and the 'material' homeland: thus, whilst the Scottish Highlands – that 'promised land of modern romance' (Marx 1970: 728) – takes on the mantle of a lost homeland for diasporic Scots, the *meaning* of that homeland is not confined to the historical circumstances of Scottish settlement and migration, but arguably acquires its significance in relation to more 'proverbial' homelands – notably that other 'promised land' which flowed, not with *uisge-beatha* ('the water of life'), but with 'milk and honey'.

A full exposition of the semantic migration which 'dynamically relates' the Scottish diaspora and homeland with the Jewish Diaspora and homeland is beyond the scope of this essay, so the following comments will necessarily be somewhat elliptical (see, however, Basu forthcoming [b]). Put briefly, one way of approaching this movement of meaning is to examine the slippage between academic and popular usage of the terms 'diaspora' and 'homeland' themselves. As Clifford observes, 'for better or worse, diaspora discourse is being widely appropriated' and is 'loose in the world' (1997: 249); but, whilst this discourse is generally employed in a neutral manner by academic commentators (e.g. Safran 1991; Tölölyan 1991; Cohen 1997), in popular culture its use is again proverbial. In other words, while academics have disarmed the victimological connotations of diaspora in their references to 'trade diasporas', 'cultural diasporas' and so forth, in popular usage 'diaspora' is still equated with 'Diaspora' and continues to carry all the connotations of forced exile, oppression and genocide. This metaphorical process is exemplified in the Scottish Highland context, where a morally ambiguous history of expansionism and colonial emigration has been displaced in popular diasporic discourse with a morally virtuous, victimo-logical history of expulsion and involuntary exile.

This is most forcefully articulated in the folk narrative of the so-called 'Highland Clearances': largely *internal* rural population displacements that accompanied the piecemeal adoption of agricultural 'Improvements' in the region between *c*.1780 and 1860, but which have become commonly perceived as the foundational trauma which caused the dispersal of the Highlands Scots from Scotland (Devine 1988; Richards 2000). In popular histories, nationalistic jingoism and countless diasporic websites, the Clearances are thus typically characterized as a 'Highland Holocaust', a genocide equivalent in all but scale to that perpetrated on the Jews and Armenians, which thus provides the diaspora with a collective (false) memory 'of the great historic injustice that binds the group together' (Cohen 1997: 23) and which appears to explain the group's fate as an exiled people. In fact, the vast majority of those who now comprise this Scottish Highland diaspora are descended from emigrants who, like millions from other European countries, were attracted by the prospect of opportunity in the New World and who chose emigration as their escape route from economic adversity (Devine 1992). This is not to deny the trauma of even voluntary emigration, but it is to recognize the 'mythic' nature of the exile which many Scottish diasporic roots-tourists appear to experience: a vague, ineffable sense of nostalgia and loss, which is given vivid form, and therefore becomes expressible, through the misappropriation of 'paradigmatic' victimiza-tion and survival narratives such as those of the Jewish Diaspora and Holocaust (cf. Novick 1999).

In a series of metaphorical displacements, the *'absent* home' consequent upon the alienating forces of modernity thus becomes transformed into the *'lost* homeland' of the Scottish Highlands, which, while acquiring all the connotations of the paradigmatic homeland of the Jewish Diaspora, also becomes, in a sense, recoverable (LaCapra 2001; Basu forthcoming [b]). The 'exile's return' to Scotland may therefore be understood as a profound homecoming at multiple levels: it may be understood, for example, as a return to the 'cradle' of a craved-for collective identity; as an existential journey to the source of the self (Taylor 1989); as the diaspora's cathartic 'mission' to reclaim its sacred sites of trauma, to re-enter its 'mythic space and time' in a manner akin to the 'Holocaust' and 'slave-route' pilgrims described by Kugelmass (1996) and Schramm (Chapter 7 this volume); or simply as the discovery of that place where one feels one most belongs. Such disparate desti-nations are, to echo Simmel, uniquely synthesized in the root metaphor of home: to find this home – materialized, perhaps, in an old family croft, at the grave of an ancestor or in the totemic sites of one's 'clanlands' – is, as one might expect, a deeply profound and moving experience.

Quest – seeking the indeterminate

The symbol of the 'Holy Grail', the object of the 'proverbial' quest, has occupied a place in the European imagination since the Middle Ages and it continues to exert a fascination today, particularly in 'New Age' and popular culture. But, as Matthews notes, 'there is no single, clearly defined image of the Grail, nor indeed evidence that it ever existed . . . yet most agree that it is a profound and mysterious thing, perhaps worth giving up the whole of one's life to find, even in the knowledge that the search may be fruitless' (1981: 5). This indeterminacy of both the destination of the quest and the chances of reaching it are actually fundamental to the motif of the quest. As F.W. Locke explains in his analysis of the thirteenth-century *La Queste del Saint Graal*:

> The truth that the quester discovers at the end of the Journey is essentially incommunicable and can be only obliquely suggested. Its multivalency reflects . . . the Home, the *Patria*, the City, the Pot of Gold, the Awakening of the Land cast into sleep, and, ultimately, the deepest secrets of the Self.
>
> (1960: 3)

Whilst remaining obscure and 'essentially incommunicable', the object of the quest is, however, 'capable of bearing a heavy burden of meaning' (Locke 1960: 5), and, like the quest itself, it 'does not "stand for" something else', but is rather an 'instrument of insight' (ibid.). Indeed, it is only in the structure of the quest that the meaning and revelatory quality of the 'mysterious object' of the quest can be explicated; and even then its wisdom is revealed only to the one who seeks it and who thereby attains the means of understanding it. Locke argues that 'until the end of the Quest is achieved, the Grail, the object of the Quest, is future. It is that which is expected, and hoped for, and striven for' (1960: 39).

Like homecoming, the metaphor of the quest is evocative for both the participant and the researcher of roots-tourism. Indeed, many roots-tourists use this same Jungian language to articulate both the meaning and *the mystery* of their journeys, discursively placing themselves in the roles of heroes seeking possibly unattainable goals. Thus, one informant from Texas explains that:

A Diasporan Scot returning to the ancestral lands is more of a traveler or pilgrim [i.e. than a tourist]. He or she is not necessarily going to the major tourist centers or popular destinations of Scotland. Usually there is a quest involved here, a quest for ancestors or the lands where the family originated. A quest for lost memories and traditions, a hunger for identity and belonging, a reaching for connections from something severed long ago. Like the quest for the Grail itself, it is a complex, convoluted and perilous journey and perhaps the Grail of ourselves is unobtainable.

Another informant, from Colorado, goes further, drawing out other correspondences between the genealogical journey to Scotland and the 'archetypal' Grail quest, including its associations between the health of the land and the health of the person, and the healing potential of the journey itself.

In the old Grail myths there is a sense that the holy object can simultaneously heal the king of his wound, as well as the land itself . . . In the old Grail tales the king is connected to the land. What happens to the king happens to the land. So, in this context, the Arthurian tales speak of the land falling into a wounded state because of the wounded king.

The knights are sent out on a quest for the only object that can restore the king and the land: the Grail. In the tales there is a guiding question that if answered truly will result in the seeker finding the true grail. The question? What ails thee? . . .

In my own participation with the Scottish landscape, and my own family's relationship to our place of origin (Argyll, the [Western] Isles and the Orkneys), the premise of the Arthurian and other Celtic tales seems to suggest a formula of sorts.

There is an old saying: 'The healing of the wound must come from the blood of the wound itself'. This denotes the biological reality that it is largely the blood of the wound that cleanses the wound. If the blood is our ancestry and cultural heritage as well as the landscape and the wound is a ripping up of foundation, a severing of connectedness, the formula suggests that it is precisely by revisiting the landscape that we begin to participate 'in the quest' for our healing and reconnection.

This informant articulates what remains implicit or at best vaguely intuited in many roots-tourists' quests. Although rarely stated as such, for many the homecoming journey *is* a therapeutic act. And if, as suggested, the journey provides the cure through reconnecting the roots-tourists with the 'bloodlines' of their ancestry and cultural heritage, then it is left for us to extrapolate the ailment: the loss of 'memories and traditions', 'a hunger for identity and belonging', a sense of being 'severed' from one's roots.

It is not, of course, only members of this posited Scottish diaspora that suffer from a sense of being alienated from the source of their 'authentic', rooted identity. As discussed in the last section, this crisis of identity is considered by many to be a consequence of modernity – part of the 'melancholy of modernity' described by Kierkegaard (Ferguson 1995). Because of a 'confluence of disorientating factors such as wars, campaigns of genocide, rapid technological and ideological change, the breakdown of moral authority, and the saturation of the mass media', the psychologist Dan MacAdams argues that the self can no longer be thought of as a unitary entity (1997: 48). Instead we have witnessed what Berger *et al.* call a 'pluralization of the lifeworld' (1973: 64) and the rise of a 'protean' self (Lifton 1993). As MacAdams explains, 'Like the Greek god Proteus, one takes on whatever forms and qualities that a particular life situation demands. One juggles multiple roles, tries on different hats, different lives, forging selves whose unity is at best tentative and provisional'(1997: 48). Whilst proteanism represents an adaptive model for how to live amid a world of perceived mobility and fragmentation, MacAdams claims that it has left the individual feeling 'few connections to the past and little faith in the future' (ibid.). This results in an inability in people to make meaningful and long-term commitments to each other, to institutions and 'to the more enduring aspects of selfhood that may reside beneath the surface of everyday role-playing' (ibid.). The individual thus hungers for a deeper, more unified, more coherent and more enduring sense of self, and the search for this elusive entity becomes a primary source of identity in its own right.

In his influential work *After Virtue*, Alasdair MacIntyre equates this contemporary search for self with the narrative of a quest. This has a number of implications: the notion, for example, that self-identity can be conceptualized as a process of emplotment, whereby 'we achieve our personal identities and self-concept through the use of . . . narrative configuration, and make our existence into a whole by understanding it as an expression of a single unfolding and developing story' (Polkinghorne quoted in Bruner 1990: 115–16). This self-narrative does not necessarily begin at birth and end at death, but rather places the self on a continuum, 'embedding' it in a more enduring 'narrative heritage' or 'tradition' which transcends the individual. As MacIntyre states:

> I inherit from the past of my family, my city, my tribe, my nation, a variety of debts, inheritances, rightful expectations and obligations. These constitute the given of my life, my moral starting point . . . The story of my life is always embedded in the story of those communities from which I derive my identity . . . What I am, therefore, is in key part what I inherit, a specific past that is present to some degree in my present. I find myself part of a history and that is generally to say, whether I like it or not, whether I recognise it or not, one of the bearers of a tradition.
>
> (1981: 205–6)

The heroic quest narrative, like that of pilgrimage, has long been used to allegorize the trials and tribulations of the 'journey of life', but what attracts MacIntyre to the quest metaphor is the particular nature of its destination. In this respect, there is, first, the very *positing* of a destination or 'final *telos*' (for example, the longed-for 'unitary' self), which motivates the quest in the first place; but, second, and more significantly, is the fact that this destination, as noted above, remains essentially indeterminate. 'It is clear', MacIntyre writes, 'the medieval conception of a quest is not at all that of a search for something already characterised'; but, rather, it is only through the process of questing that the 'goal of the quest is finally to be understood' (1981: 204). The quest is therefore 'always an education both as to the character of that which is sought and in self-knowledge' (ibid.). The 'mysterious object' at the heart of the quest – something that remains abstruse, inadequately defined, but which is nevertheless intuited and glimpsed obliquely – is, I suggest, also an essential aspect of the '*mystical homecoming*' that is roots-tourism.

Thus, whilst psychologists emphasize the *constructive* nature of self-narration, arguing that the 'true self' is not somehow retrieved from the hidden depths of the inner being, but is rather a creative project in which the self constructs a narrative of itself which is, above all, 'true' to its own logic (Spence 1984), roots-tourists typically assert the opposite, preferring to understand their genealogical quests as the divination of something present, but obscure, within the self. Rather than conceptualizing their identification with a Highland heritage as something chosen, a psycho-social construct or symbolic resource (Waters 1990: 18,

167), their sense of being Scottish is instead understood as a more mysterious, but essentially biological fact: part of their very substance. 'For me, being Scottish is not a choice,' one informant explains, 'it's in the blood. It is something which has no name, but yet lingers there within me.' This genetic connection with an ancestral identity is often also extended to places associated with these ancestors. Thus a profound 'resonance' is felt at certain sites: something strange and affecting, which is rationalized (or, perhaps, further mystified) as a 'race memory', 'ancestral memory' or 'genetic memory'. An American informant speculates:

> Do we have a genetically inherited memory for places? . . . Is this the real secret of 'déjà vu'? Is this why we bite back tears of sorrow at the sound of the bagpipes? Are we responding to memories that we have, but have no understanding of?

Another informant, from Victoria, Australia, describes her journey to her ancestral homeland in Jungian terms as a journey into the 'Scottish psyche' and, ultimately, a journey into her self: 'I come from those people, I share that psyche, therefore journeying into it is a journey into myself.'

In seeking ontological security in an era of existential anxiety, Giddens argues that the self creates coherence and continuity, through narrative, by situating the self on a 'trajectory' from the remembered past to the anticipated future. In this reflexive project, he explains, 'we are, not what we are, but what we make of ourselves' and, to these ends, 'the individual appropriates his past by sifting through it in the light of what is anticipated for an (organised) future' (1991: 75). The self thus creatively 'reworks' the past to suit its future-orientated present (1991: 85). Crucially, however, I suggest that, in order to provide that ontological security, the constructive nature of this project must remain obscure and must, instead, be misrecognized by the subject as a *re*constructive process. The narrating self may, I contend, effectively *choose* to reject choice, and continue to believe in a '"real", inner, essential [self] that lives behind the public presentation of self' (MacAdams 1997: 64). From the roots-tourist's perspective, for example, the revelation that 'we are what we make of ourselves' provides little consolation; what is sought is not a deconstruction of the myth of the self, but rather its rediscovery and revitalization. Thus, to answer those insistent questions of late modernity – 'What to do? How to act? *Who to be?*' (Giddens 1991: 75; emphasis added) – the genealogist turns to the supposedly indubitable inheritance of the blood, and seeks there the elusive grail of the 'authentic' self, the bearer of a tradition.

Pilgrimage – the sacred journey

Aside from the broad structure of the journey from 'an accustomed place towards a place or state that is held to embody ideals of importance' and back again, and the simultaneity of its 'outward and inward' trajectories (Morinis 1992a: ix; 1992b: 10), roots-tourism and pilgrimage share many characteristics. Not least among these is the practice of collecting souvenirs or relics from ancestral places: such items typically include stones, pebbles, pieces of driftwood, sprigs of heather, pottery sherds and, as in the example I mentioned at the beginning of the chapter, even flasks of water drawn from lochs, rivers and wells. Like purported fragments of the 'real cross' or ampullae of holy-water hawked outside medieval cathedrals, such objects contain the 'sacred substance' of the ancestral home, which roots-tourists can then carry back to the diaspora and display in household shrines (often mantelpieces or bookshelves devoted to Scottish memorabilia). Conversely, intimate objects such as finger rings and brooches representing the homecomer or others unable to travel (elderly parents, for example) are sometimes left at ancestral places like *ex-votos* at the shrines of saints. A Canadian informant, whom I observed depositing her ring in the loose stone walls of an iron age 'dun' during her homecoming journey to Skye, explained her actions to me as follows:

> By putting my cheap ring inside the walls, I felt I was giving a humble offering, asking, almost begging to be part of it forever . . . I wanted to leave a part of 'me' there. I did not know this before that moment, nor had I planned to do so. But when I did it, I felt extremely good, extremely relieved.

The homologies between roots-tourism and pilgrimage are also noted by Celeste Ray in her study of the Scottish heritage community in North Carolina. Discussing tours to Scotland organized by clan societies, she explains, 'I interchange the term pilgrim with heritage tourist, because community members describe their own travels as pilgrimage, and also because their travels are structured by and have meaning as pilgrimage' (2001: 134). The structure to which Ray refers is Turner's notion of 'ritual process' and, particularly, the application of this process

to touristic practices (MacCannell 1976; Graburn 1989; Cohen 1992).
Thus, according to Graburn, because the touristic journey 'lies in the
nonordinary sphere of existence', its goal is 'symbolically sacred and
morally on a higher plane than the regards of the ordinary workaday
world' (1989: 28). Pursuing this Turnerian orthodoxy, Ray explains
that the commemorative activities performed by 'heritage pilgrims'
during these tours 'have ritualistic and religious qualities' (2001: 134)
and she draws attention to the sense of *communitas* achieved among
clansfolk during such events (2001: 133). I have found much to support
this argument in my own research with roots-tourists in the Scottish
Highlands. Indeed, as roots-tourists leave behind the 'ordinary' world
of their diasporic homes and enter the 'non-ordinary sphere' of the
ancestral homeland, they do appear to enter a 'liminal' zone where they
often report supernatural occurrences and altered states of mind (feeling
ancestral presences, having premonitory dreams, etc.). Such other-
worldly experiences add to the transformative potential of these rites
of passage, and roots-tourists may return to their ordinary homes
significantly changed, sometimes experiencing difficulties re-adjusting to
domestic routines and commitments or else determined to resolve
outstanding problems.

In these terms, roots-tourism may undoubtedly be conceptualized as
a kind of secular pilgrimage (Reader and Walter 1993), but I am not
convinced that this wholly explains the sense of 'sacredness' that animates
these journeys, nor fully explores the metaphor of the roots-tourist
as pilgrim. Understanding roots-tourism specifically as a *social* drama
(Turner 1974c), Ray argues that 'heritage pilgrimage' is 'not the
individual pilgrimage of finding oneself, but that of finding one's
"people" and one's "place"' (2001: 133). I contend, however, that, in
these journeys, a more complex dialectic exists between this integrative
social identity and a more 'self-centred' individual identity. 'It is the
"soul" that yearns to return to its own land and return to its own people',
explains an Australian informant, 'it is the "soul" that needs to regain its
sense of self at the grass roots'. 'In finding our ancestors', remarks
another, 'we somehow find ourselves'. I suggest that what empowers
these journeys and imbues them with an aura of the sacred is this very
convergence of socializing and personalizing trajectories: a quasi-mystical
finding of oneself in others and others in oneself. In a transcendental
epiphany of 'connectedness', the apparent contrariness of oneself *as
another* and oneself *as being other* (Ricoeur 1992) is thus resolved, and
the 'sites of memory' and 'sources of identity', which are the destinations
of these journeys, ultimately also become 'shrines of self' (Basu 2001).

An informant from New Mexico powerfully articulates the significance of this sacred 'soul connection' to Scotland:

> Being disenfranchised, unattached to my heritage, going to Scotland was becoming connected to an origin that had never before existed. Whether the Scots themselves or anyone else acknowledged it or not, it was my connection. It was sacred to me because it was something of my soul, that part that you don't share with anyone, can't share with anyone. My 'self' has changed since that pilgrimage, whether anyone believes, acknowledges, validates or confirms it or not. Yes, to me it was sacred. I now know that my ancestors came from somewhere, and I've been there, I've breathed the same air and touched the same ground as they did.

I am not, of course, unmindful of the post-structuralist critique of the sacred that has characterized much anthropological writing on pilgrimage since Eade and Sallnow's *Contesting the Sacred* (1991). It goes without saying that the 'spiritual magnetism' (Preston 1992) which empowers the particular 'sacred centres' of roots-tourism is highly selective in its influence, drawing only those who seek it. As such, it would be foolish to suggest that there is anything inherently 'sacred' about these destinations outside the emotional, intellectual and physical journeys through which their sacredness is constructed; or to doubt that they are, if not exactly 'voids', then certainly 'vessels' into which roots-tourists 'devoutly pour their hopes, prayers and aspirations' (Eade and Sallnow 1991a: 15). However, like Rapport and Dawson's contestation of the rootedness of identity, such deconstructions prioritize 'etic' over 'emic' interpretations, and therefore do not fully engage with the subjective reality of the experiences of those we are studying. Thus, just as the practices of roots-tourism demonstrate that modern individuals continue to 'centre themselves' in a notion of home which is itself centred on the specific spatial and temporal coordinates of homeland, so they attest to the resilience of a concept of the sacred which is perceived to emanate from particular places rather than being merely projected onto such places according to the needs of each subject (cf. Eliade 1958: 369). This is surely crucial if we are to attempt to understand not only how certain places come to be regarded as sacred, but also how they acquire the capacity to effect *real* personal transformations in the individuals who experience them as such.

By widening the frame of our scrutiny to examine not only the appropriateness of our own academic use of the metaphor of pilgrimage but also the potential fruitfulness of its use by our informants, we again shift into the realms of the proverbial. Here we discover, not the formulation of 'ever more vacuous' generalizations (Eade and Sallnow 1991b: 9), but evidence for the reconfiguration of the sacred in the context of what has been characterized as a 'post-secular' age (Tacey 2000). Whether these post-secular pilgrimages are rooted in the routes of more ancient pilgrims' ways, as in the contemporary reanimation of the Camino de Santiago (Frey 1998), in New Age meccas such as Glastonbury or Sedona (Ivakhiv 2001) or, indeed, in the moral geographies of ancestral homelands, they succeed in remapping the sacred in terrains both physical and metaphysical, thus re-enchanting a world perceived to be dulled by secular rationalism with transcendent mystery. Metaphorically translated into proverbial pilgrims, roots-tourists are thus called to cross 'the boundaries of their familiar territory' and set off 'in search of the earthly home of their god' (Morinis 1992b: 1). And, if it is not God in any orthodox sense that they seek, then the question remains: to what ideals incarnate are these contemporary spiritual odysseys directed?

A clue may be found in the guidebooks that such pilgrims carry with them on their journeys: not the *Codex Calixtinus* of old, but 'personal growth' manuals such as Frank MacEowen's *The Mist-Filled Path: Celtic Wisdom for Exiles, Wanderers and Seekers* (2002) or Phil Cousineau's *The Art of Pilgrimage: The Seeker's Guide to Making Travel Sacred* (1999). As Frey notes of the motives that draw post-secular *peregrinos* to Santiago, 'the spiritual shares the stage with a wide variety of esoteric, cultic, or individualized religious practices characteristic of Western religious and New Age movements' (1998: 34). Such alternative spiritual callings often entail a rejection of religious orthodoxies in favour of 'more vaguely defined personal searches or inner journeys of transformation' (1998: 33). Thus these pilgrimages become 'personal therapeutic acts' (Morinis 1992b: 9), influenced as much by popular psychology as more institutionalized ritual practices – active responses to the perceived 'relative dearth of effective rites of passage' in the secular world of the West (LaCapra 2001: 76).

In a recent commentary on psychology as a religion, Barnard argues that religion and psychology now 'fulfill similar, if not identical, roles and functions': both may be understood as vehicles for the 'exploration of the depths of reality and consciousness', both enable healing and fulfilment 'via dynamic, experiential, living contact with a cosmic "more"' (2001: 310). In this context, it is interesting to note that at the culmination of his genealogical journey in *Roots*, Alex Haley uses the term 'the peak experience' to describe his homecoming to Juffure, the Gambian village to which he has supposedly traced his eighteenth-century ancestor. The phrase is borrowed from the founding father of transpersonal psychology, Abraham Maslow, who used it to characterize the 'dramatic, if short-lived openings of consciousness leading to feelings of awe, a sense of wholeness and connection or even union with the natural world' (Barnard 2001: 309). Maslow sought to disassociate such 'mystical illuminations', which he believed were the 'intrinsic core' of all religions, from institutional religious structures and instead incorporate them within a new naturalistic faith based on personal experience (ibid.). Along with Jungian theory, transpersonal psychology 'stresses the need to unfold the innate potentials hidden within each person', but it also emphasizes those 'aspects of the human psyche that seem to transcend personal boundaries' (ibid.). Combined with the ascendant discourse of 'genetic essentialism' associated with the new genetic sciences (Strathern 1992, 1995; Sykes 1999), this vision of cosmic connectedness in the very substance of the individual injects a new 'genealogical rhetoric' into the stolid, matter-of-fact world of family history research, transforming it into an atavistic mystery religion of sorts. The *mysterium tremendum* at its heart (that to which it makes its homecoming, its quest, its pilgrimage) is not, however, the ancestors themselves ('one's people'), nor 'their place', hallowed though that land may be, but is ultimately no more, and no less, than the self. The obfuscation is, of course, a necessary component of the mysterium – as Tersteegen writes, 'A God comprehended is no God' (quoted by Otto 1980: 25) – and the ineffable, non-rational, numinous 'peak experience' becomes an end in itself, 'something sought for its own sake' (Otto 1980: 33).

Roots-tourists in the Scottish Highlands often report feeling especially drawn to a particular ancestor they have discovered in their genealogical research. For Sharon, an informant from New South Wales, this was her great-great-grandfather, Alexander, born in 1807. Sharon explains that Alexander was 'just a name' when she first found him on an 1881 census, but by the time of her homecoming in 1999, when she visited his grave and the various places in which he had lived, she felt she had come to know him and sensed his presence beside her on her explorations. Despite this strong sense of identification with an ancestral figure, it is apparent, however, that Sharon's genealogical quest was not only about the past, but in fact more concerned with her present, about 'finding Sharon', as she put it. On her second visit to Scotland, as we wandered around the ruins of the deserted township in which her ancestors once lived, Sharon elaborated on this sense of self-(re)discovery:

When I grew up I was Betty's daughter, and then I sort of went from home to married life, so I was David's wife, and then David, Andrew and Steven's mother, and somewhere in all that Sharon got lost. And then when I came here, I had this sense of freedom, you know . . . this is mine . . . Yes. This is mine. But in this being mine, this is finding out who I am, so really it's nobody else's. Who else can you let in? I can tell you for a thousand years how I feel a sense of belonging to this area, but you can never know it because it's an emotion, not a tangible thing or something you can write on paper. There's no words to describe it, because it's in here [pointing to heart] and it's in here [pointing to head].

In this way roots-tourism may be understood as the 'outward and visible form to an inward and conceptual process' (Turner 1991: 96): past- and place-orientated practices effecting personal transformations in the present.

Conclusions – a longing for form

Sherry Ortner classifies root metaphors as 'one type of key symbol in the elaborating mode': symbols, that is, which provide 'vehicles for sorting out complex and undifferentiated feelings and ideas, making them comprehensible to oneself, communicable to others, and trans-latable into orderly action' (1973: 1340–1). By considering three such 'vehicles' in the context of roots-tourism in the Scottish Highland diaspora, I have attempted to 'probe and describe' the ways in which these particular social actions 'acquire form through the metaphors and paradigms in their actors' heads' (Turner 1974c: 13) – pre-existing forms learnt, as Turner argues, 'by explicit teaching and implicit generaliza-tion from social experience' (ibid.). I hope I have also been able to demonstrate that there is nothing banal about genealogical heritage-tourism, that Kugelmass is wrong to characterize this phenomenon as being motivated 'by something as ordinary as the desire to know who [one's] grandparents were' (1996: 212). If, indeed, we probe beneath the surface of these social actions – by examining, for instance, the 'traditional forms' they appropriate (1996: 201) – we may begin to understand the complexity of the longings (the 'hopes, prayers and aspirations') articulated therein.

Evident in Sharon's comments regarding her genealogicaal journey is a convergence in the three root/route metaphors with which this chapter has been concerned. Through a process of metaphorical triangulation, her journey, like so many journeys made by roots-tourists, is at once a homecoming, quest and pilgrimage, in which qualities of these differently symbolic 'other' genres of travel and their respective destinations are clearly 'active together' in engendering meaning and transformative potential. As with pilgrimage, roots-tourism is simultaneously a 'metaphorical journey' and a 'terrestrial journey', *per ager*, 'through the fields' (Morinis 1992b: 23); as with homecoming, it is a journey to the source, to the cradle of belonging; but as with quest, its destination remains essentially elusive and incommunicable – as Sharon explains, 'it's . . . not a tangible thing or something you can write on paper'. From an emic perspective, the 'associated implications', which migrate between the principal and subsidiary subjects of metaphor, generate meaning and structure, and may thus be said to bear fruit; from an etic perspective, this very generative capacity ought to keep us vigilant in assessing the appropriateness of our own sometimes unreflecting use of metaphor as an interpretative tool.

Given that roots-tourism is a genre of symbolic action in its own right, it may be argued that we should refrain from such interpretative translations: to equate – even through 'analogical extension' – is to risk obscuring the haecceity or 'thisness' of the phenomenon being studied (cf. Sontag 1967). But this would also be to deny the metaphorical logic that lies not only at the heart of the academic endeavour of 'intellectuals', but also at the heart of the intellectual endeavour of being human: the fact that we are cognitive as well as sentient beings. We are, after all, 'self-interpreting animals' (Taylor 1985), who live by myths and metaphors, and through other symbolic systems (Lakoff and Johnson 1980; Bruner 1990; Samuel and Thompson 1990), each perpetually engaged in a hermeneutics of the self and of the world in which we live. Our experience of the world is thus not merely enriched, but *enabled* by the analogical faculty through which one thing (let us say, roots-tourism) may be understood in terms of another (for instance, pilgrimage).

As a function of cognition as well as a linguistic device, metaphor transcends the language of words and allows us to apprehend a language of objects, a language of landscapes and a language of practices – all of which are articulated together in the phenomenon I have merely labelled roots-tourism. But, whereas homecoming, quest and pilgrimage have all long-figured in the popular imagination as particular genres of travel and have thus acquired commonplace or proverbial meanings, roots-tourism is a relatively novel and inchoate phenomenon. By implicitly and explicitly drawing on the route metaphors of homecoming, quest and pilgrimage to provide a composite grammar for roots-tourism, roots-tourists are also provided with a repertoire of appropriate actions and attitudes for their journeys (e.g. processing barefoot, kneeling, weeping, collecting relics, depositing *ex-votos*, etc.), and their vague, incommunicable longing is thus given form. Whilst it is significant that, at a proverbial level, this composite form may be defined against tourism, this is by no means the sole 'structural' rationale that explains the appropriateness and potential fruitfulness of these preferred metaphors. Indeed, the fact that each metaphor connotes a whole 'system' of meanings and therefore cannot be reduced to any simple dichotomization is crucial to the maintenance of roots-tourism as a profound, mysterious and multivalent endeavour.

Notes

1   My observations are based on multi-sited ethnographic research undertaken with roots-tourists, clan societies and other diasporic and homeland Scottish heritage groups between 1998 and 2001; during this time I participated in a great many genealogical journeys of various kinds and collected accounts from those whom I could not accompany or who had made such journeys in the past (see Basu 2002 for methodological discussion).

Bibliography

Adler, J. (1989) 'Travel as performed art', *American Journal of Sociology*, 94 (6): 1366–91.

—— (2002) 'The holy man as traveler and travel attraction: early Christian asceticism and the moral problematic of modernity', in W. Swatos, Jr. and L. Tomasi (eds) *From Medieval Pilgrimage to Religious Tourism: the social and cultural economics of piety*, Westport, Conn.: Praeger.

Allen, J.B. (1980) 'Emergence of a fundamental: the expanding role of Joseph Smith's first vision in Mormon religious thought', *Journal of Mormon History*, 7: 43–61.

Allen, L. (1995) 'Offerings at the Wall', *American Heritage*, February/March: 94.

Anquandah, K.J. (1999) *Castles and Forts of Ghana*, Accra/Paris: Ghana Museums and Monuments Board & Atlante.

Appadurai, A. (1993) 'Disjuncture and difference in the global cultural economy', in M. Featherstone (ed.) *Global Culture: nationalism, globalization and modernity*, London: Sage.

Asad, T. (1997) 'Remarks on the anthropology of the body', in S. Coakley (ed.) *Religion and the Body*, Cambridge: Cambridge University Press.

Augé, M. (1995) *Non-Places*, London: Verso.

Barnard, G.W. (2001) 'Diving into the depths: reflections on psychology as a religion', in D. Jonte-Pace and W.B. Parsons (eds) *Religion and Psychology: mapping the terrain*, London: Routledge.

Barthes, R. (1990) [1973] *S/Z*, Oxford: Blackwell.

Basu, P. (1997) 'Narratives in a landscape: monuments and memories of the Sutherland Clearances', unpublished master's thesis, University College London.

—— (2000a) 'Sites of memory – sources of identity: landscape-narratives of the Sutherland Clearances', in J.A. Atkinson, I. Banks and G. MacGregor (eds) *Townships to Farmsteads: rural settlement studies in Scotland, England and Wales*, Oxford: BAR British series 293.

—— (2000b) 'Genealogy and heritage tourism in the Scottish Highlands and Islands', report prepared for Moray, Badenoch and Strathspey Enterprise.

—— (2001) 'Hunting down home: reflections on homeland and the search for identity in the Scottish diaspora', in B. Bender and M. Winer (eds) *Contested Landscapes: movement, exile and place*, Oxford: Berg.

—— (2002) 'Homecomings: genealogy, heritage tourism and identity in the Scottish Highland diaspora', unpublished PhD thesis, University of London.

—— (2004) 'My own island home: the Orkney homecoming', *Journal of Material Culture*, 9 (1): 27–42.

—— (Forthcoming [a]) 'Macpherson country: genealogical identities, spatial histories and the Scottish diasporan clanscape', *Cultural Geographies*.

—— (Forthcoming [b]) 'Roots-tourism as return movement: semantics and the Scottish diaspora', in M. Harper (ed.) *Emigrant Homecomings*, Manchester: Manchester University Press.

—— (Forthcoming [c]) 'Pilgrims to the Far Country: North American roots-tourists in the Scottish Highlands and Islands', in C. Ray (ed.) *Scottish North America*, Lanham, Md.: Lexington.

Bauman, Z. (1996) 'From pilgrim to tourist – or a short history of identity', in S. Hall and P. du Gay (eds) *Questions of Cultural Identity*, London: Sage.

—— (2000) *Liquid Modernity*, Oxford: Polity Press.

Berdahl, D. (1994) 'Voices at the Wall: discourses of self, history and national identity at the Vietnam Veteran's Memorial', *History and Memory*, 6 (2): 88–124.

Berger, P.L., Berger, B. and Kellner, H. (1973) *The Homeless Mind: modernization and consciousness*, New York: Random House.

Bhardwaj, S.M. (1973) *Hindu Places of Pilgrimage in India: a study in cultural geography*, Berkeley: University of California Press.

Blacking, J. (1977) *The Anthropology of the Body*, London: Academic Press.

Boissevain, J. (ed.) (1996) *Coping with Tourists*, Oxford and New York: Berghahn.

Bourdieu, P. (1977) *Outline of a Theory of Practice*, Cambridge: Cambridge University Press.

—— (1989) *The Logic of Practice*, Cambridge: Polity Press.

Bowman, G. (1985) 'Theoretical itineraries towards an anthropology of pilgrimage', in M. Jha (ed.) *Dimensions of Pilgrimage: an anthropological appraisal*, New Delhi: Inter-India Publications.

—— (1991) 'Christian ideology and the image of a Holy Land: the place of Jerusalem pilgrimage in the various Christianities', in J. Eade and M. Sallnow (eds) *Contesting the Sacred: the anthropology of Christian pilgrimage*, London and New York: Routledge.

Bracht, J. (1990) 'The Americanisation of Adam', in G.W. Trompf (ed.) *Cargo Cults and Millenarian Movements: transoceanic comparisons of new religion movements*, Berlin and New York: Mouton de Gruyter.

Bruner, E.B. (1996) 'Tourism in Ghana: the representation of slavery and the return of the Black diaspora', *American Anthropologist*, 98 (2): 290–304.

Bruner, J. (1990) *Acts of Meaning*, Cambridge, Mass.: Harvard University Press.

Buerger, D.J. (1994) *The Mysteries of Godliness: a history of Mormon temple worship*, San Francisco: Smith Research Associates.

Buitelaar, M. (1993) *Fasting and Feasting in Morocco*, Oxford: Berg.

Caldwell, P. (1983) *The Puritan Conversion Narrative: the beginnings of American expression*, Cambridge: Cambridge University Press.

Callaway, B. and Creevey, L. (1994) *The Heritage of Islam: women, religion and politics in West Africa*, Boulder, Col. and London: Lynne Rienner Publishers.

Carter, D.M. (1997) *States of Grace: Senegalese in Italy and the new European immigration*, Minneapolis: University of Minnesota Press.

Carter, P. (1992) *Living in a New Country: history, travelling and language*, London: Faber and Faber.

Casey, E.S. (1993) *Getting Back into Place: toward a renewed understanding of the place-world*, Bloomington and Indianapolis: Indiana University Press.

Chouin, G. (1998) 'Looking through the forest – sacred groves as historical and archaeological clues in Southern Ghana: an approach', paper presented at the Society of Africanist Archaeologists 14th Biennial Conference, Syracuse University, 21–24 May 1998.

Christian, W.A., Jr. (1982) 'Provoked religious weeping in early modern Spain', in J. Davis (ed.) *Religious Organisation and Religious Weeping*, London: Academic Press.

The Church of Jesus Christ of Latter-Day Saints (1985) *The Book of Mormon*. Copyright 1981 by the Corporation of the President of the Church of Jesus Christ of Latter-Day Saints, Salt Lake City, Utah.

—— (1985) *Saints and Covenants*. Copyright 1981 by the Corporation of the President of the Church of Jesus Christ of Latter-Day Saints, Salt Lake City, Utah.

Clifford, J. (1997) *Routes: travel and translation in the late twentieth century*, Cambridge, Mass.: Harvard University Press.

Cohen, E. (1979) 'A phenomenology of tourist experiences', *Sociology*, 13 (2): 179–201.

—— (1988) 'Traditions in the qualitative sociology of tourism', *Annals of Tourism Research*, 15 (1): 29–46.

—— (1992) 'Pilgrimage and tourism: convergence and divergence', in E.A. Morinis (ed.) *Journeys to Sacred Places*, Westport, Conn.: Greenwood Press.

Cohen, R. (1997) *Global Diasporas: an introduction*, London: UCL Press.

Coleman, S. (2000a) *The Globalisation of Charismatic Christianity: spreading the gospel of prosperity*, Cambridge: Cambridge University Press.

—— (2000b) 'Meanings of movement, place and home at Walsingham', *Culture and Religion*, 1 (2): 153–69.

—— (2002) 'Do you believe in pilgrimage? *Communitas*, contestation and beyond', *Anthropological Theory*, 2 (3): 355–68.

—— (forthcoming) 'The charismatic gift', *Journal of the Royal Anthropological Institute*.

—— and Collins, P. (2000) 'The "plain" and the "positive": ritual, experience and aesthetics in Quakerism and charismatic Christianity', *Journal of Contemporary Religion*, 15 (3): 317–29.

—— and Crang, M. (2002a) *Tourism: between place and performance*, Oxford and New York: Berghahn Books.

— and Crang, M. (2002b) 'Grounded tourists, travelling theory', in S. Coleman and M. Crang (eds) *Tourism: between place and performance*, New York: Berghahn Books.

—— and Elsner, J. (1995) *Pilgrimage: sacred travel and sacred space in the world religions*, London: British Museum Press and Cambridge, Mass.: Harvard University Press.

—— and Elsner, J. (1998) 'Performing pilgrimage: Walsingham and the ritual construction of irony', in F. Hughes-Freeland (ed.) *Ritual, Performance, Media*, London and New York: Routledge.

—— and Elsner, J. (2003) *Pilgrim Voices: narrative and authorship in Christian pilgrimage*, Oxford and New York: Berghahn Books.

Comaroff, J. and Comaroff, J. (1991) *Of Revelation and Revolution: Christianity, colonialism, and consciousness in South Africa*, vol. 1, Chicago: University of Chicago Press.

Connerton, P. (1989) *How Societies Remember*, Cambridge: Cambridge University Press.

Copans, J. (1988) *Les Marabouts de l'Arachide*, Paris: L'Harmattan.

Coulon, C. and Reveyrand, O. (1990) *L'Islam au féminin: Sokhna Magat Diop, Cheikh de la confrérie mouride*, Bordeaux: CEAN.

Cousineau, P. (1999) *The Art of Pilgrimage: the seeker's guide to making travel sacred*, Shaftesbury: Element.

Covey, C. (1961) *The American Pilgrimage: the roots of American history, religion and culture*, New York: Collier Books.

Crang, M. (2002) 'Surrounded by place: embodied encounters', in S. Coleman and M. Crang (eds) *Tourism: between place and performance*, New York and Oxford: Berghahn Books.

Crick, M. (1995) 'The anthropologist as tourist: an identity in question', in M.-F. Lanfant, J.B. Allcock and E.M. Bruner (eds), *International Tourism: identity and change*, London: Sage.

Cruise O'Brien, D. (1971) *The Mourids of Senegal: the political and economic organization of a brotherhood*, Oxford: Clarendon Press.

Csordas, T.J. (1989) 'Embodiment as a paradigm for anthropology', *Ethos*, 18: 5–47.

—— (1994a) *The Sacred Self: a cultural phenomenology of charismatic healing*, Berkeley: University of California Press.

—— (ed.) (1994b) *Embodiment and Experience: the existential ground of culture and self*, Cambridge: Cambridge University Press.

—— (1997) *Language, Charisma and Creativity: the ritual life of a religious movement*, Berkeley: University of California Press.

D'Acquili, E.G., Laughlin, C.D., Jr. and McManus, J. (1979) *The Spectrum of Ritual: a biogenic structural analysis*, New York: Columbia University Press.

Davies, D.J. (1987) *Mormon Spirituality: Latter-Day Saints in Wales and Zion*, Nottingham: University of Nottingham Series in Theology.

—— (1989) 'On Mormon history, identity and faith community', in E. Tonkin, M. McDonald and M. Chapman (eds) *History and Ethnicity*, Association of Social Anthropologists of the Commonwealth Monographs vol. 27, London: Routledge.

Davis-Floyd, R.E. (1992) *Birth as an American Rite of Passage*, Berkeley: University of California Press.

Dean, E.T. (1997) *Shook over Hell: post-traumatic stress, Vietnam and the Civil War*, Cambridge: Cambridge University Press.

Delaney, C. (1990) 'The hajj: sacred and secular', *American Ethnologist*, 17 (3): 513–30.

Devine, T.M. (1988) *The Great Highland Famine: hunger, emigration and the Scottish Highlands in the nineteenth Century*, Edinburgh: John Donald.

—— (ed.) (1992) *Scottish Emigration and Scottish Society*, Edinburgh: John Donald.

Dolgin, J. (1974) 'Latter-Day sense and substance', in I.I. Zaretsky and M.P. Leone (eds) *Religious Movements in Contemporary America*, Princeton, NJ: Princeton University Press.

Douglas, M. (1966) *Purity and Danger*, Harmondsworth: Penguin.

—— (1970) *Natural Symbols*, Harmondsworth: Penguin.

Dubisch, J. (1995) *In a Different Place: pilgrimage, gender, and politics at a Greek island shrine*, Princeton, NJ: Princeton University Press.

Duffy, E. (2002) 'The dynamics of pilgrimage in late medieval England', in C. Morris and P. Roberts (eds) *Pilgrimage: the English experience from Becket to Bunyan*, Cambridge: Cambridge University Press.

Eade, J. (1992) 'Pilgrimage and tourism at Lourdes, France', *Annals of Tourism Research*, 19 (1): 18–32.

— (2000) 'Introduction to the Illinois Paperback' in J. Eade and M. Sallnow (eds) *Contesting the Sacred: the anthropology of Christian pilgrimage*, Urbana and Chicago: University of Illinois Press.

—— and Sallnow, M. (eds) (1991a) *Contesting the Sacred: the anthropology of Christian pilgrimage*, London: Routledge.

—— (1991b) 'Introduction', in J. Eade and M.J. Sallnow (eds) *Contesting the Sacred: the anthropology of Christian pilgrimage*, London: Routledge.

Ebin, V. (1995) 'International networks of a trading diaspora: the Mourids of Senegal abroad', in P. Antoine and A.B. Diop (eds) *La ville à guichets fernés? Itinéraires, réseaux et insertion urbaine*, Dakar: IFAN-Orstom.

— (1996) 'Making room versus creating space: the construction of spatial categories by itinerant Mourid traders', in B. Metcalf (ed.) *Making Muslim Space in North America and Europe*, Berkeley and Los Angeles: University of California Press.

Ebron, P. (1999) 'Tourists as pilgrims: commercial fashioning of transatlantic politics', *American Ethnologist*, 26 (4): 910–32.

Eickelman, D. and Piscatori. J. (eds) (1990a) *Muslim Travellers: pilgrimage, migration, and the religious imagination*, Berkeley and Los Angeles: University of California Press.

—— (1990b) 'Introduction' in D. Eickelman and J. Piscatori (eds) *Muslim Travellers: pilgrimages, migration, and the religious imagination*, Berkeley and Los Angeles: University of California Press.

—— (1990c) 'Social theory in the study of Muslim societies', in D. Eickelman and J. Piscatori (eds) *Muslim Travellers: pilgrimages, migration, and the religious imagination*, Berkeley and Los Angeles: University of California Press.

Eliade, M. (1958) *Patterns in Comparative Religion*, London: Sheed and Ward.

—— (1964) *Myth and Reality*, London: George Allen and Unwin.

Emancipation Day Programme (1998) *First Emancipation Day Celebrations Ghana. Emancipation: Our Heritage, Our Strength, 25th July – 2nd August*.

Emancipation Day Programme (1999) *The Second Annual Emanicpation Day Celebrations: Emancipation Day '99. Organized under the Auspices of the Ministry of Tourism, Ghana, July 24 – August 1 1999*.

Evers Rosander, E. (1991) *Women in a Borderland: managing Muslim identity where Morocco meets Spain*, Stockholm: Stockholm Studies in Social Anthropology.

—— (1998) 'Women and Mouridism in Senegal: the case of the Mam Diarra Bousso Daira in Mbacké', in K. Ask and M. Tjomsland (eds) *Women and Islamization: contemporary dimensions of discourse on gender relations*, Oxford: Berg.

—— (2000) 'Money, marriage and religion: Senegalese women traders in Tenerife, Spain', in T. Salter and K. King (eds) *Africa, Islam and Development*, Edinburgh: Centre of African Studies.

—— (2001) 'Mam Diarra Bousso: den goda modern i Porokhane' ('Mam Diarra Bousso: the good mother in Porokhane'), in D. Westerlund (ed.) *Levade sufism*, Sufism Alive, Falun: Nya Doxa.

Fabian, J. (1983) *Time and the Other: how anthropology makes its object*, New York: Columbia University Press.

Faroqhi, S. (1994) *Pilgrims and Sultans: the hajj under the Ottomans*, London: I.B. Tauris.

Ferguson, H. (1995) *Melancholy and the Critique of Modernity: Soren Kierkegaard's religious philosophy*, London: Routledge.

Fernandez, J. (1986) *Persuasions and Performances*, Bloomington: Indiana University Press.

—— (ed.) (1991) *Beyond Metaphor: the theory of tropes in anthropology*, Stanford, Calif.: Stanford University Press.

Franklin, A. (2003) *Tourism: an introduction*, London: Sage.

Franklin, B. (1993) *M.I.A., or Mythmaking in America*, New Brunswick, NJ: Rutgers University Press.

Frey, N. (1998) *Pilgrim Stories: on and off the road to Santiago*, Berkeley: University of California Press.

Gardner, K. (1995) *Global Migrants, Local Lives: travel and transformation in rural Bangladesh*, Oxford: Clarendon Press.

Gatewood, J. (1985) 'Actions speak louder than words', in J. Dougherty (ed.) *Directions in Cognitive Anthropology*, Urbana and Chicago: University of Illinois Press.

Gemzoe, L. (1999) *Feminine Matters: women's religious practice in a Portuguese town*, Stockholm: Stockholm Studies in Social Anthropology.

Ghana Tourist Board (2002) 'Attractions'. Online. Available at <http://www.ghanatourism.com> (accessed 25 September 2002).

—— (n.d.) *Ghana: a special Africa – a different Africa*, promotional brochure.

Giddens, A. (1991) *Modernity and Self-Identity: self and society in the Late Modern Age*, Cambridge: Polity.

Gillett, H.M. (1946) *Walsingham: the history of a famous shrine*, London: Burns Oates & Washbourne.

Ginsberg, F.D. (1989) *Contested Lives: the abortion debate in an American community*, Berkeley and Los Angeles: University of California Press.

Gold, S. (1988) *Fruitful Journeys: the ways of Rajasthani pilgrims*, Berkeley: University of California Press.

Gölpınarlı, A. (1983) *Mevlana' dan Sonra Mevlevilik*, Istanbul: Inkilap ve Aka Kitabevleri.

Graburn, N. (1989) [1977] 'Tourism: the sacred journey' in V. Smith (ed.) *Hosts and Guests: the anthropology of tourism*, Philadelphia: University of Pennsylvania Press.

Gupta, A. and Ferguson, J. (1997) 'Discipline and practice: "the field" as site, method, and location in anthropology', in A. Gupta and J. Ferguson (eds) *Anthropological Locations: boundaries and grounds of a field science*, Berkeley: University of California Press.

Haley, A. (1991) [1976] *Roots*, London: Vintage.

Halman, T. and And, M. (1992) *Mevlana Celaleddin Rumi and The Whirling Dervishes. Sufi Philosophy. Whirling Rituals. Poems of Ecstasy. Miniature Painting*. Istanbul: Dost Yayınları.

Harrison, J.F.C. (1989) 'The popular history of early Victorian Britain: a Mormon contribution', in R.L. Thorp and M.R. Thorp (eds) *Mormons in Early Victorian Britain*, Salt Lake City: University of Utah Press.

Harvey, D. (1989) *The Condition of Postmodernity*, Oxford: Blackwell.

Hass, K. (1998) *Carried to the Wall: American memory and the Vietnam Veterans Memorial*, Berkeley: University of California Press.

Hastrup, K. and Olwig, K.F. (1997) 'Introduction', in K.F. Olwig and K. Hastrup (eds) *Siting Culture: the shifting anthropological object*, London and New York: Routledge.

Holbrook, V. (1999) 'Diverse tastes in spiritual life: textual play in the diffusion of Rumi's Order', in L. Lewisohn (ed.) *The Heritage of Sufism: the legacy of medieval Sufism (1150–1500)*, vol. II, London: Oneworld Publications.

Hubert, J. (1994) 'Sacred beliefs and beliefs of sacredness', in D. Carmichael, J. Hubert, B. Reeves and A. Schanche (eds) *Sacred Sites, Sacred Places*, London and New York: Routledge.

Hummel, R. and Hummel, T. (1995) *Patterns of the Sacred: English Protestant and Russian Orthodox pilgrims of the nineteenth century*, London: Scorpion Cavendish.

Ivakhiv, A.J. (2001) *Claiming Sacred Ground: pilgrims and politics at Glastonbury and Sedona*, Bloomington: Indiana University Press.

Jackson, M. (1983) 'Knowledge of the body', *Man* (N.S.), 18 (2): 327–45.

Jean, C. (1997) 'Les sokhnas Mbacké-Mbacké: des femmes marabouts', unpublished PhD thesis, Department of Ethnology and Comparative Sociology, University of Paris X (Nanterre).

Jensen-Stevenson, M. and Stevenson, W. (1990) *Kiss the Boys Good-bye: how the United States betrayed its own POWs in Vietnam*, Toronto: McClelland and Stuart.

Kaelber, L. (2002) 'The sociology of medieval pilgrimage: contested views and shifting boundaries', in W. Swatos, Jr. and L. Tomasi (eds) *From Medieval Pilgrimage to Religious Tourism: the social and cultural economics of piety*, Westport, Conn.: Praeger.

Kafadar, C. (1992) 'Visibility of Sufism', in R. Lifchez (ed.) *The Dervish Lodge: architecture, art and Sufism in Ottoman Turkey*, Berkeley and Los Angeles: University of California Press.

Karve, I. (1962) 'On the road: a Maharashtrian pilgrimage', *The Journal of Asian Studies*, XXII (1): 13–31.

Kaur, R. and Hutnyk, J. (eds) (1999) *Travel Worlds: journeys in contemporary cultural politics*, London: Zed.

Keeble, N.H. (2002) '"To be a pilgrim": constructing the Protestant life in early modern England', in C. Morris and P. Roberts (eds) *Pilgrimage: the English experience from Becket to Bunyan*, Cambridge: Cambridge University Press.

King, C. (1993) 'His truth goes marching on: Elvis Presley and the pilgrimage to Graceland', in I. Reader and T. Walter (eds) *Pilgrimage in Popular Culture*, Basingstoke: Macmillan.

Kleinman, A., Das, V. and Lock, M. (eds) (1997) *Social Suffering*, Berkeley: University of California Press.

Knowlton, D.C. (1991) 'Belief, metaphor and rhetoric: the Mormon practice of testimony bearing', *Sunstone*, April.

—— (1994) 'The unspeakable and intellectual politics in Mormonism', unpublished paper. [An earlier version of this paper was given at the 1992

Sunstone Symposium, Salt Lake City, Utah, under the title 'Secrecy, deceit and the sacred in Mormonism'.]

Kugelmass, J. (1992) 'The rites of the tribe: American Jewish tourism in Poland', in I. Karp, C. Kreamer, S. Lavine and A. Karp (eds) *Museums and Communities: the politics of public culture*, Washington, DC: Smithsonian Institution Press.

—— (1996) 'Missions to the Past: Poland in contemporary Jewish thought and deed', in P. Antze and M. Lambek (eds) *Tense Past: cultural essays in trauma and memory*, New York: Routledge.

Kwarkeng, K.A. (1999) 'The dilemma of the Diasporan', *The Ghanaian Chronicle*, Wednesday, 26 May – Thursday, 27 May, p. 5.

LaCapra, D. (2001) *Writing History, Writing Trauma*, Baltimore: Johns Hopkins University Press.

Lakoff, G. and Johnson, M. (1980) *Metaphors We Live By*, Chicago: University of Chicago Press.

Larson, P.M. (1999) 'Reconsidering trauma, identity, and the African diaspora: enslavement and historical memory in nineteenth-century Highland Madagaskar', *William & Mary Quarterly*, 56 (2): 335–62.

Lavigne, Y. (1987) *The Hells Angels: taking care of business*, Toronto: Ballantine.

Lembcke, J. (1998) *The Spitting Image: myth, memory, and the legacy of Vietnam*, New York: New York University Press.

Levin, D.M. (1985) *The Body's Recollection of Being*, London: Routledge and Kegan Paul.

Lévi-Strauss, C. (1964) [1962] *Totemism*, London: Merlin Press.

Lifchez, R. (1992) 'The Lodges of Istanbul', in R. Lifchez (ed.) *The Dervish Lodge: architecture, art and Sufism in Ottoman Turkey*, Berkeley and Los Angeles: University of California Press.

Lifton, R.J. (1993) *The Protean Self: human resilience in an age of fragmentation*, New York: Basic Books.

Locke, F.W. (1960) *The Quest for the Holy Grail: a literary study of a thirteenth-century French romance*, Stanford, Calif.: Stanford University Press.

Lowenthal, D. (1985) *The Past is a Foreign Country*, Cambridge: Cambridge University Press.

—— (1994) 'Identity, heritage, and history', in J. Gillis (ed.) *Commemoration: the politics of national identity*, Princeton, NJ: Princeton University Press.

—— (1998) *The Heritage Crusade and the Spoils of History*, Cambridge: Cambridge University Press.

Lyon, M.L. and Barbalet, J.M. (1994) 'Society's body: emotion and the "somatization" of social theory', in T. Csordas (ed.) *Embodiment and Experience: the existential ground of culture and self*, Cambridge: Cambridge University Press.

MacAdams, D.P. (1997) 'The case for unity in the (post)modern self', in R.D. Ashmore and L. Jussim (eds) *Self and Identity: fundamental issues*, Oxford: Oxford University Press.

MacCannell, D. (1973) 'Staged authenticity: arrangements of social space in tourist settings', *American Journal of Sociology*, 79 (3): 589–603.
—— (1976) *The Tourist: a new theory of the leisure class*, London: Macmillan.
McDannell, C. (1995) *Material Christianity: religion and popular culture in America*, New Haven: Yale University Press.
MacEowen, F. (2002) *The Mist-Filled Earth: Celtic wisdom for exiles, wanderers, and seekers*, Novato, Calif.: New World Library.
MacIntyre, A. (1981) *After Virtue: a study in moral theory*, London: Duckworth.
Malkki, L. (1997) 'Speechless emissaries: refugees, humanitarianism and dehistoricization', in K.F. Olwig and K. Hastrup (eds), *Siting Culture: the shifting anthropological object*, London and New York: Routledge.
Markowitz, F. (1996) 'Israel as Africa, Africa as Israel: "divine geography" in the personal narratives and community identity of the Black Hebrew Israelites', *Anthropological Quarterly*, 69 (4): 193–205.
Marx, K. (1970) [1887] *Capital: a critique of political economy, Volume 1*, London: Lawrence and Wishart.
Massey, D. (1992) 'A place called home?', *New Formations*, 17 (3): 3–15.
—— (1994) *Space, Place and Gender*, Cambridge: Polity Press.
Matthews, J. (1981) *The Grail: quest for the eternal*, London: Thames and Hudson.
Mauss, M. (1950) *Les Techniques du corps, sociology et anthropology*, Paris: Presses Universitaires de France.
Meethan, K. (2000) *Tourism in Global Society: place, culture, consumption*, Basingstoke: Palgrave.
Messerschmidt, D. and Sharma, J. (1981) 'Hindu pilgrimage in the Nepal Himalayas', *Current Anthropology*, 22: 571–2.
Meyer, B. and Geschiere, P. (1999) 'Globalization and identity: dialectics of flow and closure: introduction', in B. Meyer and P. Geschiere (eds) *Globalization and Identity: dialectics of flow and closure*, Oxford: Blackwell.
Michalowski, R. and Dubisch, J. (2001) *Run for the Wall: remembering Vietnam on a motorcycle pilgrimage*, Brunswick, NJ: Rutgers University Press.
Mitchell, H.J. (2000) 'Belief, activity and embodiment in the constitution of contemporary Mormonism', unpublished PhD thesis, Queen's University, Belfast.
Mitchell, J.P. (1997) 'A moment with Christ: the importance of feelings in the analysis of belief', *Journal of the Royal Anthropological Institute*, 3 (1): 79–94.
—— (1998) 'A providential storm: myth, history and the story of St Paul's shipwreck in Malta', *Memory, History and Critique: European identity at the Millennium*, Proceedings of the Fifth Conference of the International Society for the Study of European Ideas (ISSEI).
Morinis, E.A. (1984) *Pilgrimage in the Hindu Tradition: a case study of West Bengal*, Delhi: Oxford University Press.
—— (ed.) (1992a) *Sacred Journeys: the anthropology of pilgrimage*, Westport, Conn.: Greenwood Press.

—— (1992b) 'Introduction: the territory of the anthropology of pilgrimage', in E.A. Morinis (ed.) *Sacred Journeys: the anthropology of pilgrimage*, Westport, Conn.: Greenwood Press.

Morley, D. and Robins, K. (1993) 'No place like Heimat: images of home(land)', in E. Carter *et al.* (eds) *European Culture in Space and Place: theories of identity and location*, London: Lawrence and Wishart.

Morris, C. (2002) 'Introduction', in C. Morris and P. Roberts (eds) *Pilgrimage: the English experience from Becket to Bunyan*, Cambridge: Cambridge University Press.

Morrison, S. (2000) *Women Pilgrims in Late Medieval England: private piety as public performance*, London: Routledge.

Myerhoff, B. (1975) 'Organization and ecstasy: deliberation and accidental communitas among Huichol Indians and American youth', in S.F. Morre and B. Myerhoff (eds) *Symbols and Politics in Communal Ideology: cases and questions*, Ithaca: Cornell University Press.

Needham, R. (1972) *Belief, Language and Experience*, Chicago: University of Chicago Press.

Netton, I.R. (1996) *Seek Knowledge: thought and travel in the House of Islam*, London: Curzon Press.

Neville, G. (1987) *Kinship and Pilgrimage: rituals of reunion in American Protestant culture*, New York: Oxford University Press.

Nora, P. (1989) 'Between memory and history: *les lieux de memoire*', *Representations*, 26 (1): 7–25.

Novick, P. (1999) *The Holocaust and Collective Memory*, London: Bloomsbury.

Ortner, S. (1973) 'On key symbols', *American Anthropologist*, 75 (6): 1338–46.

Otto, R. (1980) [1923] *The Idea of the Holy*, London: Oxford University Press.

Panafest '99 (1999) *PANAFEST '99*. Produced by the Information Services Department, Ghana for Panafest Foundation (video, 60 mins).

Parry, J. (1986) 'The gift, the Indian gift and the "Indian gift"', *Man* (N.S.), 21 (3): 453–73.

—— and Bloch, M. (1989) 'Introduction: money and the morality of exchange', in J. Parry and M. Bloch (eds) *Money and the Morality of Exchange*, Cambridge: Cambridge University Press.

Patterson, T.R. and Kelley, R.D.G. (2000) 'Unfinished migrations: reflections on the African diaspora and the making of the modern world', *African Studies Review*, 43 (1): 11–45.

Peacock, J. and Tyson, R. (1989) *Pilgrims of Paradox: Calvinism and experience among the Primitive Baptists of the Blue Ridge*, Washington, DC: Smithsonian Institution Press.

Percy, M. (1998) 'The morphology of pilgrimage in the "Toronto Blessing"', *Religion*, 28: 281–8.

Pierson, M.H. (1997) *The Perfect Vehicle: what is it about motorcycles?*, New York: Norton.

Piquet, C. and Best, R.A. (1986) *Post Traumatic Stress Disorder, Rape Trauma,*

Delayed Stress, and Related Conditions: a bibliography, Jefferson, NC: McFarland.

Pittock, M.G.H. (1991) *The Invention of Scotland: the Stuart myth and the Scottish identity, 1638 to the present*, London: Routledge.

Portes, A. (2001) 'Introduction: the debates and significance of immigrant transnationalism', *Global Networks*, 1 (3): 181–94.

Preston, J.J. (1992) 'Spiritual magnetism: an organizing principle for the study of pilgrimage', in E.A. Morinis (ed.) *Sacred Journeys: the anthropology of pilgrimage*, Westport, Conn.: Greenwood Press.

Putnam, R. (2003) 'Conclusión', in R. Putnam (ed.) *El declive del capital social: un estudio internacional sobre sociedades y el sentido comunitario*, Barcelona: Nueva Galaxia Gutenberg.

Rapport, N. (1998) 'Coming home to a dream: a study of the immigrant discourse of "Anglo-Saxons" in Israel', in N. Rapport and A. Dawson (eds) *Migrants of Identity: perceptions of home in a world of movement*, Oxford: Berg.

—— and Dawson, A. (eds) (1998a) *Migrants of Identity: perceptions of home in a world of movement*, Oxford: Berg.

—— (1998b) 'The topic and the book', in N. Rapport and A. Dawson (eds) *Migrants of Identity: perceptions of home in a world of movement*, Oxford: Berg.

—— (1998c) 'Home and movement: a polemic', in N. Rapport and A. Dawson (eds) *Migrants of Identity: perceptions of home in a world of movement*, Oxford: Berg.

Ray, C. (2001) *Highland Heritage: Scottish Americans in the American South*, Chapel Hill: University of North Carolina Press.

Raynor, S. (2002) 'Breaking the silence: the unspoken brotherhood of Vietnam Veterans', *NC Cross Roads*, Greensboro: North Carolina Humanities Council 6: 2.

Reader, I. (1993) 'Conclusion', in I. Reader and T. Walter (eds) *Pilgrimage in Popular Culture*, Basingstoke: Macmillan.

Reader, I. and Walter, T. (eds) (1993) *Pilgrimage in Popular Culture*, Basingstoke: Macmillan.

'Report of the proceedings of the Conference on Preservation of Elmina and Cape Coast Castles and Fort St. Jago in the Central Region held in the Cape Coast Castle, May 11–12, 1994' (1994) unpublished report.

Riccio, B. (2001) 'Following Senegalese migratory paths through media representation', in R. King and N. Wood (eds) *Media and Migration*, London and New York: Routledge.

—— (2003) 'L'Urbanisation mouride et les migrations transnationales sénégalaises', in A. Piga (ed.) *Islam et ville en Afrique au sud de Sahara: entre soufisme et fondamentalisme*, Paris: Karthala.

Richards, E. (2000) *The Highland Clearances: people, landlords and rural turmoil*, Edinburgh: Birlinn.

Richards, I.A. (1936) *The Philosophy of Rhetoric*, New York: Oxford University Press.

Ricoeur, P. (1992) *Oneself as Another*, Chicago: University of Chicago Press.

Robertson, G., Tickner, L., Bird, J., Curtis, B. and Putnam, T. (eds) (1994) *Travellers' Tales: narratives of home and displacement*, London and New York: Routledge.

Rojek, C. and Urry, J. (1997) *Touring Cultures: transformations of travel and theory*, London and New York: Routledge.

Rowlands, M. (1999) 'Remembering to forget: sublimation as sacrifice in war memorials', in A. Forty and S. Kuchler (eds) *The Art of Forgetting*, Oxford: Berg.

Rushdie, S. (1992) *Imaginary Homelands: essays and criticism, 1981–91*, London: Granta.

Safran, W. (1991) 'Diasporas in modern societies: myths of homeland and return', *Diaspora*, 1 (1): 83–99.

Sallnow, M. (1987) *Pilgrims of the Andes: regional cults in Cusco*, Washington DC: Smithsonian Institution Press.

Samuel, R. and Thompson, P. (eds) (1990) *The Myths We Live By*, London and New York: Routledge.

Sarr, F. (1998) *L'Entrepreneuriat feminine au Sénégal: la transformation des rapports de pouvoir*, Paris: L'Harmattan.

Schama, S. (1995) *Landscape and Memory*, London: Fontana.

Schwartz, J. (1997) '"Roots" and "mosaic" in a Balkan border village', in K.F. Olwig and K. Hastrup (eds) *Siting Culture: the shifting anthropological object*, London and New York: Routledge.

Scottish Executive (2000) *A New Strategy for Scottish Tourism*, Edinburgh: Scottish Executive.

Scruggs, J.C. and Swerdlow, J. (1985) *To Heal a Nation: the Vietnam Veterans Memorial*, New York: Harper and Row.

Sellers, R.W. and Walter, T. (1993) 'From Custer to Kent State: heroes, martyrs, and the evolution of popular shrines', in I. Reader and T. Walter (eds) *Pilgrimage in Popular Culture*, Basingstoke: Macmillan.

Sered, S. S. (1992) *Women as Ritual Experts: the religious lives of elderly Jewish women in Jerusalem*, New York and Oxford: Oxford University Press.

Shay, J. (1994) *Achilles in Vietnam: combat trauma and the undoing of character*, New York: Athenaeum.

Shipps, J. (1987) *Mormonism: the story of a new religious tradition*, Urbana and Chicago: University of Illinois Press.

Shoumatoff, A. (1995) [1985] *The Mountain of Names: a history of the human family*, New York: Kodansha.

Skog, M. (1993) 'Trosrörelsen i Sverige', *Tro och Tanke*, 87 (5): 89–138.

Smith, A.D. (1991) *National Identity*, London: Penguin.

Smith, V. (1992) 'Introduction: the quest in guest', *Annals of Tourism Research*, 19 (1): 1–17.

Solomon, R.C. (1984) 'Getting angry: the Jamesian theory of emotion in anthropology', in R.A. Shweder and R.A. LeVine (eds) *Culture Theory: essays on mind, self and emotion*, Cambridge: Cambridge University Press.

Sontag, S. (1967) 'Against interpretation', in *Against Interpretation and Other Essays*, London: Eyre and Spottiswoode.

Spence, D. (1984) *Narrative Truth and Historical Truth: meaning and interpretation in psychoanalysis*, New York: Norton.

Stirrat, R. (1991) 'Place and person in Sinhala Catholic pilgrimage', in J. Eade and M. Sallnow (eds) *Contesting the Sacred: the anthropology of Christian pilgrimage*, London: Routledge.

Strathern, A. (1999) *Body Thoughts*, Ann Arbor: University of Michigan Press.

Strathern, M. (1992) *After Nature: English kinship in the late twentieth century*, Cambridge: Cambridge University Press.

—— (1995) 'Nostalgia and the new genetics', in D. Battaglia (ed.) *Rhetorics of Self-Making*, Berkeley: University of California Press.

Stromberg, P.G. (1993) *Language and Self-Transformation: a study of the Christian conversion narrative*, Cambridge: Cambridge University Press.

Swatos, W., Jr. (2002) 'New Canterbury trails: pilgrimage and tourism in Anglican London', in W. Swatos, Jr. and L. Tomasi (eds) *From Medieval Pilgrimage to Religious Tourism: the social and cultural economics of piety*, Westport, Conn.: Praeger.

Swatos, W.J. and Tomasi, L. (eds) (2002) *From Medieval Pilgrimage to Religious Tourism: the social and cultural economics of piety*, Westport, Conn.: Praeger.

Sykes, B. (1999) *The Human Inheritance: genes, language and evolution*, Oxford: Oxford University Press.

Tacey, D. (2000) *Re-enchantment: the new Australian spirituality*, Sydney: HarperCollins.

Tall, S.M. (2002) 'L'Émigration internationale sénégalaise d'hier à demain', in M. Diop (ed.) *La Société sénégalaise entre le local et le global*, Paris: Karthala.

Talmage, J.E. (1966) *The House of the Lord: a study of holy sanctuaries, ancient and modern*, Salt Lake City, Utah: Bookcraft Publishers.

Tapper, N. (1990) 'Ziyaret: gender, movement and exchange in a Turkish community', in D. Eickelman and J. Piscatori (eds) *Muslim Travellers: pilgrimage, migration, and the religious imagination*, Berkeley: University of California Press.

Taylor, C. (1985) *Human Agency and Language: philosophical papers I*, Cambridge: Cambridge University Press.

—— (1989) *Sources of the Self: the making of the modern identity*, Cambridge: Cambridge University Press.

The Great Homecoming: the 'Door of No Return' opens . . . (1999) written and directed by Fred Daramani, produced by Visionlink Productions Ltd, Accra (video, 35 mins).

Thiam, S. (1998) *Mam Diarra Bousso: un idéal de vie*, Mémoire de maîtrise, Dakar: UCAD (Université Cheikh Anta Diop).

Bibliography 189

Tilley, C. (1994) *A Phenomenology of Landscape: places, paths and monuments*, Oxford: Berg.
—— (1999) *Metaphor and Material Culture*, Oxford: Blackwell.
Tölölyan, K. (1991) 'Preface', *Diaspora*, 1 (1): 3–7.
Tomasi, L. (2002) '*Homo Viator*: from pilgrimage to religious tourism via the journey', in W. Swatos, Jr. and L. Tomasi (eds) *From Medieval Pilgrimage to Religious Tourism: the social and cultural economics of piety*, Westport, Conn.: Praeger.
Tremlett, P. (2003) 'The problem of belief: a response to Matthew Engelke', *Anthropology Today*, 19 (4): 24.
Turner, V. (1973) 'The center out there: pilgrim's goal', *History of Religions*, 12: 191–239.
—— (1974a) 'Liminal to liminoid in play, flow and ritual: an essay in comparative symbology', *Rice University Studies*, 60: 53–92.
—— (1974b) 'Pilgrimage and communitas', *Studia Missionalia*, 23: 305–27.
—— (1974c) *Dramas, Fields, and Metaphors: symbolic action in human society*, Ithaca: Cornell University Press.
—— (1991) [1969] *The Forest of Symbols: aspects of Ndembu ritual*, Ithaca: Cornell University Press.
—— (1992) 'Foreword' in E.A. Morinis (ed.) *Sacred Journeys: the anthropology of pilgrimage*, Westport, Conn.: Greenwood Press.
—— and Turner, E. (1978) *Image and Pilgrimage in Christian Culture*, New York: Columbia University Press.
Urry, J. (1990) *The Tourist Gaze: leisure and travel in contemporary societies*, London: Routledge.
—— (1995) *Consuming Places*, London and New York: Routledge.
— (2000) *Sociology Beyond Societies: mobilities for the twenty-first century*, London and New York: Routledge.
— (2002) 'Mobility and proximity', *Sociology*, 36 (2): 255–73.
Van Alphen, E. (1999) 'Symptoms of discursivity: experience, memory, and trauma', in J. Crew *et al.* (eds) *Memory: cultural recall in the present*, Hanover, NH: University of New England Press.
Van Dantzig, A. (1980) *Forts and Castles of Ghana*, Accra: Sedco.
Van Devanter, L. (1983) *Home Before Morning: the true story of an army nurse*, New York: Warner.
Varenne, H. (1978) *Americans Together: structural diversity in a Midwestern Town*, New York: Teachers' College Press.
Vertovec, S. and Cohen, R. (eds) (1999) *Migration, Diasporas and Transnationalism*, Northampton: E. Elgar.
Voyé, L. (2002) 'Popular religion and pilgrimages in Western Europe', in W. H. Swatos, Jr. and L. Tomasi (eds) *From Medieval Pilgrimage to Religious Tourism: the social and cultural economics of piety*, Westport, Conn.: Praeger.
Waters, M.C. (1990) *Ethnic Options: choosing identities in America*, Berkeley: University of California Press.

Wells, J., Danquah, J. and Intsiful, G. (1996) *Assin Manso Historic Park Village Tourism Project: pre-feasibility analysis*, Accra: Ministry of Tourism.

Werbner, R.P. (1977) 'Introduction', in R.P. Werbner (ed.) *Regional Cults*, London: Academic Press.

Werbner, P. (2002) *Imagined Diasporas Among Manchester Muslims*, Oxford: James Currey.

—— and Basu, H. (eds) (1998) *Embodying Charisma: modernity, locality and the performance of emotion in Sufi cults*, London and New York: Routledge.

Whitehouse, H. (1992) 'Memorable religions: transmission, codification and change in divergent Melanesian contexts', *Man* (N.S.), 24 (4): 777–98.

—— (1996) 'Rites of terror: emotion, metaphor and memory in Melanesian initiation cults', *Journal of the Royal Anthropological Institute*, 2 (1): 99–116.

Williams, A. (1996) 'Foreword', in M. Warner, *Walsingham: an ever-circling year*, Oxford: Oxford University Press.

Winkelman, M. (forthcoming) 'Conclusion', in J. Dubisch and M. Winkelman (eds) *Pilgrimage and Healing*.

Wolf, D. (1991) *The Rebels: a brotherhood of outlaw bikers*, Toronto: University of Toronto Press.

Wolf, E. (1958) 'The Virgin of Guadalupe: a Mexican national symbol', *Journal of American Folklore*, 71 (1): 34–9.

Womack, P. (1989) *Improvement and Romance: constructing the myth of the Highlands*, Basingstoke: Macmillan.

Wood, N. (1999) *Vectors of Memory: legacies of trauma in postwar Europe*, Oxford: Berg.

Yamba, C.B. (1995) *Permanent Pilgrims: the idea of pilgrimage in the lives of West African Muslims*, London: Edinburgh University Press.

Young, A. (1995) *The Harmony of Illusions: inventing post traumatic stress disorder*, Princeton, NJ: Princeton University Press.

Index